# Lay and Expert Contributions to Japanese Criminal Justice



This book examines the little or not previously researched roles and contributions of non-legal professionals in Japanese criminal justice against the background of recent social and legal changes that either gave birth to or affected the roles played by these "outsiders". On the basis of a wealth of primary and secondary sources, including meeting records of policy makers and practitioners, surveys, interviews and court verdicts, the book zooms in on forensic psychiatrists' role in the disappearance of criminally insane defendants from Japanese criminal courts; social workers' new role in diverting a growing number of elderly, mentally disturbed repeat offenders from prison; the therapeutic dimension added to Japanese criminal justice proceedings with the introduction of a system of victim participation as well as the increasingly important role of forensic scientists' contributions, notably DNA evidence, in Japanese courts. Finally, it examines lay judges' contributions to sentencing practices as well as how these lay judges make sense of the other outsiders' contributions. On the basis of very recent social and legal developments the book provides an original contribution to understandings of Japanese criminal justice, as well as more general socio-legal debates on the role of extra-legal knowledge in criminal justice. The book will be of value within BA and MA level courses on and to students and researchers of Japanese law and society as well as comparative criminal justice and socio-legal theory.

**Erik Herber** is university lecturer in socio-legal studies and criminology at the Leiden University Institute of Area Studies (LIAS) as well as the Leiden University Law School. He holds a MA in Japanese Studies from Leiden University (The Netherlands) and a MA and PhD in sociology from Tsukuba University (Japan). His main research interests concern crime and criminal justice in Japan, with a particular focus on the role of citizens and other non-juridical professionals in the prevention and adjudication of crime as well as the reintegration of offenders. He is also interested in trends in policies and responses to crime in a comparative perspective, as well as human rights in Japan, in theory and practice.

# Lay and Expert Contributions to Japanese Criminal Justice

Erik Herber

Routledge
Taylor & Francis Group
LONDON AND NEW YORK

First published 2019
by Routledge
2 Park Square, Milton Park, Abingdon, Oxon OX14 4RN

and by Routledge
52 Vanderbilt Avenue, New York, NY 10017

First issued in paperback 2020

*Routledge is an imprint of the Taylor & Francis Group, an informa business*



*British Library Cataloguing-in-Publication Data*
A catalogue record for this book is available from the British Library

*Library of Congress Cataloging-in-Publication Data*
Names: Herber, Erik, author.
Title: Lay and expert contributions to Japanese criminal justice / By Erik Herber.
Description: New York, NY : Routledge, 2019. | Includes bibliographical references and index.
Identifiers: LCCN 2018049127 | ISBN 9781138063662 (hbk)
Subjects: LCSH: Evidence, Expert—Japan. | Lay judges—Japan. | Forensic scientists—Japan. | Criminal justice, Administration of—Japan.
Classification: LCC KNX1626 .H47 2019 | DDC 345.52—dc23
LC record available at https://lccn.loc.gov/2018049127

ISBN 13: 978-0-367-66213-4 (pbk)
ISBN 13: 978-1-138-06366-2 (hbk)

Typeset in Galliard
by Apex CoVantage, LLC

# Contents

# Acknowledgments

My gratitude goes out to the public prosecutors, lawyers and judges who were kind enough to take the time to answer my questions and share their knowledge, thoughts and opinions with me. Without them this book could not have been written. My colleagues at Leiden University, Lindsay Black, Kasia Cwiertka, Aya Ezawa, Saori Shibata, Bryce Wakefield and Guita Winkel have generously provided me with their input. I would like to thank them, as well as the following persons who have in different ways been of help, inspiration and encouragement: Sanae Chida, Atsushi Honjō, Makoto Ibusuki, Takeshi Izumaru, Rens Jaspers, David Johnson, Kayo Konagai, Peter Mascini, Rumi Nakagawa, Yōji Nakatani, Masahiko Saeki and Tamono Tsujikawa. I would however like to especially thank Jennifer Connelly for her invaluable help and input. Finally, to my beloved Renate and Sarah: your company and support have meant the world.

# Introduction

Much is changing in the realm of Japanese criminal justice. To name just a few developments: in 2008 a system of victim participation was introduced. The year 2009 saw the introduction of a mixed lay judge system, in accordance with which lay and professional judges now together decide on defendants' guilt and the appropriate sentence, for a specific category of serious offenses. Reforms enacted in 2017 have allowed for social workers to play an institutionalized part in providing support for often elderly and mentally disturbed repeat offenders. These and other developments have resulted in a growing involvement of legal "outsiders" – persons without legal training or background – in Japanese criminal justice. They join the ranks of other legal "outsiders" playing a part in Japanese criminal justice. These outsiders and their contributions are the focus of this book.

When legal outsiders present their own perspectives and knowledge within criminal proceedings, they do so as a part of the role they are assigned to play, by virtue of their various non-legal backgrounds, perspectives and expertise. The "outsiders" referred to here are therefore outsiders only in the sense that they do not possess legal background and expertise. Nevertheless, in spite of their role being an assigned one, its impact is unclear before it is played out. Outsiders' contributions may be the key to preventing or correcting a miscarriage of justice. They may be of pivotal importance when deciding upon the right sanction or treatment. Depending on the outsider, the information and perspectives he or she provides may also be set aside.

How and why do outsiders' contributions affect or fail to affect the legal decisions ultimately taken? How do they impact the roles as traditionally played by the legal insiders: lawyers, prosecutors and judges? These questions, which are as much about the outsiders as they are about the insiders interacting with them and their contributions, have received only little and fragmented attention. This book addresses these questions against the background of the social developments and legal reforms that translated into outsiders' new or changed roles, so as to make sense of why outsiders' roles play out the way they do, and how in practice these roles relate to the aims behind them.

Pursuing these issues will help further our understanding of Japanese criminal justice in times of change. Doing so will also have important implications, however, for more general, long-standing debates on the role of extra-legal knowledge in law in general, and the administration of justice in particular. Michel Foucault has famously argued that "today, criminal justice functions and justifies itself only by this perpetual reference to something other than itself, by this unceasing reinscription in non-juridical systems. Its fate is to be redefined by knowledge" (1978: 22). Others have highlighted the autonomy of legal thinking and practice, and that any facts will need to be legally constituted, before they can take effect within law (Luhmann, 1987, 1991; Bourdieu, 1987; Van Krieken, 2004). Still others have brought into focus different forms of hybrid knowledge within the realm of legal decision-making (Valverde, 2009; Barrera López, 2009). The knowledge and perspectives that either redefine criminal justice, or that are legally reconstituted or are blended with legal common sense – and of course: these are hardly either/or possibilities – are typically presented by legal outsiders.

The debates on these issues are important in terms of improving theoretical understandings of legal practices. Their undiminished relevance, also in a Japanese criminal justice context, further resides in the already alluded to fact that they open up a window on the knowledge and perspectives that constitute these practices, allowing also for a better understanding of the terms in which Japanese criminal justice is administered, and the "Japanese way of justice" (Johnson, 2002).

The increased involvement of legal outsiders has come about against the background of policy and legal reforms implemented in especially the past decade. In examining legal outsiders' roles, this book also addresses these reforms – reforms that have different origins: some were implemented as part of a large scale, top down overhaul of the Japanese legal system, others were driven by citizens' activism or triggered by very specific incidents and individuals' efforts. By examining to what extent and how outsiders' knowledge and perspectives have contributed to the achieving of reform goals, this book will further our understanding of the impact of the legal reforms that have been implemented (cf. Miyazawa, 2017, Foote, 2011 and references provided therein). In doing so it addresses, in other words, the question of how and how much Japanese criminal justice has changed.

This book aims to make sense of its subject – outsiders' criminal justice role within the context of legal and social change – in its own right rather than in comparison with similar or dissimilar developments or reforms implemented elsewhere, within criminal justice systems outside of Japan. Still, those advocating reform in Japan have often done so in reference to criminal justice practices outside of Japan, while developments outside of Japan have certainly played a role in the coming about of some of the Japanese criminal justice developments addressed in this book. Furthermore, the theoretical questions regarding the role of extra-legal perspectives and knowledge were inspired by non-Japanese legal contexts. And last but certainly not least: this Dutch author's assumptions about what matters and what does not have inevitably shaped the focus of this book, that is accordingly characterized by implicit or explicit comparative perspectives.

The following chapters are attentive to international trends and developments where relevant, as well as the fact that labels, concepts and ideas developed in connection with, say, New Zealand or French contexts cannot be expected to be similarly applicable to a Japanese one. Nevertheless, the departing assumption in this book is that talking through these ideas may aid us, as a heuristic exercise, when trying to make analytical sense of the issues focused on in this book. Doing so additionally allows for a rare contribution on the earlier mentioned "general" theoretical questions on the basis of findings from a Japanese context.

## Outsiders and insiders

When it comes to persons without a legal background playing an assigned role in Japanese criminal justice, especially lay judges have been receiving much attention. While there is indeed much to learn about lay judges' role within criminal justice, and this book also aims to provide an original contribution in this regard, it is important to realize that there are many other legal outsiders whose contribution to Japanese criminal justice has been receiving far less attention. The already mentioned participating victims and social workers constitute other such outsiders. But besides these there are also the contributions to the criminal process made by forensic psychiatrists and other scientific experts to consider.

These outsiders play their part both in and outside the courtroom. Participating victims' role, for example, begins long before any court hearing. The role played by forensic psychiatrists on the other hand, may begin before any court hearing but also end there, in the investigation stage. In order to be able to address outsiders' roles within Japanese criminal justice in their different facets, this book will examine these roles from the stage of the pre-trial investigation to the moment a verdict and sentence are handed down.

In fulfilling their role, the different outsiders interact with the main "insider protagonists" of these stages of criminal procedure: judges, prosecutors and lawyers. The various outsiders provide legal professionals with information and knowledge on the basis of which they, at times together with the outsiders, make their case and their decisions. It is accordingly in connection with the insider protagonists that this book addresses the roles of the legal outsiders.

## The structure of this book

The previous paragraphs only very briefly referred to the changes that translated into legal outsiders' new or changed roles. Chapter 1 presents a more in-depth introduction of the general context within which such change came about. In doing so this chapter paints a picture of the issues that are relevant and at stake when trying to make sense, in later chapters, of the impact of legal outsiders' roles. It in addition introduces the developments specifically relevant for each outsider's role, developments that are further pursued in the following chapters.

Chapters 2–6 are each focused on the contributions of a particular legal outsider, in connection with the legal professionals' striving to make sense of these contributions. Chapter 2 examines forensic psychiatrists' role within the process of establishing suspects' and defendants' criminal responsibility, or rather the extent to which such responsibility is diminished or absent, focusing in particular on the disappearance of the diminished responsible or criminally insane[1] offender from public criminal trials in Japan.

In close connection with this issue, Chapter 3 addresses social workers' role in providing "support at the entrance" – that is, in providing support for especially elderly and mentally disturbed repeat offenders, whose numbers in prison have in recent years been growing. Social workers' role here is that of providing support for such offenders to facilitate, when possible, their diversion from prison.

Chapter 4 looks into crime victims' new role and its impact on court proceedings as well as criminal justice dispositions, by examining the extent to which crime victims have been making use of the possibilities provided by the legal reforms, as well as the impact of the therapeutic jurisprudence dimension added to criminal justice proceedings, with victims' new role. Chapter 5 addresses the criminal justice contributions of forensic scientists, notably DNA evidence, but especially also what both professional and lay judges make of these contributions when they may not necessarily possess a full understanding. Chapters 2, 4 and 5 each deal with forensic psychiatrists', participating victims' and forensic scientists' roles, respectively. Given that since the introduction of the lay judge system in 2009 it is now up to professional and lay judges to jointly make sense of these outsiders' contributions, these chapters will also highlight how these judges do so. In this sense these three chapters already address different aspects of lay judges' role. Chapter 6 further pursues that role, focusing especially on how lay and professional judges go about deciding on a defendant's sentence. The book ends with a concluding discussion.

## Methodology

For this book I have made use of a variety of sources that are also outlined in this book's six chapters. I have made much use of the transcripts of meetings of policy makers, practitioners and others involved. For Chapter 1 I have made use of the meeting records of, among others, the Justice System Reform Council, on the basis of whose recommendations the lay judge system was introduced. These documents allow for insight into the motivations behind reforms such as these, which are relevant when considering the extent to which these reforms played out as planned.

For Chapters 2, 4, 5 and 6, I have made use of the transcripts of 363 "meetings for the exchange of opinions" (*ikenkōkankai*) that were held nationwide in Japanese District Courts between 2011 and 2017. These meetings, which still continue to be held today, typically lasted two hours and were led by a district court judge. Besides around 5–11 lay judges who had not necessarily participated in the same trial, participants typically also included a judge, a lawyer and a prosecutor who had participated in one of the trials. At some meetings members of

1 These are loose English translations of the Japanese terms *shinshinkōjaku* ("weakened mind") and *shinshinsōshitsu* ("loss of mind").

the press were also present to ask questions at the end. Lay judges were typically asked to first give their general impression and opinion about their participation, after which the discussions focused on various aspects of trial procedures, such as opening statements, investigation of the evidence, arguments, deliberation, verdict, etc., after which the former lay judges were asked to relay a message for future lay judges. Members of the press were often also present, and could at the end of the meetings ask questions. Recurring themes were in addition those of what had been easy or rather difficult to understand for lay judges, as well as the extent to which they had experienced their participation as a burden. Discussed in the meetings were also the contributions made by forensic psychiatrists and other forensic scientists and participating victims. These meeting records accordingly provide an impression of how especially lay judges have been dealing with the contributions of the other legal outsiders. The relevant chapters further outline how references to specific outsider roles were analyzed.

For Chapter 4 I have in addition made use of transcripts of 12 two-and-a-half-hour-long meetings organized by the Japanese Ministry of Justice in which legal professionals who had participated in victim participation trials as well as representatives of victim interest groups shared their experiences and exchanged opinions about the system of victim participation, therefore allowing for insights into both professionals' and participating victims' perspectives on victims' role in court.

Chapter 4 is furthermore based on findings from surveys on victim participation, both published and unpublished, conducted by the Japan Federation of Legal Bar Associations (JFBA) and local bar associations. Chapters 1, 4 and 6 in addition draw on surveys conducted by the Supreme Court of Japan on victim participation, lay judges' participation as well as sentencing. For especially Chapter 5 but also Chapter 6, I have made use of documents compiled by the Supreme Court Legal Research and Training Institute, the institute where all Japanese legal professionals receive part of their training. These documents are aimed at being a source of reference for legal professionals and provide an insight into the formal Supreme Court line on various topics, but here especially on the role of scientists' contributions, that is: scientific evidence in criminal trials, as well as advice for professional judges involved in lay judge trials. For the purpose of this book I have between 2011 and 2017 interviewed, corresponded and talked with prosecutors, judges, lawyers, lay judges and social workers. All chapters are informed by relevant Ministry of Justice and Supreme Court statistics and criminal trial verdicts. Translations are the author's, unless otherwise provided.

## References

Barrera López, Leticia (2009). *Performing the court: forms and practices of legal knowledge-making in Argentina*. Doctoral dissertation, Cornell University.

Bourdieu, Pierre (1987). The force of law: towards a sociology of the juridical field. *Hastings Law Journal* 38: 814–853.

Foote, Daniel H. (2011). *Law in Japan: a turning point*. Seattle: University of Washington Press.

Foucault, Michel (1978). *Discipline and punish*, trans. Alan Sheridan. New York: Vintage.

Johnson, David T. (2002). *The Japanese way of justice: prosecuting crime in Japan*. Oxford: Oxford University Press.

Luhmann, Niklas (1987). Unity of the legal system, in Gunther Teubner (ed.), *Autopoietic law-a new approach to law and society*. Vol. 8. Berlin: Walter de Gruyter: 12–35.

Luhmann, Niklas (1991). Operational closure and structural coupling: he differentiation of the legal system. *Cardozo Law Review* 13: 1419–1441.

Miyazawa, Setsuo (2017). East Asian court reform on trial: introduction to the symposium. *Washington International Law Journal* 27(1): 1–6.

Valverde, M. (2009). *Law's dream of a common knowledge*. Princeton, NJ: Princeton University Press.

Van Krieken, R. (2004). *Legal reasoning as a field of knowledge production: Luhmann, Bourdieu and law's autonomy*. University of Sydney eScholarship repository website. Available at: http://prijipati.library.usyd.edu.au/bitstream/2123/967/1/legal%20reasoning.pdf. Website last visited 31 August 2018.

# 1 Forces of change

## Introduction

In 1985, Ryūichi Hirano, emeritus law professor and former president of Tokyo University, presented what he called a diagnosis of the Japanese Code of Criminal Procedure. Comparing Japan with the United States and Europe, he found the Japanese criminal process to be "rather abnormal" and "diseased", and concluded that "criminal trials in Japan are really quite hopeless" (1989: 129, 142).[1] Coming from a highly respected expert from Japan's top university, Hirano's diagnosis provoked much discussion and debate. It also sowed the seeds of the change that was to come, change that looked like the "cure" that Hirano proposed. Still, Hirano's diagnosis was by no means the only impetus for legal change. There were in fact many different driving forces, originating both within and outside of Japan. This chapter will zoom in on those driving forces: the incidents and occurrences that either had an impact on or gave birth to the roles played by the criminal justice outsiders that are the focus of this book. Here, Hirano's diagnosis is a good place to start. Not only because of the debate it provoked, but also as a reference point to return to when assessing the impact of criminal justice outsiders' roles.

As Section 1 of this chapter will show, Hirano's diagnosis is especially relevant for discussions on the legal reforms that were implemented based on the recommendations of the Justice System Reform Council (JSRC) issued in 2001. The recommendations of this Council ushered in an era of groundbreaking legal reforms, notably the introduction in 2009 of a system of lay participation, meaning that from then on a panel of lay and professional judges was to decide on the innocence or guilt, as well as the sentencing, of those accused of crimes belonging to a category of serious offenses designated to be adjudicated on the basis of the new system. Many of these reforms were introduced in reference to "the will of the people", "the expectations of the people" and their "sound common sense". Nevertheless, as the first part of this chapter will show, these can be characterized as reforms that were planned and introduced from above through the

1 As the 1985 article is not digitally available, I have for the purpose of this chapter made use of the English translation that was published in 1989.

JSRC. On the basis of its 63 meetings, the JSRC had determined what reforms would be in the best interests of the Japanese people and of Japanese society and its economy (JSRC, 1999–2001). Section 1 will thus show how the JSRC caused lay judges to re-enter the Japanese criminal justice picture, even if there were no popular calls for their return.

The JSRC was not the only source of legal reform, however. Besides the setting up of the JSRC, Japan in the late 1990s also saw the rise of popular movements lobbying for legal change, notably higher punishments for offenders as well as more rights for victims of crime within the criminal justice system – movements that caught the attention of the media as well as politicians. Japanese society thus developed its own brand of *penal populism* (cf. Roberts et al., 2002; Pratt, 2007) as public opinion, or representations thereof, came to play a pivotal role in bringing about reforms that allowed for harsher punishment of criminal offenders.

Section 2 of this chapter will address this Japanese-style penal populism and the legal reforms that it has brought forth, notably the new criminal justice role for victims of crime as well as the reforms relevant for lay judges' sentencing decisions. The reforms addressed in these Parts 1 and 2 are two of the most talked about and highly publicized Japanese criminal justice reforms of the last decades. Addressing these reforms is important in specific connection with the criminal justice roles they directly affected or brought about, namely those of lay and professional judges and crime victims and public prosecutors. It is also important, however, in view of the more general criminal justice context that Sections 1 and 2 will in the process bring into focus, a context that is also relevant when addressing the roles of the other outsiders that are the focus of this book.

Section 3 will address developments relevant for the roles of social workers, scientific experts and forensic psychiatrists in Japanese criminal justice. It will show that technological and scientific developments have resulted in an increasingly important role for these experts especially, but not exclusively, in relation to DNA evidence. The new criminal justice role of social workers, on the other hand, has come about against the background of very different developments, namely a growing awareness of a population of repeat offenders who without social workers' help have little way of breaking the cycle of offending, getting caught and punished increasingly harshly with each offense, and then reoffending upon release from prison. Finally, it will highlight how a growing societal awareness of offenders with mental health issues has culminated in relevant legal reforms and a changed role for forensic psychiatrists. The issues addressed in Section 3 are thus more role-specific than the developments addressed in Sections 1 and 2 that also more generally pertain to the criminal justice environment in which the outsiders function. Nevertheless, as Section 3 will show, all these developments interrelate, even if only because they will eventually interact in the same lay judge courtroom.

## 1. A prelude to lay participation

Back, then, to Hirano's diagnosis of the Japanese criminal process. Hirano presented this diagnosis some 35 years after the adoption, in 1948, of a new Code of Criminal Procedure.[2] Around that time, in the mid-1980s, the way in which that Code was interpreted and applied had more or less stabilized. That being the case, the timing was right to see what in practice had become of the legal changes that the 1948 Code had introduced. That new Code, compiled and implemented while Japan was placed under the authority of the Supreme Commander of the Allied Powers, had formally changed the structure of Japanese criminal proceedings.

Under the old (1922) Code these proceedings had been shaped by inquisitorial principles, on the basis of which the state power that hands down sentences will by itself conduct the criminal investigation. Here, judges are required to actively take part in the search for the truth. In line with these principles, Japanese prosecutors were not just a party in criminal proceedings. They were also overseers of these proceedings, in which evidence was collected through the exercise of judicial power. Suspects were objects of investigation rather than carriers of rights. Formally this all changed with the new (1948) Code, that adopted so-called accusatorial, or adversarial, principles, that dictates, among other things that criminal proceedings will start when a plaintiff files a complaint against a defendant, and consequently the plaintiff and defendant will, as equal parties, oppose each other in court. Here, the judge is a passive adjudicator (Miyazawa, 2002: 1; Ito, 2012: 1246–1248; cf. van den Wyngaert, 2009: 514).

Examining how in practice the new Code was functioning, Hirano famously highlighted that in Japan courts are "places that confirm that the defendant is guilty". (Hirano, 1989: 129) Indeed, looking at Japan's famously high guilty rates of around 98%, it was hard to argue with Hirano's assessment, even though there is room to argue about the meaning of these percentages.[3] As Hirano also notes, the Japanese conviction rate is mainly the result of the very high level of suspicion that is required for prosecutors to indict a suspect, as prosecutors normally only indict when they are convinced of the defendant's guilt, as well as their ability to prove this guilt in court. The need to set the hurdle for prosecution that high has been explained in terms of the social stigma that attaches to being arrested and charged in Japan.

For Hirano the high suspicion requirement was one of the causes of the diseased and hopeless state of Japanese criminal procedure, noting that as a consequence of this requirement, the "real substance" of Japanese criminal procedure had come to lie in the pre-trial stage of this procedure, which can be characterized as an inquisitorial process performed by prosecutors and police (Hirano, 1989:

2 Code of Criminal Procedure (1948/2018). *This code of criminal procedure* (No. 131, Shōwa 23, 10 July). Available at http://law.e-gov.go.jp/htmldata/S23/S23HO131.html. Website accessed 31–8–2018.

3 Chapter 6 will further address the calculation of percentages of conviction rates. As also noted there, it is important not to translate the percentage of defendants found innocent, often less than 1%, in a conviction rate of more than 99%. The gap between defendants found guilty and those found innocent is filled with persons transferred to other courts, notably family courts, cases dropped, no jurisdiction, etc., etc. See Chapter 6 and references provided there.

131). During this process, suspects or defendants were often subjected to long hours of questioning, in order to obtain the "king of evidence", a detailed confession statement. Such statements by the suspect and witnesses, which were typically not *ad verbatim* records of interrogations, but rather carefully constructed prosecutorial representations of such interrogations, would subsequently play a pivotal role in the fact finding procedures in court. Given, however, that judges would typically study such written statements and other files outside the courtroom, fact finding procedures could be said to at least in part take place outside of the courtroom. In view of the importance attached to such dossiers, the practices have been famously characterized as "trials by dossier" (Hirano, 1989: 138). Within this process there was little room to maneuver for the defense. In fact, as it seemed that no matter what they did the result would be the same, more and more lawyers were leaving the field of criminal defense (Hirano, 1999: 2).

Unsurprisingly, prosecutors viewed Japanese criminal justice in a rather different light. For example, to prosecutors the small percentage of defendants found innocent proved that they, the prosecutors, by and large succeeded in their duty of not charging those who should not be charged, shielding them from unnecessary social sanctions.[4] Where Hirano advocated "simple investigations" and "cool and collected" prosecutions (referred to in Tsujimoto et al., 2017a: 10), Prosecutors' ethics dictated a thorough investigation and a careful prosecution, as well as a dedication to substantive truth finding.

Matsuo Kōya, the legal scholar who in JSRC meeting 43 gave the lay judge system (*saiban'in seido*) its name, famously qualified Prosecutors' investigation and prosecution practices, followed by a "trial by dossier" in which judges would carefully go over the written statements and other evidence submitted mostly by the prosecution as "precise justice" or *seimitsu shihō* (JSRC, 2001, meeting 43; cf. Tsujimoto et al., 2017b: 54; Aoki, 2013: 11). While to some this label pointed to the diseased nature of Japanese criminal justice, to others it was rather a badge of honor that showed that prosecutors and judges were living up to the expectations of the Japanese people, who would not have it any other way (cf. Katō, 2015: 20; Aoki, 2013: 25). While the expectations of the Japanese people are often referred to in explaining and justifying the Japanese precise justice, prosecutors have however also explained their practices in more practical terms. In the chaotic years directly following the end of the Second World War, crime rates had skyrocketed, causing the investigative authorities to be overburdened. In order to manage and process the large volume of cases swiftly and correctly,

4 Interviews 2011–2017; cf also Shihōkenshūjokensatsukyōkanshitsuhen, 2015: 9); Given that people who are arrested and indicted are typically found guilty, it is not all that surprising that those arrested and indicted are subjected to different kinds of social sanctions (*shakaiteki seisai*), such as media shaming and getting fired. Social sanctions may be a valid reason for cautious charging policies; they can however also be seen as a consequence of those charging policies. The problem of the burden and potential social sanctions that suspects and defendants in Japan suffer accordingly qualifies as a typical chicken and egg conundrum.

"there was no other option than to rely on dossiers". In addition, at the time many judges were still accustomed to the pre-war inquisitorial practices, based on the old Code. They after all tended to attach special importance to case files, feeling uneasy about forming their convictions on the basis of in court statements (Aoki, 2013: 26).

Even though judges' role thus should not be overlooked, "precise justice" could, depending on one's perspective, also be labeled prosecutor justice (cf. Aoki, 2013: 19; Johnson, 2012: 36). Prosecutors have the discretionary authority to decide who is to be prosecuted and who is not – an issue that will be further addressed below – but once they file an indictment, prosecutors secure convictions in around 98% of all cases. For all intents and purposes it is they who determine suspects' and defendants' fate. Be that as it may, within prosecutorial and judicial circles too there have been those pointing out the need for reforms, noting that criminal justice practices were moving away from the ideals of the reformed Code of Criminal Procedure, as criminal trials had been turned into empty shells, in which the principles of immediacy and orality had lost power (Kameyama, 1998: 13; Ishimatsu, 1989). Even though the new Code had formally introduced a Common Law approach to criminal justice, Continental, inquisitorial practices persisted. Tsugio Kameyama, a former prosecutor and judge, further notes that prosecutors have become so much focused on avoiding non-guilty verdicts, that as a result courts are robbed of the opportunity to speak out on matters of great societal interests, as the cases in which they could have done so never reach them, as a result of Prosecutors' careful prosecution practices (1998: 15–16).

Still, this was not just an academic, socio-legal debate about black letter law versus law in action. Yes, Hirano presented his diagnosis at a point in time in which the manner in which the Code was being interpreted and applied appeared "nearly stable" (1989: 129). Thus, 35 years after the enactment of this Code was a good time to reflect on what the new, post-war Code had in practice brought. This was however also a decade in which the nation was shocked by four highly publicized miscarriages of justice.

In these cases the defendants had initially all confessed guilt but had later on denied the crime of which they were accused. All four had received death sentences and had for decades been awaiting their execution. As a result of their own continued efforts as well as those of their lawyers, however, they were eventually found innocent on retrial (cf. Foote, 1992). Hirano did not specifically address these cases. He did however address the characteristics of Japanese criminal justice that allowed for miscarriages of justice such as these to happen – characteristics that were increasingly becoming topics of debate in the media, among academics as well as legal professionals.

One such topic concerned the role of confessions of guilt in Japanese criminal justice. The role that confessions of guilt played in the *big four* was not necessarily related to any specific characteristic of these cases. It was rather symptomatic of the importance more generally attached to confessions, which is explainable, first of all, in terms of their evidentiary value, as the *king of evidence* (Hirano,

1989: 135).[5] A *remorseful* confession, however, is also an act that allows suspects or defendants to show their awareness of and enduring commitment to the norms they have violated. By remorsefully confessing, they are taking the first step on the road to rehabilitation. One confession may of course be more genuinely remorseful than another. What is more, given the importance more generally attached to apologizing in Japanese social life, the act of expressing remorse could also be said to be something of an unavoidable ritual that people have to go through after having been caught doing something wrong (cf. Wagatsuma & Rosett, 1986; Obuchi, 2015; Kovacs, 2016). Genuine or ritualistic or not, remorseful confessions of guilt are in any case an important condition for Prosecutors' large scale diversion practices.

In accordance with article 248 of the Japanese Code of Criminal Procedure, prosecutors in Japan have the authority to suspend a suspect's prosecution, even if there is enough evidence available to indict. When exercising this authority, prosecutors need to decide if it is *opportune* to go forward with a prosecution, taking into account matters such as the suspect's age, the seriousness of the offense and indeed also whether the suspect has made a remorseful confession of guilt. The enshrinement of this principle of opportunity, and the fact that it is so widely applied – in 2016 56.5% of all Penal Code offenses were disposed of this way (Ministry of Justice, 2017) – could be seen as a testimony to the formal commitment to diversion, and by extension, rehabilitation and reintegration (Johnson, 2002: 107–118).

Given, however, that more than half of Penal Code offenses are disposed of this way, it is clear that the suspension of prosecution should be considered as an institutionalized practice, regardless of its seemingly informal character. Given also that this practice depends on the availability of a confession of guilt, one could accordingly also say that the smooth processing of more than half of all suspects depends on these suspects confessing guilt.

What is more, the system's dependence on confessions of guilt does not end there, but also very much applies to those cases in which prosecutors do decide to go forward with a prosecution. In such a case, confessions are, in Hirano's words, *demanded* (1989: 135). They are demanded, that is, to secure a conviction. This explains why 91.5% of the defendants tried before the District Court in 2016 had made a full confession.[6] This percentage thus suggests that confessions are something close to a necessary condition for prosecution. In other words: confessions of guilt are vital for both prosecution and the suspension of prosecution.

---

5 While confessions of guilt are in Japan indeed referred to as the king or queen of evidence (*shōko no ōsama/jyo' ō*), it is important to keep in mind that this expression is a Japanese translation of the Latin phrase *confessio est regina probationum* (the confession is the queen of evidence). Admittedly, this phrase has in and outside Japan come to be associated with an overemphasis on confessions and the coercing of confessions (cf. Langbein, 1978; Fisher & Rosen-Zvi, 2008; Tsujimoto, 2010; Kingston, 2011).

6 Here, a full confession of guilt is defined as "admitting all allegations at the final (trial) stage, while not claiming the existence of grounds hindering the legal establishment of the crime, or grounds for an exemption of punishment." (Supreme Court of Japan, 2017: 81).

This, then, explains the great lengths that police and prosecutors will go through to obtain a confession. As they go through such great lengths, even innocent people wind up confessing crimes they did not commit, as did the defendants in the "big four" miscarriages of justice.[7] In these cases, all four defendants had initially confessed guilt. As Hirano notes, however, "'voluntary, false confessions' are frequently given" (1989: 137) – leaving aside the problem of persons forced to confess a crime they *did* commit. The problem here, as already noted by Hirano (1989: 137), is that judges are reluctant to throw out a confession that appears reliable, regardless of defendants' claims of having been forced to confess, and regardless of the right against self-incrimination and the right to remain silent (Code of Criminal Procedure [CCP] art. 198.2; 291.3; 311.1; Constitution of Japan art. 38.1[8]; cf. also Foote, 1991; Johnson, 2015).[9] It is typically only when a confession is found to contain statements that are demonstrably false that its voluntariness becomes an issue in court (Hirano, 1989: 137). This way of approaching the voluntariness of a confession of guilt implies that for police and prosecutors the goal (a reliable confession) may in practice justify the means (coercion).

Foote notes that the big four led to debate and comments in the media as well from academics, prosecutors, judges and especially lawyers. The discussions addressed many topics, ranging from the imbalance in power between defense and prosecution to the mindset and role of judges in a system characterized by consistently high conviction rates, and from proposals aimed at more thorough interrogations – in order to ensure more precise and complete confessions of guilt – to proposals concerning restrictions on the procurement and use of confessions.

With regard to the role of the judiciary, there was however one topic that generated much more debate than any other, namely that of reinstating the jury system (Foote, 1992: 72–83).[10] Hirano too considers a lay judge or jury system

7 For an extensive analysis of the big four, see Foote, 1992. Foote's characterization of the way investigators went about their jobs in these cases is worth quoting at length here: "each of the cases involved, at best, lax investigations in which the police and prosecutors jumped to the unsupported conclusion that the respective defendants – who, perhaps not coincidentally, were young, rather poor men with various personal problems – had committed the crimes, and then, either wittingly or not, apparently induced confessions to fit the existing evidence. At worst, they involved suppression of exculpatory evidence and perhaps even actual fabrication of evidence to ensure the convictions" (71, 72).

8 Constitution of Japan (1946). *The text of the constitution* (Shōwa 21, 3 November). Available at: http://elaws.e-gov.go.jp/search/elawsSearch/elaws_search/lsg0500/detail?lawId=321CONSTITUTION&openerCode=1. Website last accessed 31–8–2018.

9 Johnson notes in this regard that "when a wrongful conviction occurs in Japan, a false confession is usually the primary proximate cause", while in addition highlighting some examples from the "steady stream of convictions (. . .) revealed in recent years" (2015: 4–5).

10 "Reinstatement", as from 1928 through 1943 Japan had already had a jury system. Under this system, men over 30 paying a particular (substantive) amount of income tax were eligible to take part in a jury of 12 persons, who heard the evidence and decided on defendants' guilt in trials involving serious offenses (Inouye, 2014: 442; see also Vanoverbeke, 2015: 35–88.

the cure for the "diseased state" of Japanese criminal justice (1989: 142, see also Aoki, 2013: 47–55). What is more, under the instruction of Kōichi Yaguchi, Chief Justice of the Supreme Court, the judiciary in fact in the late 1980s began researching the functioning of lay participation systems in different Western countries (Inouye, 2014: 445).

The big four thus played an important role in adding momentum to discussions on lay participation, sowing the seeds of legal change and a new role for citizens in the criminal justice process. For the purposes of this book the big four are also significant, however, in view of the important role that scientists and scientific evidence played in both the reopening of the four cases and casting doubt on the original (forensic) evidence (Foote, 1992: 68). The big four accordingly alert us to the beginning of an era in which science and scientific experts were to play an increasingly important role in criminal justice.

Coming back to the issue of lay participation: regardless of all the talk, debate and research on this topic, it was far from obvious that this would all eventually lead to actual legal change. Proposals regarding major reform normally travel the following path. First, the Minister of Justice refers such proposals to the Legislative Deliberation Council (LDC), which is established under the Ministry of Justice. Or to be more precise: the Minister of Justice refers the proposals to one of the LDC's different subcommittees. These include subcommittees on for instance sex offenses and juvenile law. Members include representatives of the Ministry of Justice, the judiciary as well as other governmental agencies, practicing attorneys, but also academics, typically law professors. All in all, many of the members share a mainstream perspective on criminal justice, in line with that of the establishment. These subcommittees draft recommendations that, when approved by the LDC, are presented to the Minister of Justice as the LDC's final recommendation (Miyazawa & Hirayama, 2017: 154–155). This way of making criminal justice policy implied that any policy change would be conditional on the approval of the establishment players. Vanoverbeke in this regard however also refers to the polarization that characterized the relations between the different key players in policy making, notably prosecutors (represented by the Ministry of Justice [MOJ], judges[represented by the General Secretariat of the Supreme Court], and practicing attorneys [represented by the Japan Federation of Bar Associations {JFBA}]) As a result of such polarization and the pro-establishment bias in policy making, legal change had until the 1970s been only been incremental (Vanoverbeke, 2015: 17–19).

The next two decades, however, saw a convergence of factors conducive to legal change breakthroughs. In the 1980s, for example, then Prime Minister Nakasone's political leadership allowed for an increase in influence of non-bureaucrats on policy making processes, made possible especially by the participation in deliberative councils of academics, opinion makers hand-picked by Nakasone himself. Nakasone's approach did not only allow for increased Prime Ministerial control over these councils, but also for more active leadership on the part of business leaders and academics (Vanoverbeke, 2015: 21).

Especially important as a force for legal change, however, was the Keidanren, the Japan Business Federation. The Keidanren is an organization with a membership that now comprises 47 regional economic organizations, 109 industrial associations and 1,376 representative companies of Japan (Keidanren, 2018). The Keidanren has been an important player in the political field, as it has continuously provided support to the Liberal Democratic Party (LDP), the party that has ruled almost uninterrupted from 1955 on, and "consequently, the LDP usually accommodated *Keidanren* interests" (Miyazawa, 2013: 314). The Keidanren had from the 1960s on already been lobbying for deregulation of business activities, increased transparency and legal accountability of administrative agencies that had for a long time exerted influence on (big) business practices, with minimal judicial oversight (Miyazawa, 2013: 314; Ginsburg, 2001: 591–596). These lobbying efforts finally paid off when in 1993 the Administrative Procedure Act and other transparency increasing measures were introduced (Ginsburg, 2001: 599). In the late 1990s, against the background of Japan's economic crisis, the Keidanren again pushed for reforms, issuing a statement of opinion regarding judicial reform in which it emphasized the importance of a fully functional legal system for the protection of people's rights and the stable pursuit of economic activities, and that this was in fact a necessary condition for Japan to be trusted by the international community (Keidanren, 1998). In this regard the Keidanren proposed, among other things, an increase in judges allowing for a speedier handling of the civil and administrative cases that had increased explosively since the burst of Japan's economic bubble, as well as a reform of the legal education, so that it would be more in line with the needs of Japan's economic society (Keidanren, 1998). In the meantime, the LDP was preparing its own report on legal reform. Differences in tone and emphasis aside, the proposals presented in this report were very similar to those of the Keidanren.[11]

The proposals presented by the LDP and the Keidanren were very much about legal reforms that would be beneficial to business interests. The Keidanren report does in fact not touch upon issues of criminal justice, while the LDP in this regard only notes that "appropriate attention should be paid also to the criminal defense system, in connection with the protection of the people's rights through appropriate defense activities", and that measures to effectively deal with specific forms of crime are indispensable (LDP report, 1998: 5 and 7). These proposal are nevertheless of great importance for the present discussion, as they created opportunities for other forms of reform (cf. Miyazawa, 2013: 316) – reforms that had been heavily discussed and debated, but that had never materialized – reforms such as reintroducing a system of lay participation in criminal justice.

---

11 The report compiled by the LDP special research committee on the legal system, which is a subcommittee of the LDP Policy Research Council, is available at: www.veritas-law.jp/ronbun_doc/20090929133643_1.pdf. Website last visited 30–8–2018.

### *1.1 Establishment of the Justice System Reform Council*

As legal reform was becoming more and more of a political priority and expectations for reform were rising, the government established the Justice System Reform Council (JSRC), on the basis of legislation enacted by the Diet in July 1999.[12] According to that legislation, the main task of JSRC was to "consider fundamental measures necessary for justice reform and justice infrastructure arrangement by defining the role of the Japanese administration of justice in the 21st century. The agenda of the Council may include the realization of a more accessible and user-friendly justice system, *public participation in the justice system*, redefinition of the legal profession and reinforcement of its function" (Act Concerning the Establishment of the Justice System Reform Council, art. 2 – my emphasis).

In order to guarantee that it would be able to operate independently, the JSRC was established under the Cabinet rather than the MOJ. In addition, among its 13 members there were only three *former* legal professionals, in addition to three professors at law and seven members of academic standing in various fields, which included business people, representatives of labor and consumer organizations as well as a novelist, the aim being that the voice of people of every class in Japan would be fully reflected (JSRC, 1999). This last aim was in line also with the JSRC objective that "every person shall grow out of the sense of being a governed object and shall participate in making a free and fair society in mutual cooperation as an autonomous governing subject with social responsibility in hand" (JSRC, 1999). The JSRC aims were thus about much more than reforming the law so that it might more easily serve people's individual and business interests. They were also about providing opportunities for citizens to play an active role in society as responsible citizens.

At the same time, an important and recurring theme in the 63 JSRC meetings was that of reforming the legal system in such a way that this system would meet people's expectations.[13] Here, it was not obvious to the different members that with regard to criminal justice reintroducing lay participation would be an effective way to pursue this goal. Not all members were enthusiastic about the idea of a jury system, in view of the burden that such a system would in their view place on citizens, the question of whether a system of lay participation would actually suit Japanese society, but also in view of the risk of miscarriages of justice that might come with having such a system (JSRC meeting 31). Former JSRC member Masahito Inouye writes in fact that lay participation had been put on the

12 To be more precise: the Act Concerning the Establishment of the Justice System Reform Council (Act No. 68, promulgated on 9 June 1999. See: https://japan.kantei.go.jp/policy/sihou/singikai/991221_e.html. Website last visited 30-8-2018.

13 The transcripts (in Japanese) of all 63 meetings are available at: www.kantei.go.jp/jp/sihouseido/gijiroku-dex.html. Website last visited 30–8–2018.

agenda "mainly on the initiatives of bar association people who had been longing for a jury system" (Inouye, 2014: 447)[14] In the end, however, these people were to get what they longed for. How this came about is a question that Inouye struggles to answer. His description of the JSRC's deliberative process on the issue of lay participation is worth quoting at length here:

> Although I engaged myself in the JSRC's discussion as one of its thirteen members and served as a reporter on the subject at the final stage, it is not evident or easy to specify what really made this [the reintroduction of lay participation – EH] happen. At the beginning, there seemed to be a sharp division of opinion between several members of the JSRC who were enthusiastic for a jury system and the others who were cautious or negative about it. Most of them, however, shared a view that the existing justice system, which was too exclusive to professionals, should reflect regular citizens' sense and feelings more keenly and that increased public involvement in some form or other should help not only for that purpose but also for the people themselves to identify with the justice system. After twists and turns, the JSRC reached the conclusion that an own style of popular participation in criminal trials should be adopted in order to improve the quality of justice done by the court in terms of effectively reflecting "the sound social common sense of the public". Evaluating positively the general quality of existing criminal trials by professional judges, the JSRC thought that citizens' collaboration with them should make it much better.

It is however important to keep in mind here, as Inouye also notes in the same article, that besides the "legal bar association people", within the judiciary too the interest in the idea of reintroducing lay participation had been growing. Furthermore, through its Judiciary Committee the House of Representatives had instructed the JSRC to "thoroughly deliberate on important issues regarding the justice system under debate such as (. . .) public participation in the justice system" (quoted in JSRC, 1999). Inouye's quote nevertheless illustrates how divided the JSRC was on this issue.

In its statement, "The Points at Issue in the Justice Reform", the JSRC in addition links its own mission to previous efforts at reform, notably to movements "for institutional reforms that took place since the end of the 1980s", noting that "based on the efforts and results made, it is the mission of the JSRC to create an overall picture of the reform and a specific process to realize it as an answer to the criticisms and expectations of the people for administration of justice". (1999).

The JSRC was to eventually recommend the instatement of a system of lay participation in which professional judges and citizens, as lay judges, would

14 The characters used to write this name, 井上, are usually transcribe as Inoue. As Professor Inouye has however himself chosen a different transcription, this is the transcription that is used in this book.

together deliberate and decide on both a defendant's guilt and the appropriate sentence (JSRC report, 2001: 103). The founding of the JSRC itself and the fact that lay participation was so prominently put on the JSRC agenda are matters that cannot be understood separately from the various developments and debates that took place in the preceding years – especially also the debates on lay participation, for which Hirano's diagnosis planted one of the seeds.[15]

When it came to the reasons why lay participation should be introduced, however, the focus of the JSRC mission and discussions were somewhat different from that of Hirano's diagnosis. As Inouye's earlier quote also shows, the JSRC was first of all concerned with the issue of people's ability to identify with the justice system. From this perspective, the idea of directly involving people in the criminal justice process, and thereby allowing for criminal justice decisions to reflect "regular citizens' sense and feelings" is understandable.

Be that as it may, introducing a system of lay participation would of course necessitate changes in the way criminal trials were conducted. Lay judges could, for example, not be expected to commit themselves to trials that would last years, as criminal trials could do in Japan. Given the limitations in the time available to lay judges, they could also not be expected to carefully read all the often voluminous case files that judges had up until then studied between hearings (cf. JSRC, 2001, meeting 53). So, by necessity the involvement of lay judges would seem to imply an end to "trials by dossier". As the reliance on dossiers would have to become less, and the more immediate fact finding practices in court would have to become more important, the performances of the different players in court might also take on a bigger importance in trial proceedings. In this sense lay participation seemed to imply the promise of change with regard to various characteristics of Japanese criminal justice addressed in Hirano's diagnosis. Chapter 6 of this book, which will be focusing specifically on lay judges' roles, will accordingly also bring into focus to what extent lay participation delivered on its promise of change.

Returning to the JSRC reforms: besides reforming criminal justice into something that people could more easily relate to, the JSRC also endeavored to bring about change that would allow for the criminal justice system to more generally meet their expectations and to be trusted. The JSRC reforms accordingly were not just about lay participation, but also about, for example, increasing the speed with which criminal justice trials were conducted and consolidating a system that would guarantee suspects' access to a public defense counsel,

15 In its statement "The Points at Issue in the Justice Reform", the JSRC links its own mission to previous efforts at reform, notably to movements "for institutional reforms that took place since the end of the 1980s", noting that "based on the efforts and results made, it is the mission of the JSRC to create an overall picture of the reform and a specific process to realize it as an answer to the criticisms and expectation of the people for administration of justice." (quoted in The Points at Issue in the Justice Reform, 1999).

as Japanese law had up until then guaranteed such a right after indictment.[16] Importantly, the JSRC also acknowledged, in its final recommendations, that "it cannot be denied that there are in reality some cases where questioning lacks propriety, arising out of an excessive emphasis on confessions of suspects. Insofar as the mission of the Japanese criminal justice system is to get to the truth of cases under the guarantee of due process of law, questioning of suspects must not be improper, and measures to prevent improper questioning naturally are necessary". In this regard the JSRC report does refer to the possibility of audio and video recordings of interrogations, but it does not go so far as to explicitly recommend recordings, in view of the "significance of the questioning of suspects in the whole structure of criminal procedure", accordingly leaving these matters to be decided in the future (JSRC, 2001). In the years following the JSRC recommendations the issue of recording interrogations has indeed been put on the agenda, and the police and public prosecutors have been videotaping interrogations on an experimental basis.[17] In acknowledging the importance of defense council from the moment a person is suspected of a crime as well as the overemphasis on confessions of guilt in Japanese criminal justice, these JSRC recommendations thus also very much spoke to Hirano's diagnosis – even if they did not do so explicitly.[18]

In any case, especially important here, of course, is that these recommendations translated into the introduction, in 2009, of the so-called *saiban'in* system, Japan's lay judge system. For a specific category of serious offenses, five Japanese citizens would from then on decide, together with three professional judges – or three citizens together with one judge in simple cases – on a defendant's guilt or innocence, and on the sentence this defendant should receive. Chapter 6 will further address the specifics of this system, and how the lay judges, together with

16 Under the "lawyer on duty system" (*tōban bengoshi seido*) detained *suspects* could already apply for one time free legal advice from a lawyer on standby for this purpose. This system was first set up by the legal bar association of Oita Prefecture in 1990, but was quickly adopted by other bar associations after that. As of 2006, those suspected of a crime belonging to a limited category of relatively serious crimes too were eligible for a state appointed lawyer. In 2009 that category of offenses was expanded. For an overview of the different support systems, see www.nichibenren.or.jp/activity/criminal/reforming/kokusen_touban.html. Website last visited 30-8-2018.

17 Discussions on the issue of recording interrogations have been triggered especially by scandals surrounding police and prosecutorial misconduct, however, rather than as a following up on the JSRC recommendations. See in this regard Miyazawa & Hirayama, 2017: 158–165.

18 In several JSRC meetings Council members did however explicitly refer to Hirano's ideas, in discussing, among others, "what criminal justice should look like" ("*aru beki sugata ha nan nanoka*") and in connection with issues of substantive or rather juridical truth finding (cf. JSRC meeting 25; see also meetings 12 and 43 – in Japanese). The records of JSRC meeting 33 further note that Professor Hirano had sent all JSRC members a copy of an article in which he, Hirano, argued in favor of adopting a system of lay participation. This article, "Advocating the Adoption of a System of Lay Participation" (*sanshinsei saiyō no teishō*), was published in 2005, two years after Professor Hirano's death.

their professional counterparts, have fared, and whether the lay judge system presented the solution that Hirano had been hoping for.

## 2. The advent of penal populism, victim participation and sentencing reform

Previous paragraphs already noted that the JSRC-led reforms were not driven by popular calls for change, even if these changes did not follow the regular path of criminal justice policy making. Different polls and surveys conducted before the implementation of the new system showed, for example, that respondents were generally not very supportive of the new system of lay participation. A survey held in 2009, the year in which the new system came into effect, showed that 62% of the respondents were "against the system", while 34% were "in favor". A different survey by Jiji Press Ltd. in 2006 (Central Research Services, 2006) showed that 38.3% thought that the new system was "not necessary", while 38% expressed the opinion that it was. Furthermore, a majority of respondents (70–80%) consistently indicated being unwilling to participate in criminal trials (Central Research Services, 2006). It should in addition be noted that even now opposition against the system continues, though at a small scale.[19] This section, then, addresses the developments that would lead to bottom-up legal change, driven by citizens' movements. These developments are particularly important here, because they would translate into a new role in criminal justice for crime victims. In addition, they would lead to amendments of the Criminal Code that will be highly relevant for lay judge decision making.

The qualification "bottom-up" legal change requires some nuancing, however. As this section will show, citizens', notably crime victims', activism played an important part in some of the legal changes that were to be implemented. Much of the legal change discussed here, however, came about on the basis of policy makers' *perceptions* of the people's will and their sense of justice. In this sense, the process leading to these legal changes, changes that had in common that they all allowed for a more punitive way of dealing with offenders, is reminiscent of the *penal populism* seen in for instance the United States, Canada, the United Kingdom and New Zealand (Roberts et al., 2002; Pratt, 2007). As Francis Pakes explains, such populism is characterized by "an excessive concern with the attractiveness of policies to the electorate (. . .), the intentional or negligent disregard for evidence concerning the actual effect of such policies, and (. . .) a tendency to make simplistic assumptions regarding the nature of public opinion on matters of sentencing and punishment" (2010: 145). It should be noted that the reason for referring to this concept here is not to prove that the developments in Japan can or cannot be qualified as penal populism, but rather to make analytical use of the penal populism lens to bring into focus important characteristics of the developments in Japan.

---

19 The website of the main opposition movement can be found here (in Japanese): http://saibanin-iranainko.com/. Website last visited 30–8–2018.

In pinpointing the beginning of these developments, the origin of Japanese style penal populism, different scholars highlight the impact of one event that shocked the nation, namely the very gruesome double murder of two children by a 14-year-old boy who in the media came to be known as young person *A.* (*shōnen* A.), and that occurred in the city of Kobe in 1997 (Miyazawa, 2008a: 122, 2008b: 48; Fenwick, 2013: 218). Young person *A.* shall here be referred to with the pseudonym of Atsushi.

Atsushi had beheaded one of his victims and had left his head at the main gate of a junior high school with a message stuffed in his mouth. In this message Atsushi taunted the "dim-witted" police to try and catch him, while alluding to more killings to come, as he also did in a letter that he sent to a Kobe newspaper. Atsushi was arrested three days later. He confessed not only to this murder, but also to murdering a girl and injuring two others in the three months before.

The case had held Japan transfixed, generating a vast amount of media attention, also from foreign media. Atsushi's arrest was announced during a police news conference for which television networks interrupted their regular programming, "shocking announcers and audiences alike" (*New York Times*, 1997). This, however, would be only the beginning of a prolonged period of media attention for this case. While the mainstream media would report on "young person *A.*", there were also publications in which Atsushi's name along with other personal information was revealed. In March 1998, the *Bungei Shunjū*, a monthly magazine not commonly known for sensationalist reporting, came out with a special issue in which use was made of seven statements given by young person *A.* to the public prosecutor. *Bungei Shunjū* journalist Ryū Tachibana had received these materials from persons belonging to a radical left wing group who were convinced that Atsushi was not the real killer and who suspected a conspiracy behind this case. The publication of these statements, as well as other publications revealing Atsushi's name, provoked strong protests from among others the JFBA, who condemned this as well as other publications as these would hinder Atsushi's rehabilitation and future return to society (Tachibana, 1998; JFBA, 1998; Tokyo Bar Association, 1998). These events illustrate the attention that the Kobe case received, and the widespread commotion it caused. The JFBA response to the publications not only points to the general public attention that the case generated, but also to the role of this case as a trigger for societal debates on juvenile law.

The JFBA's protests against the reporting practices of different magazines, and its reference to rehabilitation directly relates to the distinction made between juvenile and regular criminal justice. In news reports on crime, publicizing a suspect's or defendant's picture in addition to his or her name, age, place of residence and occupation, along with other details of a person's life, is common practice. This practice of public shaming explains, in part, the social stigma that follows from becoming a crime suspect or defendant. Crimes committed by juveniles are different, however, as a result of the restrictions on media reporting on juveniles laid down in the Juvenile Act. Article 61 of this Act states in fact "with regard to a young person who has been referred to the family court, or who was prosecuted at the time he or she was a young person, newspapers and other media forms are not allowed to publish articles or pictures that would make it possible to infer who the person involved in a case was, through his or her name, profession, place of residence, appearance, etc". This restriction follows from the Act's main goal of "juveniles' wholesome and healthy upbringing" (art. 1), meaning that the Act is aimed at education and reform, not at punishment. Keeping their identity a secret is in this regard part of an effort to give a juvenile more space for a second chance. It was also this goal that the JFBA protests alluded to. The existing law thus forbade the media from publishing about the case as they would about a case involving an adult. But on the basis of the same law Atsushi could also not be criminally prosecuted as the minimum age for such prosecution was, at the time, 16. Instead, Atsushi's case would be handled by a Family Court, behind closed doors. The public, but also victims and bereaved families could accordingly not see for themselves how the Family Court handled the case.

While article 61 could in practice be ignored without any repercussions beyond people's protests,[20] the ignoring of a basic principle of Juvenile law was of course a different matter, regardless of the enormous outcry that the case provoked. The case did however trigger a nationwide debate on this and other Juvenile Act issues as well as a reform process culminating, in 2000, in an amendment that lowered the minimum age at which juveniles can be held criminally responsible for their acts from 16 to 14 (Fenwick, 2013: 218; Miyazawa, 2008a: 49).[21] The amended Act in addition granted victims and bereaved families the right to access case records and to obtain information about the disposition.

The Kobe case was accordingly not only important because of its impact on the legal treatment of juvenile offenders, but also because it furthered the cause of victims' rights in Japanese criminal justice, an issue that will be further addressed in Chapter 4. Here it is in any case important to note that the case marked the beginning of an era of increased attention for victims and their rights that contributed not only to the already mentioned changes in juvenile law, but also legal change allowing for victims to give a statement of opinion in court (in 2000), and ultimately also in the coming about of a victim participation system (*higaishasankaseido*) enabling victims to participate in criminal justice proceedings in various other ways (in 2008). This expanded role for victims in court did not just come about as a result of more societal attention for crime victims, but also as a result of the victim activism that started after 1997. Especially since the

20 It is important to note here that the Act does not contain any provisions to punish those who do publish information on a juvenile offender, something which is linked to the freedom of expression guaranteed in article 21 of the Japanese Constitution. As a result, the honoring or not honoring of Juvenile Act article 61 becomes a matter of journalism ethics (Tsukamoto, 2013).

21 Juveniles are first referred to the Family Court. On the basis of the revised Juvenile Act, the Family Court can, but is not obliged to, send the case back to the prosecutor for a regular criminal prosecution. The revised Act does however oblige the Family Court to do so when the juvenile is 16 or older and committed a crime resulting in a person's death (Miyazawa, 2008a: 49).

foundation, in 2000, of the National Association of Crime Victims and Surviving Families (NAVS) victims and bereaved families would in fact play a role on criminal justice policy making (Miyazawa, 2008a: 48; Hamai & Ellis, 2006: 172).

Finally, the Kobe double murder case was also important in terms of its impact on perceptions of public safety and the image of Japan as a safe country in which low crime rates were a self-evident fact of life. This image had already been damaged by the nerve gas attack on the Tokyo subway system that had injured around 5,500 people and had left twelve people dead (Ohtani et al., 2004: 624).[22] It was however further damaged by other violent, headline-making cases that often involved young offenders (Miyazawa, 2008a: 51–53). These cases served to strengthen perceptions of out of control youths, rising violent crime and importantly also of a failing police.[23] Facing heavy criticism for not taking citizens' complaints seriously enough, the police changed its crime registering policies. While before the recording of a crime could depend on police discretion, now all ***reported*** incidents would also be ***recorded*** (Hamai & Ellis, 2006: 164). This change in registration practices caused an explosive growth in registered crime, helping to further strengthen the perception that Japan was no longer the safe country it once was (Kawai, 2004).

These different developments would ultimately translate into various amendments of the Criminal Code,[24] allowing for a harsher treatment of not only juvenile but also adult offenders. The Code was amended to for example include new categories of crime, among which the offenses of stalking (2000), dangerous driving resulting in death or injury (2001) and gang rape (2004). The amendments provided for extensions of the statute of limitations for different categories of offenses. These last amendments were made in view of, among other things, the increased importance of DNA technology, and the role that this technology could play in solving cases that had long remained unsolved.

Most relevant for the present discussion is that the 2004 amendments also specified longer prison sentences for different categories of offenders, that

22 In a book compiled by the Legal Research and Training Institute (LRTI), the institute at which all legal professionals-to-be receive their training, this attack is actually highlighted as the moment in which the turn toward increased punitivism in Japanese criminal justice started (2012: 136).

23 Two cases were particularly important in that regard, namely one in which a young man in Tochigi was murdered by a group of teenagers, the "Tochigi lynch case", and another in which a woman in Saitama was killed by her former boyfriend, who had for a long time been stalking her, the Okegawa stalker case. In the Tochigi case the offenders had abducted the young man, assaulted him and forced him to borrow large sums of money from consumer loan firms. The young man was killed two months after being abducted. After his disappearance, the young man's parents had asked the police repeatedly to look into the disappearance of their son, but to no avail. In the Okegawa stalker case too the police had failed to intervene despite the repeated pleas for help from the victim and her family.

24 Criminal Code (1907/2017). The text of this Code (No. 45, Meiji 40, 24 April) is available at: http://elaws.e-gov.go.jp/search/elawsSearch/elaws_search/lsg0500/detail?lawId=140AC0000000045&openerCode=1. Website last accessed 31-8-2018.

affected 104 different offenses.[25] When it comes to the way in which these different amendments came about, it is important to note the impact of crime victims to the policy making process, facilitated by the media attention that crime victims received and the powerful political lobby that in particular the NAVS was able to generate. But what about the role of "the popular will", or "popular opinion" – or perceptions thereof – in the policy making process? In order to understand this role it is fruitful to briefly zoom in on the meeting records of the Legislative Deliberation Council Subcommittee on Matters Related to Heinous and Serious Crimes (LDC, 2004), on whose conclusions the 2004 amendments of the Criminal Code were based.[26]

## *2.1 The LDC and sentencing reforms*

In the Subcommittee's first meeting it was first noted that this committee had been assembled against the background of a rise in serious crimes and people's worsened sense of safety that this had resulted in. This worsened sense of safety necessitated, so it was noted, the taking of legal measures. In close connection with issue, there was also the question of whether the Criminal Code and the provisions of the Code of Criminal Procedure were in line with people's *sense of justice* (*seigi kannen*). It was furthermore noted that the Subcommittee's efforts were part of a bigger plan aimed at creating a society in which people could lead safe and secure lives. More specifically, the Subcommittee would bring the punitive provisions for serious crimes in line with this aim.

From the beginning there were committee members stating that especially the rules on sentencing were not in line with people's sense of justice: "taking into account the people's sense of justice, it is thought that they are simply too low" (LDC, 2004, meeting 1). How exactly members had formed that opinion was not clear. It was also not clear what exactly the concept of "people's sense of justice" stood for. In reference to claims regarding this sense of *justice*, committee members in any case referred to different government surveys on people's sense of *safety* (*taikan chian*). Their moral sense of justice and the sense of safety they had in leading their lives became intertwined in the discussion.

The surveys referred to certainly showed that people's sense of safety had in recent years worsened as a result of the rise in crime. Committee members did however also refer to surveys conducted by newspapers in which "the view was presented that overly lenient sentences had contributed to the worsened sense of safety". These newspaper surveys hardly provided conclusive proof of a popular

25 Among other things, the amendments raised (*a*) the upper limit of prison sentences for single crimes from 15 to 20 years and (*b*) the upper limit of combined sentences for multiple crimes as well as the upper limit of aggravated prison sentences for repeat offenders from 20 to 30 years. For a more comprehensive overview see Miyazawa, 2008a: 59.

26 The records, in Japanese, of the five meetings of this subcommittee can be accessed here: www.moj.go.jp/shingi1/shingi_keiji_kyouaku_index.html. Website last visited 30-8-2018.

call for harsher punishment.[27] The repeated reference that the committee members made to such representations and perceptions of the popular will, does however illustrate that the committee discussions on ways to deal with serious crime centered on "what the people would want".

When it came to the question of whether changing the law to allow for harsher punishment would be an effective way to address the rising crimes rates, committee members did not make use of reference materials, as they had when discussing people's sense of safety and justice. Evidence on the direct deterrence impact of harsher punishment did however not seem necessary. The following quote is telling in this regard:

> When it comes to making sentences heavier . . . there is this awareness that crime is rising, and that we have to reduce that crime. Regardless of whether that [making sentences heavier) has a direct effect or not, the people as a whole are thereby saying that this is a serious crime that has to be deterred. That, in my view, is what a crime resistant society looks like.
>
> (LDC, 2004, meeting 1)

The seriousness of the sentence would thus express people's sentiments with regard to the wrong committed. Such a Durkheimian condemnation of a rule infraction is then in turn expected to have the effect of strengthening people's sense of norms, something which in turn is expected to have a general deterrent effect.

From committee members' own perspective, the idea of harsher sentences was thus justified in terms of more or less classical ideas on sentencing and its deterrent effect, apparently making evidence on these issues superfluous. From the people's perspective, as represented by the committee members, harsher sentences would bring the law more in line with people's sense of justice, something which would also serve to improve their sense of safety, in view of the effect on crime that people expected from such harsher sentences.

It was on the basis, mainly, of such reasoning that the LDC arrived at its recommendations, which ultimately translated into the 2004 amendments of Criminal Code, raising the minimum and maximum sentences for 104 offenses. Given the limited and selective use made of surveys on popular attitudes on sentencing practices and policy on one hand and the haphazard manner in which the issue of

27 A survey conducted in 2004 by the Asahi Shimbun, a few months before the Subcommittee held its first meeting shows in fact that in response to the question: "What do you think would be effective, to reduce crime (only 1 answer possible)? 27% of the respondents chose "a better sense of morals;" 18% thought that "bonds between people in the community" would help, while 17% thought that economic recovery and measures to stimulate job opportunities would be effective, followed, finally, by 16% who chose the option of "strengthening punitive measures" (Asahi Shimbun, 2004 – NB: the word *shinbun* (newspaper) is here transcribed as *shimbun*, in view of the fact that this is the transcription used by the newspapers cited.

deterrence was discussed on the other, the records provide a striking illustration of "a tendency to make simplistic assumptions regarding the nature of public opinion on matters of sentencing and punishment", as well as an "intentional or negligent disregard for evidence concerning the actual effect of penal policies" (Pakes, 2010: 145.

Still, the Committee based its final recommendations on more than people's sense of justice or safety and the (not to be) expected effect of harsher sentences. It in fact also took into consideration that in today's society people live much longer than they did compared to when the Criminal Code was enacted (1907 – LDC, 2004, meeting 1), as well as the increasingly harsh sentences that judges had in recent years been meting out. Raising the legally prescribed sentences would give them more room to maneuver. Even if it was by no means clear that they in fact needed such room, there was anecdotal evidence suggesting they would welcome it (meeting 1).[28] The question that presents itself here is, of course, whether judges and especially lay judges, as the people's representatives, have indeed felt the need to make use of the extra room provided for by these amendments. This question will be addressed later in this book.

The developments and currents of reform presented in parts I and II provide part of the context necessary to make analytical sense of the different criminal justice roles that will be addressed in the following chapters. The general characteristics of Japanese criminal justice and the two currents of reform addressed here are points of reference that will resurface in later chapters, in connection also with Hirano's diagnosis. Did lay judges present a cure to the "disease"? What effect, if any, did participating victims and the sentencing reforms addressed in the previous sections have in this regard? These too are questions to which we will return in the following chapters.

## 3. Issues of criminal responsibility, recidivism and DNA

In introducing the first of the remaining outsiders, forensic psychiatrists, it is best to here zoom in on one final shocking episode. In 2001 Mamoru T. entered a primary school and randomly killed eight children and wounded another 15 children and adults. Amid already increasing fear of and concern about crime, this was yet another violent crime that was to dominate media headlines. Still,

28 One Committee member remarked in this regard: "This time around we're adjusting the legally prescribed sentences for the sake of the people's sense of justice and their sense of safety, and so on, but when it comes to the question of whether judges in their actual work are in fact having real problems when making their sentencing decisions, because of these legally prescribed sentences of 15 and 20 years and so on, as a lawyer I have the feeling that they're not experiencing any problems. I'd like to ask to what extent this has been considered and looked into." In this regard another member stated that he had been "asking around a bit" within the courts (*saibansho no naibu de jakkan iken wo kiite mita*), and that there were almost no voices opposing the proposed raise, and that he thought that most would in fact welcome the extra room to decide (meeting 1). It was in such anecdotal terms that judges' position was represented.

this case was different from those other crimes, in view of the T.'s profile. After his arrest it soon became clear that T. had a long history of mental illness. In view of this history and the gruesome randomness of his crime it was decided that T. should be psychiatrically evaluated in order to determine if he could be held criminally responsible for what he had done (Okae, 2013: 92–129).

Article 39 of the Japanese Criminal Code (CC) states that the acts of a criminally insane person – literally: a person who has lost his mind, *shinshinsōshitsu* – shall not be punished (art. 39.1), and that the punishment of acts committed by a person with a diminished mental capacity, *shinshinkōjaku*, shall be reduced (art. 39.2). Article 39 does not mention psychiatrists. Nevertheless, their expertise is normally invoked in order to determine whether article 39 applies or might apply.

The forensic psychiatrists performing T.'s evaluation concluded that he suffered from a personality disorder that, according to the Court, did not affect his criminal responsibility. T. was sentenced to death and executed in 2004. T.'s case is significant here because it was perceived to highlight the danger of mentally ill, violent offenders, and as a result provided the impetus for the Medical Treatment and Observation Act (MTOA) that was compiled in 2003 and implemented in 2005 (Konishi & Hokama, 2011: 19; Tomita, 2009: 243).[29] This law targets those who committed an act that caused serious harm to others, as T. did, while in a state of criminal insanity, unlike T. Ironically, the new law would thus not have applied to the person whose act triggered the making of this law.

Be that as it may, the MTOA in any case expanded the possibilities available to legal professionals to deal with mentally disturbed offenders, and for legal professionals to be involved in their forcible admission to a mental hospital. The MTOA would thus seem to be in line with the other laws and amendments introduced in the early 2000s aimed at, among others, improving social defense at times in which society seemed to be under siege. Still, this law is also only the last in a long history of legal and public health measures directed at people with mental disturbances in Japan. Such measures are of course not only shaped by specific events such as T.'s heinous crime but also by changing scientific and societal understandings of mental illness – based, for example, on increased and improved ways of treating certain illnesses.

Changes in how mental illness is understood have also very much impacted assessments of criminal responsibility. Forensic psychiatrists play a key role in such assessments. They are the ones who in first instance determine whether or to what extent a person *suspected* of a certain crime was able to distinguish right from wrong and to act accordingly *at the time of this crime*. It is this factual determination that prosecutors and lay and professional judges need to take into account when deciding on defendants' criminal responsibility. Against the background of the developments sketched in the previous section, the adoption of the MTOA as

29 The official name of this law is as follows: Act on Medical Care and Treatment for Persons Who Have Caused Serious Harm to Others Under the Condition of Insanity (Act No. 110 of 2003). For a general overview of the law (in Japanese), see www.kansatuhou.net/01_nyumon/01_nanika.html. Website last visited 30–8–2018.

well as changing perceptions of mental illness, the question is what role forensic psychiatrists' contributions currently play in decisions on criminal responsibility.

Besides being relevant within the general framework of this book, this question is also a timely one in view of the fact that the criminally insane offender has in the past 20 years virtually disappeared from the Japanese courtroom. That is to say: nowadays defendants are hardly ever found criminally insane, or of diminished responsibility. This disappearance was not the direct result of the MTOA, although as of 2005 this law does of course play its part. It has rather come about as a consequence of a much longer history. Chapter 2 will trace that history, and the role that forensic psychiatrists have played in it.

The criminally insane offender may have virtually disappeared from court. That does not mean, however, that defendants with serious mental health problems, defendants such as T., are not tried and convicted. In fact, from the early 1990s on the influx of prisoners with a mental disturbance started rising, going from 3.4% in 1992 to 14.3% in 2016. These statistics did not put the problem on the map, but the prison memoirs of Jōji Yamamoto (2003) did. Yamamoto, a former member of the House of Representatives, had in 2001 been convicted of fraud and sentenced to 18 months in prison. Once in prison Yamamoto became aware of the fact that many of his fellow inmates suffered from mental and intellectual disabilities, and that many of them were elderly repeat offenders for whom the prison gates were revolving doors. He also became aware of how ill-equipped the prison was to address the needs of these offenders, especially once he was given the task of seeing after the physical care and hygiene of some of them, a task that he vividly and graphically describes. Relevant here is that Yamamoto's memoirs fanned the flames of a debate that ultimately translated in the institutionalization of "support at the entrance" (*iriguchishien*). Those offered such support are at the pre-trial stage ("the entrance") put in contact with social welfare workers who work together with other legal professionals to bring about the diversion of an offender from trial or prison. With this new form of diversion another legal outsider, the social welfare worker, thus enters the stage.

Yamamoto's memoirs played an important part in raising awareness of the issue of elderly and mentally disturbed repeat offenders, trapped in a cycle of offending, being sent to prison only to reoffend upon release. The institutionalization, in late 2017, of support at the entrance and the social welfare worker's new role was however also part of broader plans formulated by the Cabinet Crime Committee (CCC). This committee was established in 2003 when crime rates were peaking by then Prime Minister Koizumi with the aim of "restoring Japan's status as the safest country in the world" (CCC, 2003).[30] One of the principles on which the CCC plans were based was that of supporting the Japanese people in securing their own safety.[31] One important element of the CCC plans, therefore,

30 See www.kantei.go.jp/jp/singi/hanzai/. Website last visited 30–8–2018.

31 See records from meeting 1 in 2003; CCC meeting records and other materials are available (in Japanese) on the CCC website: www.kantei.go.jp/jp/singi/hanzai/. Website last visited 30–8–2018.

was to emphasize the role of the local community in preventing crime in general and recidivism in particular. This is where among others volunteers, local NPOs and also social welfare workers would later enter the picture. The institutionalization of "support at the entrance" should thus be understood in connection with bigger community involvement in preventing the (re)occurring of crime. It is also in this connection that Chapter 3 will pursue social welfare workers' criminal justice role.

We now turn to the last legal outsider of this section: the scientific expert. Much like the forensic psychiatrist, this outsider is a familiar face with a role of changed significance. That changed significance has been the result of advances in technology, notably DNA technology. DNA technology presents immense opportunities in terms of not only identifying offenders, but also in exposing wrongful convictions. The number of DNA tests conducted by the police as part of a criminal investigation has in the past years exploded, going from 24,562 in 2005 to 299,805 in 2016, in spite of the fact that crime rates have been going down as of 2004 (NPA White Paper on Police, 2017).

The increased importance of scientific evidence, and by extension of the scientists producing such evidence and explaining it in court, has also been noticed by the Japanese judiciary. In March 2013 the Legal Research and Training Institute (LRTI), the Supreme Court run institute where all Japanese legal professionals are trained, published a book on the nature of scientific evidence and the criminal trials making use of it, "for all (. . .) involved in legal practice" (2013: preface). In its introduction the book notes not only the increased importance of scientific evidence, but also that such evidence has been receiving much attention in view of its potential "to increase the trustworthiness and certainty of criminal trials" (2013: 1). Increased trustworthiness and certainty follow from the fact that scientific evidence is more objective, certain and reliable than people's observations and memories. Scientific evidence, therefore, would "make it possible ***to avoid the tendency to rely too much on confessions of guilt*** given at the investigation stage" (2013: 6).

The question is accordingly: does the increased importance of scientific evidence and scientists' role indeed translate into less emphasis on confessions of guilt? Is scientific evidence taking over as the king of evidence, making Japanese criminal justice a little less about trial by dossier? These questions point to the potential that scientific evidence has of changing Japanese criminal justice practice. But this of course depends on how the legal professionals make use of the information and insights presented by the scientists. In its introduction, the LRTI presents an interesting observation in this regard that is here also very much to the point:

> Those who establish the facts in criminal trials by making use of such scientific evidence are jurists who are no experts in the field of science. And if one then takes into account that in lay judge trials lay judges are also involved in the process, the question is if in the end they are able, on the basis of a correct understanding of matters belonging to fields of advanced

> technology, to appropriately evaluate and determine the probative value of such evidence
>
> (1)

The LRTI book here points to a question central in this book: how do legal professionals – alongside lay judges – go about incorporating such outside information? How does the LRTI book answer this question, and what does legal practice tell us? These are some of the questions that will be pursued in Chapter 5. While Chapters 2 and 3 will thus address the connected roles of forensic psychiatrists and social workers, and Chapters 4 and 5 address participating victims' and forensic scientists' roles, respectively, lay judges' roles will be the focus of Chapter 6, even if their role will also be discussed in connection with those of forensic psychiatrists, crime victims and forensic scientists.[32] Given that social workers' role has been institutionalized only very recently (late 2017), data on lay judges' perspectives on this role are as yet not available.

## Conclusion

This chapter has outlined the developments that have led to outsiders' new or changed roles. In a general sense the following chapters will address the role that outsiders' perspectives, knowledge and information play in the criminal justice practices concerned. But as the previous sections have shown, each outsider's role also presents its own questions, while bringing into focus very different aspects of Japanese criminal justice; different determinants pointing to different connections. Outsiders' roles, in other words, draw attention to the myriad perspectives, points of reference and aims making Japanese criminal justice into a complex, internally differentiated whole, whose different elements are nonetheless interrelated (cf. Garland, 1990: 279).

As this chapter has shown, "people's trust", and "the will of the people" are recurring points of reference in criminal justice policy making. Yet it took the involvement of the Keidanren, the Japanese Business Federation, to provide the decisive push for legal reforms in which people's trust was so emphatically referred to and represented. In reference to the popular will the criminal justice infrastructure was changed to allow for more punitivism, while elsewhere in Japan's penal realm rehabilitation remains an important criminal justice objective, and a remorseful confession an important practice referent, are social workers called upon to expand existing diversion practices to improve recidivism rates, are psychiatrists enlisted in *defense sociale* and scientists in making criminal trials more certain and trustworthy, or at least representing them as such.

32 As also noted in the introduction, the distinction between these last two is not meant to suggest that forensic psychiatrists are not also scientific experts. The distinction is rather one of convenience, related to the fact that the forensic psychiatrists focused on here are specifically involved in assessing suspects' and defendants' criminal responsibility, while in this book the scientific experts are those who within the criminal justice context provide their natural scientific insights on material evidence.

Here criminal justice policy and practice shows itself to be shaped by economic, political and emotive forces, as well as matters of custom, representing shared morals and sentiments, imagined or not, while increasingly grounding itself in objective, scientific knowledge, pursuing the management of potentially dangerous populations and enlisting communities in its crime control efforts. In line with an acknowledgment of the multifaceted complexity of the Japanese criminal justice realm, the following chapters will not strive to determine a single principle that would somehow serve to explain this realm, but rather to in the end bring together outsiders' very different perspectives and contributions into one collaged picture.

## References


Aoki, Takayuki (2013). *Keijishihōkaikaku to Saiban'in Seido*. Tokyo: Nihon Hyōronsha.

*Asahi Shimbun* (2004). Chian, anzen takamaru kanshin chi'iki nadode jieisaku: Asahi Shimbunsha kokumin ishiki chosa, 27 January. Accessed via Asahi Kikuzō Database.

Cabinet Crime Committee (hanzaikakuryōkaigi) (2003). Cabinet Crime Committee website. Available at: www.kantei.go.jp/jp/singi/hanzai/. Website last visited 30 August 2018.

Central Research Services (2006). Available at: www.crs.or.jp/backno/old/No590/5902.htm and *Yomiuri Shimbun*. Available at: www.ac.auone-net.jp/~inolaw/kainaihaifu0905-2.pdf. Website last visited 30 August 2018.

Fenwick, Mark (2013). 'Penal populism' and penological change in contemporary Japan. *Theoretical Criminology* 17(2): 215–231.

Fisher, Talia and Issachar Rosen-Zvi (2008). The confessional penalty. *Cardozo Law Review* 30: 871–916.

Foote, Daniel H. (1991). Confessions and the right to silence in Japan. *Georgia Journal of International & Comparative Law* 21: 415–488.

Foote, Daniel H. (1992). From Japan's death row to freedom. *Pacific Rim Law & Policy Journal* 1: 11–103.

Garland, David (1990). *Punishment and modern society: a study in social theory*. Oxford: Oxford University Press.

Ginsburg, Tom (2001). Dismantling the "developmental state"? Administrative procedure reform in Japan and Korea. *The American Journal of Comparative Law* 49(4): 585 625.

Hamai, Kōichi and Tom Ellis (2006). Crime and criminal justice in modern Japan: from re-integrative shaming to popular punitivism. *International Journal of the Sociology of Law* 34: 157–178.

Hirano, Ryūichi (1989). Diagnosis of the current code of criminal procedure. *Law Japan* 22: 129–142.

Hirano, Ryūichi (1999). Sanshinsei no saiyō ni yoru 'kakushinshihō' wo: keiji shihō kaikaku no ugoki to hōkō (tokushū keiji soshōhō gojūnen). *Jurisuto* 1148: 2–5.

Hirano, Ryūichi (2005). *Keijihō kenkyū saishūkan*. Tokyo: Yūhikaku.

Keidanren (1998). *Shihōseidokaikaku nit suite no iken*. Available at: www.keidanren.or.jp/japanese/policy/pol173.html. Website last visited 30 August 2018.

Keidanren (2018). *About keidanren*. Available at: www.keidanren.or.jp/en/profile/pro001.html. Website last visited 30 August 2018.

Konishi, Yoshiro and Junya Hokama (2011). *Iryō kansatsuhō ni kansuru ichikōsatu: Okinawa-ken no jirei nimo furete*. Available at: http://okinawa-repo.lib.u-ryukyu.ac.jp:8080/handle/okinawa/9601. Website last visited 30 August 2018.

Inouye, Masahito (2014). Introduction of the saiban-in system and reformation of criminal procedure in Japan. *Seoul Law Journal* 55(2): 441–475.
Ishimatsu, Takeo (1989). Are criminal defendants in Japan truly receiving trials by judges. *Law Japan* 22: 143–153.
Ito, Kazuko (2012). Wrongful convictions and recent criminal justice reform in Japan. *University of Cincinatti Law Review* 80: 1245.
Japan Federation of Bar Associations (JFBA) (1998). *"Bugeishunji" "Shinchō" kakushi ni taisuru kaichō seimei.* Available at: www.nichibenren.or.jp/activity/document/statement/year/1998/1998_3.html. Website last visited 30 August 2018.
Johnson, David T. (2002). *The Japanese way of justice: prosecuting crime in Japan.* Oxford: Oxford University Press.
Johnson, David T. (2012). Japan's prosecution system. *Crime and Justice* 41(1): 35–74.
Johnson, David T. (2015). Wrongful convictions and the culture of denial in Japanese criminal justice. *The Asia-Pacific Journal* 13(6).
Justice System Reform Council (JSRC) (1999). *The points at issue in the justice reform.* Available at: https://japan.kantei.go.jp/policy/sihou/singikai/991221_e.html. Website last visited 30 August 2018.
Justice System Reform Council (JSRC) (1999–2001). *Gijiroku.* Available at: www.kantei.go.jp/jp/sihouseido/gijiroku-dex.html. Website last visited 30 August 2018.
Justice System Reform Council (JSRC) (2001). *Hōkokusho.* Available at: www.kantei.go.jp/jp/sihouseido/report-dex.html. Website last visited 30 August 2018.
Kameyama, Tsugio (1998). Keijishihōshisutemu no saikōchiku ni mukete, in *Matsuo Kōya hakase koki shukka ronbunshū.* Tokyo: Yūhikaku: 1–24.
Katō, Yasuei (2015). Keiji shihō ni okeru kensatsukan no yakuwari (2). *Nihon Hougaku* 81(3): 553–603.
Kawai, Mikio (2004). *Anzen shinwa hōkai no paradokkusu.* Tokyo: Iwanami Shoten.
Kovacs, Emese (2016). *Shakaiteki kinou toshiteno media "shazai": media event to shiteno "shazai" no jishōteki hikaku kenkyū.* Dissertation, Musashi University.
Kingston, Jeff (2011). Justice on trial: Japanese prosecutors under fire. *Asia-Pacific Journal* 9(10).
Langbein, John H. (1978). Torture and plea bargaining. *The University of Chicago Law Review* 46(1): 3–22.
Legal Research and Training Institute (LRTI) (2013). *Kagakutekishōko to sore wo mochiita saiban no arikata.* Tokyo: Hōsōkai.
Legislative Deliberation Council Subcommittee on Matters Related to Heinous and Serious Crimes (LDC) (2004). *Meetings.* Meeting records. Available at: www.moj.go.jp/shingi1/shingi_keiji_kyouaku_index.html. Website last visited 30 August 2018.
Liberal Democratic Party (LDP) (1998). *Jiyūmishitō shihōseido tokubestu chōsakai hōkoku: 21 seiki no shihō no tashikana hōshin.* Available at: www.veritas-law.jp/ronbun_doc/20090929133643_1.pdf. Website last visited 30 August 2018.
Ministry of Justice (MOJ) (annual) (2017). *White paper on crime.* Available at: http://hakusyo1.moj.go.jp/en/nendo_nfm.html. Website last visited 30 August 2018.
Miyazawa, Setsuo (2002). Introduction: an unbalanced adversary system – issues, policies, and practices in Japan, in context and in comparative perspective, in Malcolm M. Feeley and Setsuo Miyazawa (eds.), *The Japanese adversary system in context: controversies and comparisons.* Houndmills: Palgrave Macmillan: 1–11.

Miyazawa, Setsuo (2008a). The politics of increasing punitiveness and the rising populism in Japanese criminal justice policy. *Punishment & Society* 10(1): 47–77.

Miyazawa, Setsuo (2008b). Will penal populism in Japan decline? (symposium: globalized penal populism and its countermeasures). *Japanese Journal of Sociological Criminology* 33: 122–136.

Miyazawa, Setsuo (2013). Successes, failures, and remaining issues of the justice system reform in Japan: an introduction to the symposium issue. *Hastings International & Comparative Law Review* 36(2): 313–348.

Miyazawa, Setsuo and Mari Hirayama (2017). Introduction of videotaping of interrogations and the lessons of the imaichi case: a case of conventional criminal justice policy-making in Japan. *Washington International Law Journal* 27: 149.

National Police Association (NPA) (2017). *White paper on police*. Available at: www.npa.go.jp/hakusyo/h29/pdf/pdfindex.html. Website last visited 30 August 2018.

*New York Times* (1997). 14-Year-old arrested in Japan for the brutal slaying of a child, 29 June. Available at: www.nytimes.com/1997/06/29/world/14-year-old-arrested-in-japan-for-the-brutal-slaying-of-a-child.html. Website last visited 30 August 2018.

Obuchi, Kenichi (2015). *Shippai shinai ayamarikata*. Tokyo: CCC Media House.

Ohtani, Toshiyuki et al. (2004). Posttraumatic stress disorder symptoms in victims of Tokyo subway attack: a 5-year follow-up study. *Psychiatry and Clinical Neurosciences* 58(6): 624–629.

Okae, Akira (2013). *Takuma Mamoru seishin kanteisho*. Tokyo: Akishobō.

Pakes, Francis (2010). *Comparative criminal justice* (second edition). London: Routledge.

Pratt, John (2007). *Penal populism*. London: Routledge.

Roberts, Julian V. et al. (2002). *Penal populism and public opinion: lessons from five countries*. Oxford: Oxford University Press.

Supreme Court of Japan (2017). *Keiji tsūjō daiisshin jiken no gaikyō*. Available at: www.courts.go.jp/vcms_lf/hokoku_06_03keiji.pdf. Website last visited 30 August 2018.

Tachibana, Ryū (1998). Hanzai no zenbō. *Bungei Shunjū* 76(3). Tokyo: Bungei Shunjū Shinsha.

Tokyo Bar Association (1998). *Bungeishunju sangatsugō no shougakusei sasshōjiken kyōjutsusho keisai ni tsuite*. Available at: www.toben.or.jp/message/seimei/3-1.html. Website last visited 30 August 2018.

Tomita, Mikio (2009). Shinshin sō shitsusha tō iryō kansatsuhō ni tsuite. *Psychiatria et neurologia Japonica* 111(3): 243.

Tsujimoto, Norio (2010). Ronsetsu: yakusoku ni yoru jihaku no shōko nōryoku. *Kinki Daigaku Hōgaku* 57(4): 33–58.

Tsujimoto, Norio et al. (2017a). Ronsetsu: Hirano Ryūichi riron to keijisoshōhō – kyōdō kenkyu·keijisoshōhō no kisoriron (dainikai). *Kinki Daigaku Hōgaku* 64(3:4): 1–73.

Tsujimoto, Norio et al. (2017b). Ronsetsu: Matsuya Kōya kyōju to keijisoshōhōriron. *Kinki Daigaku Hōgaku* 65(2): 51–118.

Tsukamoto, Seijirō (2013). Shōnen hanzai hodo to senmonshoku riron: seichōhattatsuken wo tegakari toshite. *Ōyō Riron* 7: 3–15.

Van den Wyngaert, Christine (2009). *Strafrecht, strafprocesrecht en internationaal strafrecht in Hoofdlijnen*. Antwerpen: Maklu.

Vanoverbeke, Dimitri (2015). *Juries in the Japanese legal system: the continuing struggle for citizen participation and democracy*. London: Routledge.
Wagatsuma, Hiroshi and Arthur Rosett (1986). The implications of apology: law and culture in Japan and the United States. *Law and Society Review*: 461–498.
Yamamoto, Jōji (2003). *Gokusōki*. Tokyo: Shinchō Bunko.

# 2 Psychiatrists and criminal responsibility

## Introduction

In recent years the issue of "potentially dangerous, mentally disturbed offenders" has been discussed in connection with some high profile serious incidents, such as the case of Mamoru T. presented in the previous chapter. But while the issue of these offenders appeared prominently in public discussions, ultimately leading to legal change, Japanese courts today find virtually all defendants fully criminally responsible regardless of their mental condition. That is, defendants who are "criminally insane" or of diminished responsibility have all but disappeared from the juridical landscape. This chapter will look into this virtual disappearance and the various actors who are involved in some way: police officers, prosecutors, lawyers, forensic psychiatrists, judges and since 2009, *lay* judges as well. These different persons together decide on a suspect's or defendant's capacity to distinguish right from wrong and to act accordingly, the legal standard for assessing criminal responsibility and what accordingly should be done with this suspect or defendant. Should he or she be prosecuted, punished or receive medical treatment? This chapter examines how the persons involved go about answering these questions, focusing especially on forensic psychiatrists' role. By doing so it will not only shed light on this role, but also on the disappearance from court of the defendant who is criminally insane or of diminished responsibility. In doing so it in addition brings into focus the engagement between juridical knowledge and outside knowledge, expert and lay, implicated in this disappearance.

### *The case of Kazuhiro O. and the issues at stake*

In view of the fact that it so strongly brings into focus the issues at stake, the case of Kazuhiro O. is a good place to start. Kazuhiro O. (41) stopped going to school when he was 11 years old, as he had become too afraid to go outside where he might run into children from school. Much of the next 30 years he spent indoors, living at his mother's place. He had wanted to go to some place faraway, to a new school where he could make a fresh start, but his parents had refused. For this Kazuhiro blamed his sister Mari, who had once moved out but had then moved back home again. Thirty years later, Mari, by now 46 years old and with a family of her own, came to bring Kazuhiro groceries at their mother's place, where Kazuhiro still lived. She did this because their mother, who would normally have bought the groceries, was hospitalized as a result of physical abuse from Kazuhiro. As she had done before, Mari tried to talk Kazuhiro into being more independent and she left a note, saying: "you should pay for food and other things yourself. I'll do the shopping". Kazuhiro interpreted this note as another attempt on Mari's part – one of the many he believed to have suffered over the years – to pester him, and decided to kill her, which he did the next time she came to deliver the groceries. Even though he had planned to also kill himself – Kazuhiro had been expressing a desire to kill himself since his 20s– he did not, and was soon arrested.

After his arrest a forensic psychiatrist diagnosed Kazuhiro with Asperger's syndrome. This was the first such diagnosis Kazuhiro had received; neither he nor his family had been aware of his condition. Kazuhiro was charged with murder, which meant that six lay and three professional judges now had to decide what should be done with Kazuhiro. Should he be found innocent, not to be held criminally accountable in view of his condition? Should Kazuhiro be punished like any "regular" defendant, or should that punishment be less harsh, considering his condition, or . . . should society rather be protected from him, in view exactly of that condition?

Kazuhiro's case provokes the questions that more regularly arise in debates about serious crimes committed by those with a mental disease or disturbance. The previous chapter has shown that those with a disturbance who commit light offenses such as petty theft and do so repeatedly, are increasingly diverted away from formal criminal procedures. For those who commit more serious, violent offenses, there are different rules, resulting from different types of discussions.

Japanese courts very rarely find that such defendants should be found innocent. For the past 10 years, they have each year only found between one and ten defendants not guilty by reason of insanity, while 60–80 received a sentence reduction because of diminished criminal responsibility (*shinshinkōjaku*). These numbers obviously represent only a minute percentage of the number of the persons yearly adjudicated in court (51,622 in 2014 – see Ministry of Justice, 2015).

This small percentage does not imply, however, that the issue of (diminished) criminal responsibility is somehow a minor one. After all, the small percentage of persons found innocent does also not render the issue of guilt or innocence marginal. Furthermore, courts do generally take into account the circumstances of the offender, including matters such as a person's mental disturbance in sentencing. They just do not easily apply the labels of "criminal insanity" (*shinshinsōshitsu*) and "diminished responsibility" (*shinshinkōjaku*). Nevertheless, criminal responsibility remains a topic of in court discussions, as well as ongoing debates in the media, among academics as well as those involved in the criminal process. In fact, the issue was also discussed in 64 of the 363 meetings organized by district courts in all 48 prefectures of Japan, in which participants in lay judge trials exchanged opinions with legal professionals[1,2] (from here: lay judge meetings).

Let us now first return, however, to the six lay and three professional judges that handled Kazuhiro's case, as their reasoning and decisions will bring more sharply into focus what is at stake in both practical and theoretical terms. Together the lay and professional judges concluded that Kazuhiro's condition had certainly played a part in how the murder and the motive to commit that murder had come about. They also noted, however, that Kazuhiro was aware that he had committed an utterly unacceptable act, and that this act, which had been consciously planned, was nothing less than a vicious murder. The victim's relatives, who were also Kazuhiro's relatives, had furthermore indicated that they wanted Kazuhiro to never get out of prison. Weighing these different factors, on 30 July 2012 the court's lay and professional judges concluded that 20 years' imprisonment would be more appropriate than the 16 years demanded by the prosecution. The court's reasoning is worth quoting at length here:

> Even though the defendant has committed this act, he is still not sufficiently remorseful. Admittedly, his inability to show a remorseful attitude results from Asperger's syndrome, and one can therefore not ethically criticize him in the same way one would criticize the average person. However, regardless of how much he is influenced by his mental disorder: from the perspective of wholesome common sense one has to fear that if the defendant were to return to society without sufficient remorse, and in his social circle there would be people who would go against his wishes, he would wind up committing an act similar to his crime in this case. (. . .)
>
> The present circumstances are such that within society there is no place for him to go to that can accommodate for his condition, and there are no prospects that there will be such a place. Given that this is the case, it has to be said that the concern that the defendant might reoffend becomes all the more serious, and this is something that also has to be emphasized in sentencing. It is necessary to deepen the remorse of the defendant by keeping him in prison for as long as possible. Doing so will also contribute to the social order.
>
> (Osaka District Court, Heisei 23 (wa) no. 6063, verdict of 24.7.30)

1 As of 2011 District Courts have been organizing meetings in which former lay judges and others who participated in lay judge trials, judges, prosecutors and lawyers, can exchange opinions. A judge, who has also taken part in lay judge trials leads the meeting. Meetings still continue to be held. Records have been checked until December 2017. See the introductory chapter for more details. The lay judge meeting records are available at: www.saibanin.courts.go.jp/ikenkoukan/index.html. Website last visited 30–8–2018.

2 In 64 meetings the issue of diminished responsibility (*shinshinkōjaku*) was discussed, including 25 meetings in which the issue of criminal insanity (*shinshinsōshitsu*) came up. In 40 meetings the issue of psychiatric evaluations (*seishinkantei*) was discussed in connection with that of criminal responsibility (*sekininnōryoku*).

This verdict caused quite a stir as well as a debate. Some media questioned whether the judges had actually understood the meaning of the term "developmental disorder" that had played such an important part in this case. Others noted that this verdict amounted to punishing people for their disorders, as well as for society's failure to provide for adequate support.[3]

Through its president's statement the Japan Federation of Bar Associations (JFBA) stated that by referring to the defendant's disorder in justifying a higher punishment the verdict went against the principle of responsibility (JFBA, 2012). This is also what the defense argued, when it appealed to the High Court. The defense argued in fact that (1) the defendant's condition justified a lower punishment, (2) that the punishment imposed was in any case unreasonably high and (3) that the District Court had unjustly concluded that there were no institutions where the defendant could be looked after, without providing the defense the opportunity to prove otherwise (Osaka High Court, Heisei 24 (u), no. 1159, verdict of 26.2.2013).

On appeal the High Court recognized that Asperger's syndrome had played a part in the process through which Kazuhiro's motive had been formed. While certain aspects of this motive were for an "ordinary person" (*tsūjōnin*) hard to understand, the whole process that had led to this murder was not. The original verdict's conclusion that Kazuhiro was criminally responsible was accordingly correct. The High Court did find, however, that the imposed sentence was too high. The defendant's condition did affect the extent to which he could be blamed for his act. The Court also noted that Kazuhiro's expression of remorse was not *so* insufficient as to justify a presumption of recidivism, and that institutions that could support people with Asperger's syndrome do in fact exist, and meted out a prison sentence of 14 years, six years lower than the original sentence.

Kazuhiro's case was unusual in terms of its initial outcome: trials in which the court metes out a sentence higher than the prosecution demands are rare. The High Court verdict also shows that the conclusions of the lay and professional judges of the District Court had been based on faulty premises. But what if these premises had not been faulty? What if there in fact was a shortage of institutions that could look after Kazuhiro? What if Kazuhiro's lack of remorse did point to a risk of recidivism and the threat that Kazuhiro could pose to those around him? Would that have justified the lay and professional judges' initial conclusion? What role do expert and lay forms of knowledge play in the process of deciding on these issues and answering such questions?

Within the framework of this book these are especially salient questions. After all: besides the "wholesome common sense" referred to in Kazuhiro O.'s trial, the process of judging suspects' and defendants' (diminished) responsibility will often also include or imply a medical assessment. One could argue in fact that any punishment to be meted out requires the implicit or explicit medical assumption

---

3 See www.arsvi.com/d/hmc.htm (website of the Ritsumeikan University Center for Ars Vivendi), for an overview of the various media responses to this case. Website last visited 30–8–2018.

that the defendant is at least partially sane, even if no medical expertise is called upon to establish that defendant's sanity.

When those involved – typically: police personnel, prosecutors or lawyers – find that there are doubts in this regard forensic psychiatrists will be asked to provide their opinion as to how the actions of the person in custody or on trial can be understood. At the same time, decisions about criminal responsibility are decisions about the applicability of a legal concept, and are therefore first and foremost *legal* decisions, embedded in jurisprudence and legal doctrine. Decisions regarding criminal responsibility are accordingly taken at a nexus of common sense, medical and legal understandings of suspects' and defendants' behavior. As we will see, an examination of this nexus will especially bring into focus the role played by (1) forensic psychiatrists in connection with those of (2) professional and (3) lay judges as well as (4) public prosecutors.

In doing so this chapter will address an aspect of Japanese criminal justice on which virtually no sources in English are available. By zooming in on forensic psychiatric knowledge and forensic psychiatrists' contributions to legal decision making this chapter however also contributes to the literature on the role of "extra-legal" knowledge in legal processes. The previous paragraph already noted how decisions on criminal responsibility are taken at a nexus of different forms of knowledge.

Such decisions are here accordingly assumed to come about on the basis of hybrid, merged forms of knowledge – in line with Valverde's findings, who on the basis of US and Canadian legal contexts has argued that inquiries into the truth of immoral doings are based on a hybrid of, among others, science, common sense, intuitive and partly archival knowledge. Law's claim to enacting justice, so Valverde shows, depends on little facts known to individual witnesses, the general facts known to experts, but crucially also the universal resource of common knowledge (2009: 133–134 – see in this regard also the introduction and Chapter 5). Nevertheless, the assumption of hybridity does here not by itself explain how this hybrid form of knowledge is in practice constituted and how it informs legal decision making. By addressing the roles of the four players involved in the disappearance of the criminally insane and diminished responsible defendant, this chapter aims to elucidate just that, namely how within the context of specific Japanese criminal justice decision making practices different forms of knowledge become merged. And in doing so it aims to further our understanding of the role of "extra-legal" forms of knowledge within legal decision-making processes. This chapter is based on relevant jurisprudence and criminal justice statistics, records of the 64 lay participation meetings in which issues of criminal responsibility were discussed – see notes 1 and 2 – supplemented with information gathered through semi-structured interviews and personal communication with district court judges ($n$ = 11) and prosecutors ($n$ = 14) during 2011–2017 (see in this regard also the book Introduction).

Before examining the present day roles of these four players, however, it is necessary to briefly examine the historical background against which present day conceptions of criminal responsibility have come about, and can accordingly be understood. After this brief history the focus will be on developments in the post–World War II period that eventually culminated in a new role for citizens as lay judges.

## 1. A brief history of criminal responsibility in Japan, 701–1945

From as early as the year 701 Japanese legal codes have provided for a lighter sentence for crimes committed by people with a mental disorder. Codes in the following centuries did not always contain specific clauses on this issue, but under these codes too offenders with a mental disorder were treated more leniently (Fujino, 2005: 202; Takimoto, 2010: 9–11).[4] The Osadamegaki code of the Tokugawa period (1603–1867) again clearly stipulated (in article 78) a special treatment for mentally deranged people (*ranshinsha*). The application of this article varied, however, in accordance with the type of crime and the social class of the persons involved, in accordance with Confucian principles.[5] Still, there are also examples of *ranshinsha* who wounded a "higher" family member – that is: a familial ascendant – and were pardoned on the basis of requests for leniency submitted by family members and others. Whether a person was in fact recognized as a *ranshinsha* or not was something that depended especially on the number of persons who would testify to that effect (Takimoto, 2010: 16).

Police constables and magistrates did also call upon the expertise of medical doctors, however, especially in connection with the treatment a *ranshinsha* should get.[6] These doctors' diagnoses were based on medical knowledge derived

4 The Taihō code of 701 and its revised version, the Yōrō code of 757, for example, are said to have provided for sentence reductions for handicapped offenders, including those with a mental handicap. It is thought that under later codes too (up until the Osadamegaki code of the Tokugawa period) offenders with a mental disorder received a similarly lenient treatment (Takimoto, 2010: 11).

5 The Osadamegaki code of the Tokugawa period, a two-volume book of rules for public officials, was highly influenced by the Chinese criminal code compiled in 624 during the T'ang dynasty, and as such is very much based on Confucian ethical principles. In line with such principles the code prescribed higher punishments for criminal acts against familial ascendants. These principles have remained influential for a long time, as until 1973 Japanese criminal law stipulated (in article 200) a higher punishment for murdering familial ascendants. In that year the Supreme Court decided in a landmark ruling that such a stipulation was in violation of article 14 of the Japanese Constitution, in which the principle of all Japanese citizens' equality before the law is enshrined. Supreme Court Shōwa 45 (a) 1310, verdict of 4.4.1973. The text of this ruling (in Japanese) is available at: www.courts.go.jp/app/hanrei_jp/detail2?id=51807. Website last visited 30–8–2018.

6 *Ranshinsha* could be (1) put in prison, either as a form of punishment or upon the request of the family, who as guardians were responsible for his or her actions. Similarly, to prevent them from committing acts for which their family would be held responsible, they could be (2) put in a cage within their family's house, or (3) be put in a jail used for, among others, vagrants, juvenile delinquents and petty criminals, in case their symptoms worsened when locked up in either prison or at home.

from especially Chinese as well as Dutch sources (Takimoto, 2010: 44, 17). The recognition of a person as having a mental disorder would place him or her in a special social class, something which, as noted, did not guarantee a lenient treatment.

While this treatment thus varied in accordance with the nature of the crime and the relationship between the offender and the victim, until the first decades of the Meiji period (1868–1912) the treatment of offenders with a perceived mental disorder also generally varied in accordance with social and political circumstances. Takimoto notes in this regard that peaceful periods with little migration were characterized by a more lenient treatment of those with a suspected mental disorder (however defined), while punishment was generally harsher in periods with more migration and urbanization (Takimoto, 2010: 20).

The start of the Meiji period did not signal a clear change. From especially the 1880s on, however, Japan started a large, quick paced remodeling of its legal system on the basis of different Western models.[7] This development culminated in 1882 in the enactment of, among others, a "Western style" Criminal Procedure Code as well as a Criminal Code,[8] which in article 78 stipulated that "the crime of a person who through a loss of their mental faculties cannot distinguish right from wrong will not be judged".

Accordingly, the question to be answered was no longer that of whether an offender suffered from a mental condition, that is: whether this person had lost his or her mental faculties, and therefore belonged to the "social class" of those with a disorder. There now also was a more psychological question to be answered: at the time of the crime, was the offender able to distinguish right from wrong? Under the influence of both German law and German psychology the assessment of a person's mental sanity accordingly changed from something that was thought to be visible and easily distinguished by the average person, to something more complex that required a specialist's assessment (Takimoto, 2010: 33).[9]

7 During the better part of the Tokugawa period, when Japan was ruled by Shōguns, Japan had closed its borders to foreigners. Nevertheless, during this period Japan did trade with Chinese and Korean traders, as well as the Dutch, who had a trading post on an artificial island off the coast of Nagasaki. These contacts also provided a windows on especially these parts of the world. Toward the end of the Tokugawa period the Japanese interest in Western law grew. Under the threat of force from American gunboats Japan started opening up from the 1850s on and concluded different unfavorable treaties with different Western countries, such as France, Great Britain and the United States. When in 1867 the rule of the Shōguns ended, the emperor was "restored" to power and the Meiji period started, the Meiji leaders also looked at Western law as a means to be able to both "catch up" and be able to better resist the Western nations, with whom the unfavorable treaties were concluded. Having a modern legal system was in fact one condition for the renegotiation of these treaties.

8 Meiji 13 (1880) Daijōkanfukoku no. 36 (criminal law), and Meiji 13 (1880) Daijōkanfukoku no. 37 (criminal procedure law, officially named Chizaihō, or Crime Control Law. These laws, promulgated in 1880 and enacted in 1882, were both based on French models.

9 The influence of both German law and psychiatry should again be understood against the background of the unequal treaties referred to earlier. The introduction of an expert who

This requirement was codified in the 1882 Criminal Procedure Code that stipulated that an examining judge could during the pre-trial examination order a psychological evaluation of the suspect, to be conducted by an "expert" (*kanteinin*).[10] Takimoto, who conducted an examination of criminal cases from this period shows, however, that much like they had done before, criminal justice officials would still draw their own conclusions about "self-evident madness" and "self-evident sanity", while also assessing a suspect's mental condition on the basis of the testimony of those around him or her, as well as his or her life habits, et cetera.[11] The novelty of the field of forensic psychiatry also implied that there were simply very few persons who could perform a psychiatric evaluation.[12]

When the psychiatric evaluation pointed out any "mental abnormality", this would in an overwhelming majority of the cases result in a dismissal of the charges. Psychiatric evaluations accordingly formed a strong limitation on judges' freedom to form their own convictions and conclusions. A dismissal or a verdict of not guilty by reason of insanity (in accordance with the psychiatric evaluation) did not mean, however, that the defendant would go free. It rather meant that the defendant would for an unlimited amount of time be kept under home surveillance, in order to protect society from the threat the mentally disturbed persons we perceived to form.[13]

---

would base his judgments on insights heavily influenced by German psychology was part of a general effort to fulfill the requirements necessary for the revision of these unequal treaties (Takimoto, 2010: 107).

10 Article 191. This article 191 required, to be precise, that the person or persons who performed the evaluation were capable of doing so on the basis of their scientific profession.

11 That such practices continued is according to Takimoto indicative of the fact that criminal justice officials at the time may have had little awareness of relevant psychiatric and psychological knowledge, given also that at the time these subjects were not being taught at Japanese universities (2010: 110). This was about to change, however, thanks to scholars returning to Japan after having studied abroad. Especially influential within the field of forensic psychiatry were Hajime Sakaki (1875–1897) and Shūzō Kure (1865–1932).

12 While there appear to be hardly any records of the cases in which the criminal responsibility of the defendant was disputed, Yamagami nevertheless claims that within criminal proceedings psychiatric evaluations were "regularly conducted" (1999). He does not, however, provide a concrete number.

13 A treatment not unlike that which *ranshinsha* received in earlier times (see note 6). Home surveillance (*shitaku kanchi*) was a measure applied under the 1900 Act for the Care and Custody of the Mentally Ill. This measure obliged the family members of a mentally ill person to take care of and watch over this person by keeping him or her in a special room or a cage built within the family members' home. While it was first of all the responsibility of the family to make sure that their mentally ill member would be watched, the police were in turn charged with supervising families with a mental ill member, thereby ensuring that social order safety would be maintained (Fujino, 2005: 202). Mentally ill persons were thus regarded as a potential threat to social safety as is also illustrated by the fact that if in Tokyo, for example, a person with a mental disorder was found to be walking on the street, he or she could be taken into custody on the basis of police orders (on the basis of article 29 of the so-called Tokyo guardian rules, issued in 1873 by the Great Council of State). See in this regard Fujino, 202; National Institute of Mental Health, 2011: 20; Nakatani, 2000: 590.

The Criminal Code of 1881 was in 1907 replaced by the current Criminal Code, which was very much influenced by a German rather than a French model. This Code's provisions on criminal responsibility accordingly form the foundation upon which current practices are still based. The 1922 Code of Criminal Procedure furthermore stipulated that it was up to the court, rather than an examining judge, to order a suspect's evaluation – like it also is in the current Code. Under these Codes (diminished) criminal responsibility is established as follows. Article 39 of the 1907, *current* Criminal Code first of all contains the following provisions:

> "The actions of a person not of sound mind will not be punished"; and:
> The punishment for the acts of a person of diminished capacity will be reduced.

The question then becomes: how to define "a person not of sound mind" and "a person of diminished capacity"? The answer to this question was provided by a verdict pronounced by the Daishin'in[14] on 3 December 1931 (Daishin'in Keishū 10: 682), thereby setting the standard, *still in use today*, for the establishing of a complete lack of criminal responsibility or a diminished level thereof. This standard, then, was formulated as follows:

> Not of sound mind refers to a state of not being capable to distinguish right from wrong and not being able to act in accordance with that distinction by reason of a mental disorder,

while diminished capacity was defined as:

> a state in which the disorder has not reached a level so that this kind of capacity [of distinction) is absent, but in which this capacity is considerably diminished.

The difference between these two states was thus one of degree. When establishing this degree judges would in the pre–World War II period follow the lead of the forensic psychiatrist. In making this decision psychiatrists would especially focus on biological, rather than on psychological aspects. That is, whether a person was or was not of sound mind was decided predominantly on the basis of a diagnosis of defendants' "biological condition", rather than their motives or ways of accounting for their actions. This approach thus shows similarities to earlier approaches, where offenders would be categorized as belonging to a "class" of people with a mental disorder.

14 The *Daishin'in* was the predecessor of the current Supreme Court and was operational from 1875 to 1947. It was modeled after the imperial German Reichsgericht. As the Daishin'in was perceived as insufficiently independent from the legislature and executive, it was in 1947 abolished on the basis of the 1946 Constitution and the 1947 enacted Court Act (no. 59).

The focus on a defendants' biological condition was in fact so strong that judges' decisions did not necessarily acknowledge that the concepts of "a person of sound mind" and "a person of diminished capacity" were *legal* concepts, rather than medical diagnoses (Takimoto, 2010: 42). In any case, whether a defendant was to be held criminally accountable or not was thus effectively decided by the psychiatrist, rather than the judge. It was on the basis of especially psychiatrists' findings that defendants could be found not guilty, or that their sentence could be diminished.[15] Extra-legal knowledge and expertise were thus called upon to distinguish mentally disturbed offenders from "ordinary offenders", to accordingly provide for different criminal justice sanctions.

It is important to note here that such consideration for mentally disturbed offenders went hand in hand with various oppressive rules and laws that mentally disturbed people were generally subject to, for the sake of "maintaining public safety". That is: a defendant judged to be not (fully) of sound mind and hence not (fully) criminally responsible would nevertheless still be subject to various measures that severely restricted his or her movements (see Takimoto, 2010: 42 and note 13).[16]

After World War II, when in 1950 the Mental Hygiene Act[17] replaced the Act for the Care and Custody of the Mentally Ill, these measures would be abolished. The criteria for establishing diminished criminal responsibility or an absence thereof as defined in the 1931 verdict of the Daishin'in, were maintained. In other words: whether an offender was to be held criminally responsible or not still depended on his or her ability to distinguish right from wrong, and to act in accordance with this distinction. That does not mean, however, that courts and others involved went about establishing (diminished) criminal responsibility the same way they did before.

## 2. Criminal responsibility in the post–World War II period; the shift from *fukachiron* to *kachiron*

In the era preceding World War II the reigning line of thought had leaned toward the so-called *fukachiron*, often translated as agnosticism. Within the realm of

15 It should nevertheless be noted that even though judges typically followed forensic psychiatrists' lead, judges were not bound by the forensic psychiatrists' findings. An explicit recognition existed, in fact, of the fact that it was a matter of judges' discretion whether a psychiatrist's conclusions would be adopted or not. See 1933 Daishin'in Keishū 12, page 1796. Judges were however obliged to explain why they would adopt or rather set aside the conclusions of the forensic psychiatrist.

16 Mentally ill offenders who had committed a crime and were thought to be dangerous could on the basis of the 1919 Mental Hospital Act (*seishinbyōhō*) and a psychiatrist's recommendation furthermore be (forcibly) admitted to a mental hospital. The outbreak of the Sino-Japanese war (1937–1945) and World War II wound up interfering with mental hospital building plans, as a result of which only six hospitals were built, instead of the projected 47, resulting in a very limited capacity for patients to be (forcibly) admitted. As a consequence until the end of World War II the home surveillance system – see note 13 – continued to prevail (Fujino, 2005: 204).

17 Mental Hygiene Act, Shōwa 25 (1949), no. 123.

forensic psychiatry this word refers to the idea that it is impossible to establish whether actors possess free will or not. Accordingly, it is also impossible to establish whether a person was able to distinguish right from wrong. The only thing a forensic psychiatrist can hope to do, is to establish (diagnose) the biological condition that constitutes the basis for a person's actions. Given that it is impossible to know what moves an actor and certainty only exists with regard to his or her biological condition, the forensic psychiatrist's diagnosis would essentially determine a defendant's criminal responsibility, based on conventions with regard to the legal consequences of a psychiatrist's diagnosis. In accordance with such conventions a psychiatrist's diagnosis of schizophrenia, for example, should automatically result in the conclusion that the defendant was not criminally responsible. The fact that judges in the pre–World War II period would typically follow forensic psychiatrists' lead accordingly has to be understood in terms of the prevalence of this theory at that time (Okae, 2008; Ozawa, 2009).

The *kachiron* theory of Gnosticism, however, was to gradually become more influential. In other words: psychiatrists and judges increasingly based their conclusions on the assumption that the nature of an actor's will was amenable to their understanding. More and more judges would draw their own conclusions as to whether a suspect or defendant was able to distinguish right from wrong and act accordingly, regardless of any formal diagnosis.[18]

As we have seen (see note 15) judges had always had the authority to either adopt or set aside a psychiatrist's conclusions. As such, they had never *formally* subscribed to either the *fukachiron*, or the *kachiron*, for that matter. In 1984, however, the Third Petty Bench of the Supreme Court handed down a decision that shifted the balance in favor of the *kachiron*. This decision concerned a case in which the defendant who had been diagnosed with schizophrenia had killed five and had severely wounded two more persons. This defendant, a former naval officer in the Japanese Self Defense Forces (SDF), had fallen in love with the younger sister of a high school friend. Even though they had never dated and there was no romantic relationship between them, the defendant proposed to marry her. She and her family refused. As a result of both this refusal as well as the fact that the girl and her brother (the high school friend) had once at a party expressed their lack of sympathy for the SDF, the defendant developed a deep grudge against the girl and her family. It was this grudge that eventually motivated the defendant to do what he did.

In court one of the main questions to be answered was that of whether the defendant could be held criminally responsible for his actions. Both the District Court and on appeal the High Court decided that the defendant could indeed be held responsible. The Supreme Court to which the lawyers then appealed

18 A study by Noda, referred to by Okae (2008) however, also shows that between 1963 and 1970 judges would typically adopt the forensic psychiatrist's conclusion, suggesting that at least up until the 1970s psychiatrists' conclusions to a very great extent shaped judges' conclusions with regard to criminal responsibility. Psychiatrists' position on the *fukachiron* and *kachiron* will be addressed later.

ordered the case back to the High Court, in view of the existing possibility that the defendant should be considered diminished criminally responsible. The High Court concluded that that was indeed the case, and imposed a sentence of life imprisonment, instead of the death sentences originally meted out. On appeal the Supreme Court confirmed the High Court judgment.

This case is important as it confirmed that a psychiatrist's diagnosis (notably that of schizophrenia) does not automatically translate into a finding of diminished or no criminal responsibility. In the process it furthermore provided a range of criteria relevant for the finding of criminal responsibility, which were to have a huge impact on the way judges would from then on find criminal responsibility. This case is also important, however, as it points to some key aspects of legal conclusions about criminal responsibility and the way these come about.

During the course of the different stages of his case, the defendant was psychiatrically evaluated five times. The forensic psychiatrists who carried out these evaluations all concluded that the defendant suffered from schizophrenia.[19] What is remarkable, but as we will see not unusual, about these evaluations, however, is that in spite of the similar diagnosis of schizophrenia, the different psychiatrists reached different conclusions about the defendant's criminal responsibility. One, for example, emphasized the abnormality of the defendant's actions, which should be seen as symptomatic of his schizophrenia and general criminal insanity. Another highlighted the fact that up until his crime the defendant had had the ability to function within society, and that the motive for his crime contained elements that were not entirely incomprehensible. These different evaluations accordingly provided the judges with a multifaceted whole of information, expert findings and opinions, on the basis of which they could reach very different conclusions.

The final decision of the Supreme Court was also in line with such diversity in expert opinion. It held that when establishing defendants' criminal responsibility, judges should take into account the following four points: (1) the condition of the defendant at the time of the offense; (2) his or her lifestyle before the offense took place; (3) his or her motive, and (4) the nature of the crime. Of course, judges should also take into account the forensic psychiatrist's evaluation. The Supreme Court reconfirmed, however, that judges make their decisions in line with legal goals and on the basis of legal concepts, and that the judgment with regard to criminal responsibility is theirs and theirs alone.[20] Besides reconfirming their decision making authority, the Supreme Court here thus provided judges

19 A psychiatrist of the self-defense (naval) forces, the defendant's former employer, had also arrived at this diagnosis, something which had led to the defendant's dismissal from the SDF.

20 Supreme Court Third Petty Bench Showa 58 (a) 1761, verdict of 3.7. 1984. This verdict was accordingly in line with a Supreme Court verdict handed down in the previous year (1983), in which the Supreme Court confirmed exactly that "whether (the concepts of) criminal insanity and diminished criminal responsibility as defined in the Criminal Code article 39 apply to the defendant's mental condition: that constitutes a legal judgment that should be left exclusively (*moppara*) to the judge", and while this judgment is based on biological and psychological elements, in its connection with the assessment of the defendant's criminal

with very specific criteria on the basis of which they should reach their own conclusions regarding defendants' criminal responsibility (while also taking psychiatrists' opinion[21] into account).

The assumption underlying these criteria and any conclusion based upon them is that clearly, whether a defendant was able to distinguish right from wrong and to act accordingly is something that judges are able to assess (in reference to points 1–4). As such, the Supreme Court decision is very much in line with the *kachiron*, the theory of Gnosticism that holds that the nature of an actor's will was amenable to the understanding of others (beyond the actor him- or herself), such as psychiatrists and judges. Before going into how judges put these Supreme Court instructions into practice, and where these instructions leave the forensic psychiatrist, one question that needs to be addressed is this: how can the shift from *fukachiron* to *kachiron* be explained?

Different developments are relevant in this regard. First of all: schizophrenia or "integration function syndrome" changed from being perceived as an untreatable illness to one for which treatment was possible. This meant that those who received this diagnosis also were no longer automatically condemned to a life inside mental hospitals. This change also relates to another one that had started in the 1960s, when mental hospitals had started opening up, gradually shaking off their character as institutions that helped secure public safety by protecting society from people with mental illnesses or handicaps. More and more people in addition no longer lived in hospitals. As they increasingly received treatment or support while living in local communities, leading their lives much like any other citizen, it made sense for them to also have duties and responsibilities as such – as citizens.[22] Those with a mental illness or handicap were thus less defined by their illness or handicap, while increasingly being perceived as having civil duties. Against the background of such developments it also makes sense that when a person with a mental illness or handicap commits a crime, those in charge would proceed to examine the potential responsibility of this persons, rather than assume a lack of responsibility, on the basis of the label "mental handicap" or "mental illness". It is against the background of such developments, that the shift from *fukachiron* to *kachiron* has taken place.[23] Of course, one could also

---

responsibility this judgment too is ultimately a matter for judges to evaluate (Supreme Court Shōwa 58 (a) 753, verdict of 13.9.1983).

21 This word "opinion" (*iken*) is in fact the word that the Supreme Court has been using in reference to this issue. The implications of the use of this word, rather than the word *kantei*, which has a connotation of expertise and professionalism, will be further addressed later.

22 Symptomatic of this development is also the 2006 Ministry of Health, Labor and Welfare (MHLW) plan aimed at promoting the "normalization" of those with a mental handicap. Based on this idea of normalization the aim is for "both those with a mental handicap and those without one, to mutually support each other (. . .), with the goal of a society in which they can lead full, cheerful and rich lives, promoting the independence and social participation of those with a mental handicap (2006).

23 See Okae, 2008, 2013: 22–28; see also the account of this development provided in Tokyo High Court, Heisei 20 (u) 1097, verdict of 5.25.2009; Tokyo Bengoshikai, 2013: 156–159.

offer a more prosaic explanation: under the *fukachiron* judges in practice, even if not formally, deferred judgment on a defendant's criminal responsibility to the forensic psychiatrist. Here psychiatrists' expertise – that is extra-legal scientific knowledge – had a determinative influence on judges' decision making. The shift to *kachiron* allowed judges to reassert their authority to independently make their legal decision on a defendant's criminal responsibility, converting psychiatrists' contribution into one that stands more explicitly in service of judges' legal decision making, and that is in the more literal sense *forensic*.

## *2.1 The shift from* fukachiron *to* kachiron *in practice*

What, then, did this shift mean for the way in which judges addressed defendants' criminal responsibility? How did it impact the role of the forensic psychiatrist, or the role of the other players in criminal procedure, for that matter? As we have seen before, the Supreme Court has on one hand stated that the finding of criminal responsibility concerns a legal rather than a medical judgment. It is up to judges and judges alone, to make that judgment. They should, however, pay due respect to forensic psychiatrists' opinion, unless there are clear rational grounds not to do so.[24] In order to better understand what it means to implement a *kachiron* perspective in judgments of criminal responsibility, however, we need to return to the criteria for such judgments specified in the 1984 Supreme Court ruling. As we have seen, the Supreme Court notes that when making their assessment, judges should take into account the condition of the defendant at the time of the offense, his or her lifestyle before the offense took place, his or her motive

---

On the term schizophrenia: it should be noted that in 2002 the Japanese Society of Psychiatry and Neurology (JSPN) decided to replace the term *seishinbunretsubyō* (literally: mental split illness), a term for schizophrenia that had been in use since 1937, with the term *tōgōshicchōshō* ("integration function syndrome"). The change resulted from a growing perception that this term hindered patients' participation in society and possibly also their recovery, while in addition lacking accuracy. Having come to this conclusion the JSPN petitioned the MHLW to also start using the new term, which it did in 2002. The courts followed suit in the same year (for a full explanation see www.jspn.or.jp/modules/activity/index.php?content_id=78, and www.mhlw.go.jp/shingi/2004/06/s0621-5f.html#01. Websites last visited 30–8–2018.

24 While the Supreme Court noted in 1983 that it is up to the judge, and the judge alone to assess a defendant's criminal responsibility, in a later case in 2008 it would qualify this statement by reaffirming (after all) the importance of the psychiatric evaluation. In this case the Supreme Court notes (in true Supreme Court style): "with regard to the existence and the extent of a mental disorder (*seishinshōgai*), which is the biological element of criminal responsibility, and the extent to which this had an influence on the psychological element, bearing in mind that the *diagnosis* thereof is the task of clinical forensic psychology: in case a forensic psychologist's *opinion* is offered as evidence in the shape of an evaluation, then it should be said that this opinion should be acknowledged and sufficiently respected, unless there are rational grounds not to do so, in view of doubts concerning the psychiatrist's impartiality or skill, or problems regarding the presuppositions on which the evaluation is based, and so on" (Supreme Court Second Petty Bench, Heisei 18 (a) 876, verdict of 25.4.2008. See also Hayashi, 2013: 284–285).

as well as the nature of the crime. How, now, does this work out in practice, and where does the psychiatrist's evaluation fit in?

Factors 1–3 provide criteria to establish how normal, average or standard the person of the defendant, his or her lifestyle as well as the reasons for doing what s/he did are. "Normal" here accordingly refers to what from the perspective of the average person (*ippanjin*) and from the perspective of common sense (*ippanjōshiki*) can be considered normal, or understandable.[25] Proof of normal behavior, or of purposive, planned action then becomes an indication of the defendant's sanity and his or her condition at the time of the crime. Prior to his or her crime, had the defendant been able to function in society? Had he or she been living by him or herself, independently? Did the defendant have a job? Affirmative answers to these questions are taken as possible indications that the defendant was not governed by his or her illness or disturbance, and that the defendant had in fact been able to control his actions. These are "possible indications", as parties do typically argue about whether seemingly normal patterns of behavior are not in fact also understandable in terms of the defendant's illness.[26] Incidentally, this way of assessing a defendant's condition is not just employed by the juridical professionals. Forensic psychiatrists too may apply a similar reasoning, as the following forensic psychiatrist's quote also illustrates:"the seriousness of a defendant's illness, or lack thereof, is not directly related to the presence or absence of delusions and hallucinations or whether the illness is chronic, but is rather determined by the question of *whether [the person) can function in society*" (my emphasis).[27] Especially important in assessing the "normality" of the

25 Hayashi, 2013: 265, 275; see also Tokyo High Court, Heisei 20 (u) 1097, verdict of 25.5.2009.

26 Take the example of a defendant who was on trial for trying to kill his neighbors as their voices had in his head been taunting him. The fact that before his crime the defendant had been looking at apartments to move into and that he had taken his bike to ride to the center of the city he lived in: such acts were according to the prosecution indicative of the fact that the defendant's case of schizophrenia was not severe, and that his criminal responsibility was diminished, but not absent. The defense, on the other hand, emphasized the strangeness in his behavior, while providing a different perspective on actions that looked "normal". The fact that the defendant had been looking for a new apartment, for example, was still linked to his schizophrenic paranoia: he had wanted to move to get away from his neighbors' voices, not necessarily realizing he heard these voices only in his head (see Osaka District Court, Heisei 18 (wa) 6978, verdict of 26.5.2008). In reference also to two psychiatric evaluations, the court in this case went along with the defense rather than with the prosecution's reasoning. While the outcome of this case is not necessarily representative of how Japanese courts deal with the problem of "normal behavior mixed with abnormal behavior" (or vice versa) the argumentation is illustrative of the way in which the parties concerned look for signs of a defendant's normality or abnormality.

27 Quoted in Fukuoka High Court Heisei 23 (u) 122, verdict of 18.10.2011. This psychiatrist's statement is in line with the current juridical consensus as to how a defendant's "normality" can be assessed. In courts the implications of a person's ability to function in society while still exhibiting signs of a (severe) mental illness very much depend on the case. That is: much like a mental illness does not automatically translate into an absence of criminal responsibility, does "normal behavior" also not automatically translate into finding the

defendant and his or her actions, however, is also the defendant's motive. How understandable was this motive? Did that motive come about as a direct result of the defendant's illness, or did it rather result from the defendant's various life circumstances and his or her personality?

In practice, "understandable" does not necessarily refer to what is understandable from the judge's or the average person's point of view. Instead it may refer to what is understandable in the defendant's very subjective terms, as the following case also illustrates.

Sunao T., a 48 year old man, had set fire to a pachinko parlor, thereby causing the deaths of five people. Another 10 people were injured. In the original verdict the District Court that handled the case in first instance notes that the defendant believed to be haunted by a female person with paranormal powers, called Mihi, who belonged to a group called Mark. From about 10 years before his crime Sunao had been hearing Mihi's voice on and off. Sunao mostly ignored the things she told him to do, but he did believe that Mihi caused him pain and discomfort. Sunao also believed that Mihi and Mark together were responsible for things that went wrong in his life. Other people knew about this, but pretended not to know, and in fact helped Mihi. To take revenge on them and Mihi, Sunao had once damaged a number of cars with a screwdriver, for which he had received a 50,000 yen fine.

Sunao had been working as a taxi driver and had also driven trucks and heavy motor vehicles for different companies. Due to bankruptcies and other company misfortunes, however, Sunao had never been able to work for one company for long. For this misfortune Sunao blamed Mihi. He had in fact started thinking that if in the future there was something that would hinder him in his daily life, he would take revenge on Mihi and on the people around her, their helpers, by indiscriminately killing a number of them. When after his latest job Sunao was unable to find a new one, he decided to finally get his revenge by setting fire to a pachinko parlor. He thought that by indiscriminately killing a number of people, who had after all left Mihi and Mark free to do whatever they wanted, the world would be less easy on Mihi and Mark. This would be Sunao's revenge on them. After proceeding as planned, Sunao turned himself in, so that Mihi and Mihi's helpers would know it was he who had taken revenge on them.

In making sense of the implications of this motive for Sunao's criminal responsibility, the District Court – in this case: a panel of six lay and three professional judges – first established that Sunao suffered from delusions that were part of a kind of stimulant psychosis triggered by his methamphetamine use, years earlier. It also noted that he had been able to function without any problems, in his own

defendant responsible. When addressing this issue courts assess not only whether the (seemingly) normal behavior exhibited was in fact normal (and not after all, explainable in terms of the defendant's illness), while paying special attention to the direct influence of the illness on the defendant's behavior at the time of the crime (see e.g. Tokyo High Court, Heisei 20 (u) 1097, verdict of 25.5.2009; Supreme Court Second Petty Bench, Heisei 18 (a) 876, verdict of 25.4.2008.

way understanding the situations he had found himself in. On the basis of two psychiatric evaluations the Court in addition noted that Sunao had through his own thinking actively constructed his own delusions, as a way to adapt to his daily life – a daily life in which he had functioned without any problems. These delusions were therefore not part of his stimulant psychosis, but were the product of Sunao's own mind. The Court finally remarked that Sunao's crime might very well have been prevented had he found a job. Sunao's "revenge on Mihi" motive was thus nothing more than the defendant's own anti-social, ego-centrist response to specific life circumstances. In this sense Sunao's motive was after all understandable, so the lay judge Court reasoned (Osaka District Court, Heisei 21 (wa) 6154, verdict of 31.10.2011).

This was an exceptionally serious case. When it comes to the way in which motive figures into the assessment of a defendant's criminal responsibility, however, this case is still very much illustrative of judges' reasoning. Lay and professional judges take into account a range of factors, placing the defendant's act within the context of his or her circumstances, examining the continuity between the personality and circumstances of the defendant and his or her act. Assessing criminal responsibility implies that judges attempt to also look at these circumstances from the defendant's perspective. The rationality found in defendants' actions may here accordingly be a rationality in the defendant's terms. Doing so, however, has as a consequence that almost any motive may become understandable, making a finding of criminal responsibility more likely. So it can come to pass that a defendant who took revenge on the products of his delusions by causing the deaths of five of their "helpers" is held fully responsible and sentenced to death.[28]

The notion that a defendant's actions are amenable to judges' analysis and understanding (*kachiron*) thus in practice facilitates their increased responsibilization, in line also with the general societal trend toward responsibilization outlined earlier. But how has this notion affected forensic psychiatrists, and how do they contribute to the finding of criminal responsibility? We have already seen that different psychiatrists may reach very different conclusions. Some forensic psychiatrists in addition still present evaluations on the basis of a *fukachiron* stance.[29]

What to make of the criminal responsibility of a defendant with a mental disorder who also exhibits "normal behavior" is a question that is still being debated. Such debate, and the fact that some forensic psychiatrists still present evaluations from a *fukachiron* perspective are indicative of the fact that among psychiatrists there is still no consensus regarding issues of criminal responsibility (Okae, 2013: 33; Hirata, 2009: 87).

28 After two appeals from the defense the Supreme Court on 23 February 2016 upheld the death verdicts pronounced by both the District and High Court. For more examples of cases, see Ogata, 2013: 10.

29 See e.g. Osaka High Court, Heisei 25 (a) 729, verdict of 25.5.2015; Tokyo High Court, Heisei 20 (u) 1097, verdict of 25.5.2009.

In an effort to standardize psychiatric evaluations, then, psychiatrists are now expected to follow the guidelines provided by a psychiatric evaluation manual (*Evaluation Manual*) developed between 2006 and 2008 by psychiatrists from the Study Group on the Evaluation of the Criminal Responsibility of Persons who Harmed another Person. Besides leading to standardized evaluations, this manual is also expected to help produce psychiatric evaluations that are short and easy to understand for lay judges (Study Group, 2009: 2–3; Yoshikawa, 2009: 80). In practice the manual is said to have led to evaluations that are oriented toward legally relevant criteria, such as premeditation and the comprehensibility of the suspect's motive, and to a further responsibilization of mentally disturbed suspects (Yoshikawa, 2009: 80; Tokyo Bengoshikai, 2013: 104, 162; Nakatani, 2009a: 1367).

That does not mean that psychiatrists are invited or expected to draw legal conclusions on the basis of their own findings, even if doing so is a not uncommon practice that the Supreme Court is actually trying to put a stop to (Legal Research and Training Institute, 2009: 42; Okada et al., 2012: 15). It does mean that psychiatrists present their specialist findings so that legal implications are easily deduced. The criteria employed, however, bring about a (further) narrowed focus on criteria that are part of a (*kachiron*) perspective that, as we have seen, facilitates an increased responsibilization of defendants.

## 3. Responsibilization or social defense?

The aligning of psychiatrists' perspective with the *kachiron* perspective employed in court thus facilitates a further responsibilization of defendants with a mental disorder. The available statistics are in line with these developments (see Graph 2.1). That is: they show decreasing numbers and percentages of defendants found diminished criminally responsible or not criminally responsible by reason of insanity. Graph 2.1 also shows that this downward trend in findings of diminished criminal responsibility had started well before 1984. Accordingly, important as the 1984 ruling may have been (as a formal recognition of the *kachiron*), it should be seen as a symptom or confirmation of already occurring change, rather than an initiation of such change. This change, then, could be qualified as a process of responsibilization of mentally disturbed persons, of which the shift from *fukachiron* to *kachiron* was a part. The increasing standardization of psychiatric evaluations further contributed to this process and these statistics.

Since especially the late 1990s, however, this change is said to have been reinforced especially by penal populist trends that have contributed to the development of an increasingly harsh criminal justice climate. The public demands for harsher criminal justice policies – or at least: policy makers' perceptions thereof – also included the demand that mentally disturbed persons would be punished like "regular" offenders (Kanai, 2010; Ichinose, 2008, see also generally Okae, 2013: 22–38; Nakatani, 2009b: 17 and generally Chapter 1).

Interestingly enough, and as also remarked earlier, this virtual disappearance of persons not held criminally responsible in court went hand in hand with an increased recognition of the fact that many suspects and defendants suffer from

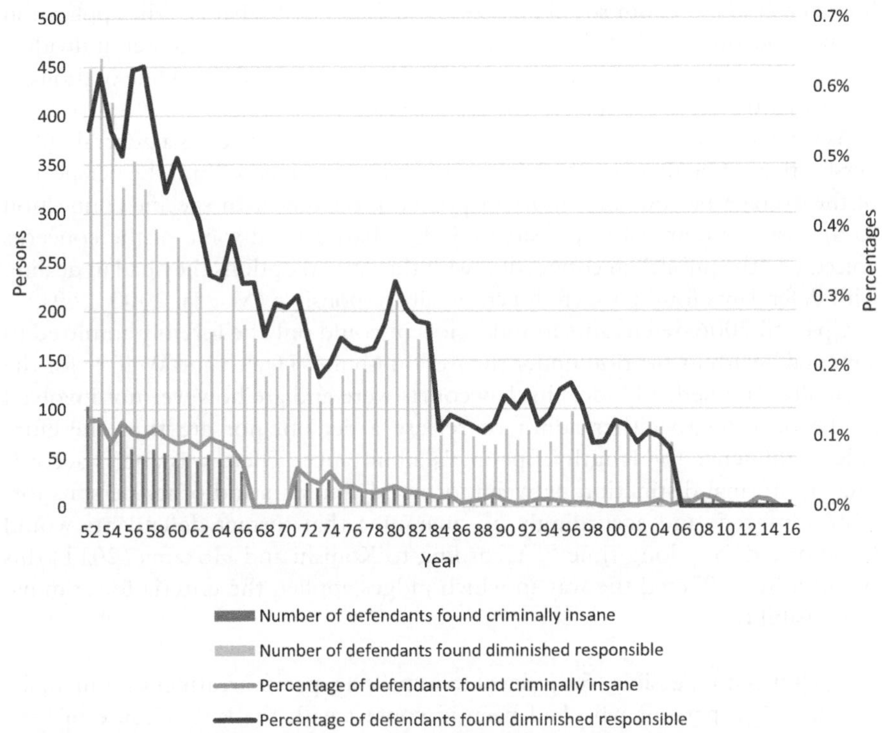


*Graph 2.1* District Court findings of criminal responsibility 1952–2016[30]

Source: Graph generated on the basis of data from the 1953–2017 MOJ White Papers on Crime.

Note: The percentages presented are the percentages of the total number of defendants who stood trial in District Courts for both General Penal Code and Special Code offenses.

some form of mental disturbance. Chapter 3 will further address this development and its consequences for criminal justice practice. Here it is in any case important to note that the gradual disappearance from court of the criminally insane or offender of diminished responsibility has been going hand in hand with increasing numbers and rates of registered crime committed by mentally disturbed offenders, translating into higher numbers and rates of such offenders going to prison.

Like the disappearance of the diminished criminally responsible actor, the increased presence of the responsible yet mentally disturbed offender could be understood in terms of processes of responsibilization, as mentally disturbed persons have increasingly been held accountable and incarcerated for their actions.

30 Between 1967 and 1970 the MOJ White Papers on Crime do not provide any data on defendants found innocent due to a finding of criminal insanity. From the year 2006 on, these Papers do not provide data on diminished criminal responsibility.

Increased accountability and incarceration is not just about responsibilization, however. It is also about social defense, or *defense sociale*, that is: "the application of safety-measures to individuals because of and in proportion to their individual capacity for doing harm" (Ancel, quoted in Dando, 1970: 519), a line of thought that was introduced in Japan in the early 1900s.

As we have also seen, judges take into account what they see as a general public perspective. After all, matters of "wholesome common sense" and the perspective of the average person are important points of reference. In specific connection to the issue of criminal responsibility judges have shared some of the concerns voiced by "the public" in connection with the limited options they had in dealing with defendants found not (fully) criminally responsible (Maeda, 2000: 269).

Up until 2006 defendants found innocent could only be forcibly admitted to a mental health institution under the Act on Mental Health and Welfare for the Mentally Disabled.[31] Under this law courts were and are however not involved in the decision to either admit or release a person, nor are they therefore able to influence the length of people's admittance. There was and is accordingly no formal distinction between former defendants and other persons forcibly admitted, and accordingly no guarantee that former defendants would be admitted for a long time.[32] According to Konishi and Hokama (2011) this situation too affected the way in which judges applied the criteria for criminal responsibility:

> [I]t was not possible (for judges) to impose a separate treatment for mentally disturbed persons who had been in contact with the law. Because of that, one would often come across cases in which (judges were) forced to find (defendants) fully criminally responsible, even when defendants were at least of diminished responsibility.
>
> (9)

Similarly, a Tokyo Bar Association guidebook for lawyers defending mentally disturbed clients notes:

> Courts have had the tendency to rarely find defendants (. . .) criminally insane. At the most they would find (a defendant) to be of diminished responsibility, even when in the psychiatric evaluation a severe mental disorder was recognized. This was, so it is said, because not punishing a person who committed an illegal act (. . .) would mean that victims' feelings of retribution would remain unsatisfied and because in our country no facilities existed where mentally disturbed offenders could be both punished and treated.
>
> (Tokyo Bengoshikai, 2013: 141)

31 This law, no. 123, adopted in 1965, was a greatly revised version of the Mental Hygiene Act addressed earlier.

32 See www.kansatuhou.net/07_genzai/01_kongonokadai.html; Act on Mental Health and Welfare for the Mentally Disabled, available at: http://law.e-gov.go.jp/htmldata/S25/S25HO123.html. Websites last visited 30-8-2018.

The judges I spoke to on this issue ($n = 11$) rejected this assessment, in wordings much like those of this district court judge: "I look at the facts, I look at the psychiatrist's assessment. I apply the law, keeping legal precedent in mind, and I come to a conclusion on the basis of all these things combined. I don't concern myself with the nature of the sanction (*shogū*) to be imposed". They also noted, however, that judges agonize about decisions regarding criminal responsibility, especially when finding somebody either criminally insane or criminally responsible may mean the difference between a death sentence and a not guilty verdict. Such agonizing suggests that judges are mindful of the consequences of their conclusions during the process of drawing these conclusions.[33] Similarly, in an article published in the Japanese law journal *Hanrei Taimuzu*, Tokyo District Court judge Mikio Miyoshi expressed the expectation that new possibilities to forcibly admit mentally disturbed offenders to a mental hospital would have the secondary effect of mollifying the standards of criminal responsibility (Miyoshi, 2008: 35).[34]

Lawyers' and academics' observations on one hand and judges' remarks on the other thus together suggest that findings of criminal responsibility have been affected by the availability of an acceptable treatment or sanction. Within the limits allowed by the evidence, considerations regarding the consequences of judges' legal conclusions may affect the nature of the legal conclusions drawn. Within these limits, room to maneuver does exist, even if it cannot be formally acknowledged or integrated into legal reasoning. It is as such an unacknowledged form of discretion, an unchartered "hole in the doughnut".[35] While many legal actors within Japanese criminal justice enjoy a certain amount of officially acknowledged discretion – as judges also do when it comes to sentencing, for example – the idea that the available sanction affects the choice of legal labels applied to facts found is from a legal reasoning viewpoint problematic.

At the same time, in criminal justice practice this phenomenon is far from unusual. Johnson (2002) notes, for example, that prosecutors routinely

> assess culpability and character so as to select a charge that 'makes the crime fit the punishment' (. . .). Indeed, after constructing "the truth" about an

33 During one talk, over lunch, one judge did in fact explicitly note that judges are conscious of the consequences of not finding a defendant criminally responsible, in terms of its impact on the sanction to be imposed, and that such consciousness plays a role in deciding on defendants' criminal responsibility. The following day he however emailed to reaffirm that judges evaluate a defendant's criminal responsibility in accordance with Supreme Court jurisprudence, that "as far as judges' way of thinking goes the assumption is that assessments of criminal responsibility are not affected by the seriousness of a case."

34 In reference to the adaption of the Medical Treatment and Observation Act, which allows for the (forced) treatment of mentally disturbed offenders (Miyoshi, 2008). When hypothesizing over this possibility, Tokyo District Court judge Mikio Miyoshi explicitly linked the strictness of existing standards to insufficient facilities to treat mentally disturbed offenders (Miyoshi, 2008: 35). I will come back to the Medical Treatment and Observation Act later.

35 Dworkin famously compared discretionary authority to the hole in a doughnut, as it "does not exist except as an area left open by a surrounding belt of restriction (1977: 52). I will come back to the hole in the doughnut in Chapter 6, when addressing the ways in which lay judges make use of their discretion in sentencing.

> offense and offender, the prosecutor has discretion to choose from a number of crimes a charge that both "fits the facts" and "fits the punishment". The Japanese prosecutor normally selects a charge that reflects her appraisals of desert and correctability.
>
> (185)

When it comes to the connection between facts and sanctions in case of criminal responsibility, however, for now the remarks and observations of academics, lawyers and judges at this point only provide *indications.*[36]

### *3.1 Introduction of the Medical Treatment and Observation Act*

In any case, as of 2005 both judges and prosecutors have had more options when dealing with mentally disturbed offenders, as a result of the introduction of the "act regarding the medical treatment and observation of those who committed a serious act harmful to others whilst in a state of criminal insanity", in discussions usually shortened to the Medical Treatment and Observation Act (Iryōkansatsuhō, here: MTOA). As also explained in Chapter 1, this law was introduced in the wake of a violent crime committed by a man with a long history of mental health issues, targeting those who committed an act that caused serious harm to others while in a state of criminal insanity.[37] Ironically, the MTOA would thus not have applied to the person responsible for the incident that triggered the making of this law, raising doubt also about the potential of this law to prevent similar incidents from happening.

Be that as it may, the law's aim is to treat those who committed a serious act harmful to others whilst in a state of criminal insanity and prevent them from committing a similar act and to promote their return to society (MTOA, art. 1). But given that an assessment of the risk of reoffending is one of the criteria of its applicability, the law is obviously also aimed at keeping society safe from "dangerous mentally disturbed persons". The MTOA in any case expands the options available to judges, as it allows for those found innocent by reason of insanity or

36 When considering the effect that ideas about the appropriate sanction may have on the way in which a case against a defendant is built, it is also important to remember that when in the past greater numbers of defendants were still being found innocent by reason of insanity, these defendants would still be subject to various measures that severely restricted their movements (see note 13). In other words: the verdict of innocent by reason of criminal insanity did not have the consequences it would have in the post-war period.

37 I will return to this issue below. The law in any case only applies to (1) those whose prosecution was dropped by reason of diminished criminal responsibility or criminal insanity; (2) those who were in court found innocent by reason of criminal insanity, as well as (3) those who in court were given a suspended (and reduced) sentence in view of their diminished criminal responsibility. The specified harmful acts are: murder, arson, robbery/robbery resulting in death, rape/rape resulting in death, indecent sexual assault/indecent sexual assault resulting in death and bodily harm (art. 2, par. 1–5).

given a suspended sentence in view of diminished criminal responsibility to still be dealt with within a criminal justice framework.[38]

In the case of acts and persons who fit the MTOA profile, prosecutors are required to file a petition to the District Court, unless there is "clearly no need for treatment" (art. 33). Thereupon a hearing will be held at which one judge and one psychiatrist will decide on the need for treatment of the person concerned, who at this hearing is accompanied by a lawyer. At the hearing the judge ascertains both whether the suspect has in fact committed an act as specified by the MTOA and whether this person was in fact criminally insane at the time of the act.[39]

The need for treatment and the nature of that treatment are assessed by (1) considering a person's disorder, (2) the possibilities of treating that disorder and (3) the chances that the person concerned might commit a similar act if he or she were to return to society without treatment. Treatment here takes place either after forcible admission to a mental hospital or through regular visits to such a hospital as an outpatient. Institutions generally aim at a treatment of 18 months. Having said that, there is no legal limit regarding the duration of the forcible admission (the maximum length of outpatient treatment is five years, however). Treatment can be prolonged for periods of six months, on the basis of petitions filed to the District Court. The decision to end treatment is again made by the District Court, on the basis of petitions filed by the treating institutions or the guardian or lawyer assisting the person being treated.

Given that the disorder of the person concerned and the possibilities of treating that disorder form two important pillars on which decisions regarding treatment rest, psychiatric expertise necessarily plays an important part in the making of these decisions. The third pillar, which concerns the chances of reoffending, obviously requires a very different kind of assessment. How are judges or psychiatrists to predict these?

Those critical of the law have been pointing out that chances of reoffending are in fact impossible to predict, and that is accordingly problematic for such a prediction to figure into a decision concerning a person's medical treatment. The law furthermore treats the risk of reoffending as given, even though for the type of serious crimes targeted by the law the risk of recidivism remains unclear, while the law obviously does not address the risk of a first offense. Given that a

38 It is important to note here that this law and the possibilities for treatment it offers come on top of the already existing Act on Mental Health and Welfare for the Mentally Disabled (see notes 31 and 32).

39 Among those for whom a petition is filed are also persons who at trial are found criminally insane and accordingly found innocent as well as those found to be of diminished responsibility, who were given a suspended sentence. Court findings on their criminal responsibility are at the hearings not disputed. In 99.7% of the cases the judge finds that the suspect did commit an "MTOA act", while finding around 3% of the suspects not criminally insane or of diminished responsibility. These suspects will then after all be standing trial.

risk assessment plays an important role in the decision to forcibly admit people to a mental hospital, the MTOA is often characterized as a segregation measure, where segregation is in fact used as a means to after all punish mentally disturbed persons for what they have done. The law is furthermore said to help perpetuate the misrepresentation of mentally disturbed persons as dangerous.[40]

Prosecutors are the ones who decide whether to file a petition to the District Court for a suspect to be dealt with on the basis of the MTOA. This fact accordingly brings into focus the importance of examining the practices of legal insiders and outsiders during the *pre-trial* stage. Up until now we have focused on the practices and practitioners involved in finding criminal responsibility during the trial stage, and the results of these practices as represented in Graph 2.1. Important as these practices are, Graph 2.1 cannot be understood without taking into account what goes on before that stage. We have seen in Chapter 1 that prosecutors will only prosecute when they are convinced that they can secure a guilty verdict in court. Their prosecution policies and practices also determine which defendants' criminal responsibility psychiatrists and judges get to assess during trial. How have prosecution practices been affected by the societal and judicial trends toward responsibilization, punitiveness and concerns of social defense? What role do psychiatrists play in this regard? How have pre-trial practices been affected by the introduction of the Medical Treatment and Observation Act? By addressing these questions in connection with recent legal change the following section will also help make more sense of the trend of the disappearance of the diminished or not criminally responsible defendant.

## 3.2 *Psychiatrists, prosecutors and the question of criminal responsibility – on and off stage*

Forensic psychiatrists' role within the criminal process starts when a public prosecutor asks him or her to provide an evaluation of a suspect whom the police have apprehended and sent on to the public prosecutor.[41] Prosecutors may have different reasons for doing so. They may feel that the way a suspect speaks or

40 For an overview of the various criticisms directed at the law, see www.kansatuhou.net/02_mondai/index.html (a website run by mental health professionals, dedicated to thinking about the MTOA – last visited 30-8-2018). See in this regard also Konishi and Hokama (2011).

41 It is important to keep in mind here that in cases involving a person with a mental disturbance where the victim is a family member, "the police have a tendency to not make things official", unless the case is too serious to do so (Yoshikawa, 2009: 72). When they do encounter a person who, according to their judgment, might inflict harm on him or herself or on others, they are obliged to notify the governor of their prefecture. On the basis of this investigation the governor may order a psychiatric evaluation on the basis of which persons who are judged to be a danger to themselves or others may be forcibly admitted to a state psychiatric institution. For the conditions of such forcible admission and further information, see Yoshikawa (2009). As we have also seen in Yoshikawa, in the past two decades incidents involving mentally disturbed persons have been increasingly dealt with through formal

acts is unusual (*ijō*) or find that a suspect does not (fully) remember what he or s/he has done (interviews, *n* = 14). The nature of the crime committed or the motive provided[42] may be reason enough for a psychiatric evaluation, as is also a suspect's psychiatric history (interviews; Yamauchi, 2001: 1394). In the words of one prosecutor: "to put it plainly: when you get the feeling: this isn't normal, is it? When you have the feeling that there's something wrong, sometimes you immediately ask for a full evaluation, but at times you first just go for a simple evaluation, and look at the results, and if those are ok, you don't do a full evaluation. But if it looks like it's better to do some more tests, you have the person admitted and have them do an official evaluation".

When a public prosecutor thus finds that there are good reasons to do so, he or she will thus in most cases request that the forensic psychiatrist performs a "simple evaluation" (***kan'i kantei***, in accordance with Code of Criminal Procedure (CCP) article 223.[43] Prosecutors may do so on their own accord, that is: they do not require a judge's permission or warrant. Suspects will need to consent to an evaluation, however. Prosecutors may also request a judge to issue a warrant for a "full evaluation" (***honkantei*** or (***shokutakukantei***), conform CCP article 224 and 225), for which suspects' consent is not required.

Besides the issues of judges' approval and suspects' consent, the main difference between these two types of evaluation is their length and thoroughness. Full evaluations usually take around two months, during which the suspect will be (forcibly) admitted to a psychiatric institution. Simple evaluations, on the other hand, typically only take a few hours (Kudo, 2016). During these "one to three hours" psychiatrists will have to familiarize themselves with the case and tentatively diagnose the suspect.[44]

The most important way for psychiatrists to familiarize themselves with the case is that of examining the evidence shown to them by the prosecutor, and in particular: reading the statements provided by the suspect. The psychiatrist may accordingly very well read statements that the prosecution will not submit as evidence to the court, or that will not be admitted into evidence (Okae, 2008). While psychiatrists' task is obviously not that of establishing a suspect's guilt or innocence, it is nevertheless important to note that when psychiatrists make their diagnosis, this diagnosis is typically colored by the assumption that the person being evaluated indeed did what he or she is being suspected of.

---

adjudication. In (very) recent years, however, efforts are being made to change that, and to increasingly divert mentally disturbed persons away from formal criminal procedures.

42 Such observations are obviously based on the assumption that the suspect has indeed committed the crime s/he is suspected of.

43 According to Hirata (2009) 91% of the pre-trial evaluations are simple evaluations (93).

44 "Tentatively" because, as Okae, a forensic psychiatrist with over 30 years of experience notes, the psychiatrist obviously cannot reach a diagnosis the way he or she normally would, i.e. a diagnosis based on his or her own observations and questions (etc.), but has to rely on information provided by the suspect or defendant on his or her state at the time, or "secondary sources", such as records of treatment or information provided by a treating physician (2008). On this issue, see also Hirata, 2009: 87–88.

A notorious example of how the assumption that the suspect is the actual offender colors psychiatrists' perceptions is the evaluation that was presented in a murder case that happened in Ashikaga city on 12 May 1990. In this case the suspect was accused of murdering a four year old girl. This suspect, Toshikazu Sugaya, initially confessed. Half-way through his trial he however recanted and professed his innocence. Based on his initial confession and especially DNA evidence found at the scene Sugaya was found guilty and sentenced to an indeterminate prison sentence. Some 20 years later, in 2010, Sugaya would ultimately be found innocent, as the DNA evidence against him was judged to have been produced by means of an unreliable method, and his confession judged to be false. Chapter 5 will further address this case as it is highly significant when thinking about the role of scientific evidence and experts in criminal justice. What is especially important here is that the psychiatrist who evaluated Sugaya found him to be a pedophile, and explained his motives in terms of experiences of sexual failure in his marriage, that had led him to substitute adult women with little girls as sexual objects. As also shown by Onuki and Matsuki (2003), this conclusion and the general gist of the evaluation were totally dependent on the assumption that Sugaya had indeed killed a little girl.[45]

When confronted with a confessing suspect, and having been informed about the evidence against this suspect, such mistakes may be hard to avoid. Psychiatrists are of course aware of this problem – and the Ashikaga case certainly helped raise that awareness – as well as the problem of "objective information", when also confronted with different, often conflicting sources of information, such as that provided by the public prosecutor on one hand, and the information provided by the suspect on the other (Nakatani, 2001, 2007: 882; Yoshikawa, 2009: 74–75). Be that as it may, on the basis of their findings they will write an evaluation in which they indicate if at the time of his or her act the suspect was able to distinguish right from wrong and to act accordingly.[46]

While the time available to come to an assessment of the suspect's state of mind at the time of his or her (alleged) offense is thus very limited, the importance of this simple evaluation for the suspect's fate cannot be overstated. Hirata has found that when psychiatrists concluded that the label "criminal insanity" was appropriate ($n$ = 337), or conversely, that their findings justified the conclusion

45 Curiously enough, in recognizing the *validity* of the psychiatric evaluation the High Court that upheld Sugaya's conviction in 1996 actually acknowledged as much: "*when departing from the assumption that the defendant is the offender,* it is sufficiently convincing and justified for the evaluation to have concluded that the defendant is a (. . .) pedophile" (Onuki & Matsuki, 2003: 76 – emphasis in original).

46 We noted earlier the lack of consensus that existed among psychiatrists concerning issues of criminal responsibility, a situation that has also affected pre-trial evaluations. When studying simple evaluations Hirata (2009) and Yamagami (1997) furthermore discovered that these differed enormously in form, content and scope, while the number of evaluations also greatly differed, depending on the district. While some evaluations are only a few sentences long, others are very extensive and not necessarily all that different from a full evaluation. The evaluation manual discussed earlier is also intended to help remedy this problem.

"fully criminally responsible" ($n$ = 849), prosecutors in around 98% of the cases went along with the psychiatrist. Only when psychiatrists' findings suggested a conclusion of diminished responsibility ($n$ = 429), did prosecutors steer a more independent course, as they prosecuted around 60% of these suspects while suspending prosecution in around 40% of the cases (Hirata, 2009: 93).[47]

The Ministry of Justice's annually published White Papers on Crime present the number of prosecutions dropped by reason of criminal insanity, and they also show that over the years registration practices have changed a few times.[48] As a result it is unfortunately not possible to present an overview of long-term trends in prosecution practices in a single graph. Between 1949 and 1991 the *numbers* have fluctuated without showing a clear trend that might have correlated with Court practices. Graph 2.2 shows that numbers from the period from 1991 to 2016 – during which registration practices remained constant – in any case show that from 1997 on percentages of offenders not prosecuted by reason of insanity started dropping slightly, from the already small percentage of 0.6% of all non-prosecutions in 1997 to 0.3% in 2004, i.e. before the introduction of the MTOA. Since then percentages have risen somewhat, but they have not returned to the levels of the 1990s.

Since the introduction of the MTOA prosecutors have thus been dropping cases by reason of insanity at a slightly higher rate than in the few years before the MTOA, but the impact in terms of numbers and percentages of dropped prosecutions has been limited. Prosecutors file a petition for 60–70% of the cases they drop by reason of insanity. These cases in turn constitute 85–90% of the cases for which a petition is filed. In other words, the MTOL procedure is for 85–90% used to deal with persons whose case prosecutors would otherwise have dropped. The remainder are almost exclusively cases of defendants who at trial were found to have diminished responsibility and were given a suspended (diminished) sentence. Prosecutors thus in practice do not file petitions for suspects they find to

---

47 Hirata's findings are based on a study of the 2,014 evaluations conducted in Japan in the year 2000. In 1,670 of these the decisions taken were based on psychiatrists' simple evaluations (in the remaining cases prosecution was dropped for other reasons). Three hundred thirty-seven simple evaluations justified the conclusion "criminally insane", resulting in about 330 dropped or suspended prosecutions (Hirata does not provide a precise number). The 2001 MOJ White Paper on Crime notes that in the year 2000 prosecutors dropped the cases against 480 suspects by reason of criminal insanity (representing 0.6% of the total of cases dropped). These numbers thus suggest that the findings of simple evaluations translate into a little over two-thirds of all prosecutions dropped by reason of insanity.

48 For example: between 1981 and 2005 the MOJ White Papers differentiate between offenders not prosecuted by reason of criminal insanity and offenders whose prosecution was suspended in view of diminished responsibility. Starting in 2006 numbers of offenders receiving a suspended prosecution are no longer listed. An overview of the numbers of offenders not prosecuted by reason of insanity between 1991 and 2014 presented in the 2015 MOJ White Paper shows that "in retrospect" these numbers have been recalculated, as this overview presents different numbers for the period 1991–2005. That is: the numbers of suspects not prosecuted by reason of insanity published in the separate issues 1991–2005 do not match the numbers in the 2015 overview that includes this period.

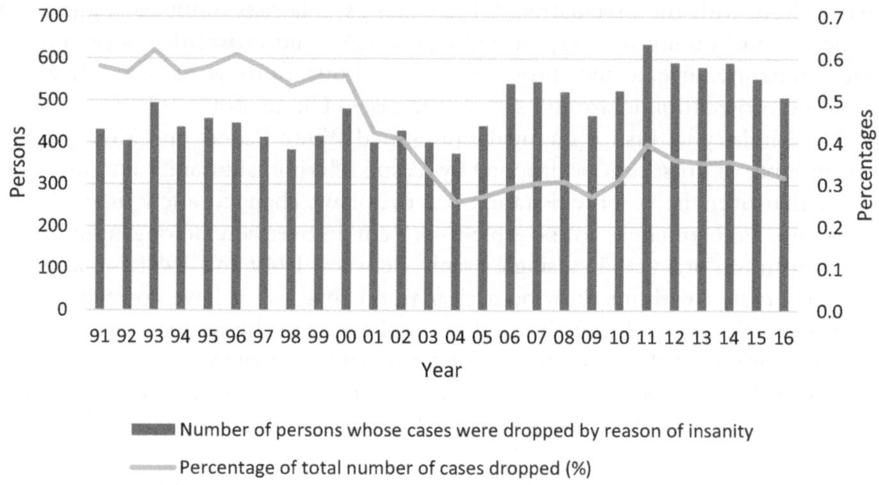


*Graph 2.2* Numbers and percentages of cases that prosecutors dropped by reason of insanity

Source: Graph generated on the basis of data from the 1992–2017 MOJ White Papers on Crime.

be of diminished responsibility. These are either prosecuted or they receive a suspended prosecution.[49]

This graph does not show that the availability of the "alternative option" to deal with offenders on the basis of MTOA has translated into clearly higher numbers of persons found criminally insane, and accordingly they also do not lend support to the idea that the availability of an alternative way to deal with mentally disturbed offenders, as provided by the MTOA, affects the likelihood that a person is found (suspected to be) criminally insane at the pre-trial investigation stage. This graph does show that Prosecutors' practices have remained relatively stable and unaffected by societal preoccupations with social defense.

Graph 2.3 shows the numbers of persons whose case was dealt with on the basis of an MTOA hearing and who were either forcibly admitted or given an outpatient treatment. This graph thus shows how the MTOL redirects persons whose case would otherwise be dropped to hearings headed by a judge, as such

49 Since the prosecution office as of 2006 no longer publishes statistics differentiating between suspects found to be of diminished responsibility and those found criminally insane. Trends in dispositions regarding diminished responsibility accordingly can no longer be ascertained. Thanks to statistics on the functioning of the MTOA we do know how many persons who committed MTOA acts are each year found to be of diminished responsibility and dealt with under the MTOA, based on the number of persons who received a suspended sentence. We do not know, however, how large the total number is of persons found diminished criminally responsible. These persons have thus largely gone off the map.

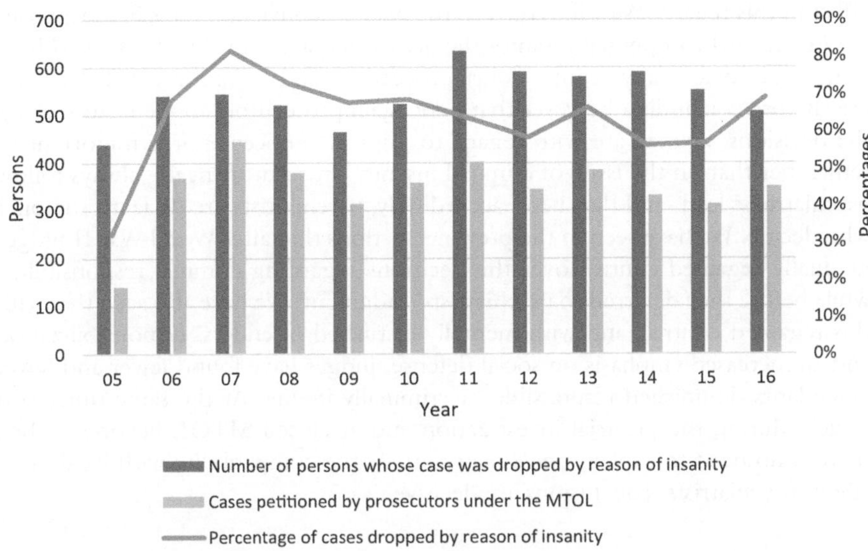


*Graph 2.3* Prosecutions dropped and petitions filed under the MTOA
Source: Graph generated on the basis of data from the 2006–2017 MOJ White Papers on Crime.

making criminally insane offenders visible again to the Courts. But while in regular trials the defendant is virtually always found criminally responsible, in these hearings the person at the center of the hearing is typically found criminally insane: since the introduction of MTOA the percentage of petitions denied because persons were found not criminally insane or the court did not recognize that the person had committed an MTOL act was on average 3% (White Papers on Crime, 2006–2017). Characteristic for both types of proceedings is thus that with the exception of a small percentage of cases, beforehand it is already clear what findings the proceedings will produce: criminal insanity in MTOA hearings, criminal responsibility in regular trials. In regular trials judges very much steer their own course. In closed MTOL hearings however psychiatrists' conclusions de facto shape most of the final decisions, keeping in mind that at the pre-trial stage prosecutors follow psychiatrists' findings on criminal insanity in 98% of the cases, and when they file a MTOL petition, the court in about 97% of the cases grants the petition.

That does not mean that in regular criminal trials responsibility is no longer an issue. Lawyers do of course still dispute their clients' responsibility when it is appropriate for them to do so. The cases of Kazuhiro O. and Sunao T., for example, happened *after* the MTOA was implemented. But while lawyers do dispute their clients' criminal responsibility as they did in these cases, they thus very rarely (0.1% of the cases) succeed in convincing the Courts, much like they very rarely succeed in convincing the Courts of their clients' innocence. The introduction of the lay judge system in 2009 does not appear to have had any clear statistical effect in this regard. We will return to the issue of conviction rates in Chapter 6.

With regard to criminal insanity the actual decision can thus be said to have been made before any regular court proceeding and before any MTOA hearing. Before concluding however that here again prosecutors are de facto making the decisions, as they are with regard to guilt or innocence, it is important to remember that on the issue of criminal insanity prosecutors nearly always follow psychiatrists' lead, and that here, accordingly, psychiatrists are de facto the ones who decide. We have seen in the previous sections that after World War II judges gradually regained control over the decisions regarding criminal responsibility, while before they deferred to psychiatrists' judgment. We have also seen that with this regained control, and with mentally disturbed offenders' responsibilization and an increased emphasis on social defense, judges have found fewer and fewer defendants diminished responsible or criminally insane. At the same time, "off stage", during the pre-trial investigation and at closed MTOL hearings, when there is no need to explain one's reasoning or the compatibility with legal precedent, psychiatrists' conclusions are decisive.

## *3.3 Lay judges and criminal responsibility*

The statistics presented in Graph 2.1 show that the numbers of defendants found criminally insane have since the introduction of the lay judge system in 2009 not gone up.[50] Nevertheless – and as also noted before – the significance of lay judge trials cannot be solely expressed in terms of criminal justice output. Regardless of this output, decisions on criminal responsibility have since May 2009 been taken in ways different from before, given that professional and lay judges now together decide on this issue. Furthermore, lay judges do of course bring their own perspective and understandings of actors and events to the deliberation room, as they also did in the case of Kazuhiro O. – exceptional as that case may have been. Given, in any case, that one aim of this chapter is to pursue the ways in which decisions on criminal responsibility come about, it is fruitful to examine more in depth lay judges' role in this decision making process.

In the previous section we already discussed the role that forensic psychiatric expertise plays in the making of legal decisions on criminal responsibility. We also noted that when it comes to the legal criteria applied to determine criminal responsibility, frequent reference is made to "the average person". The (ab)normality of the defendant's lifestyle or reasons for doing what he or she did, for example, are assessed by considering an average person's lifestyle as well as the perspective of the average person. Lay judges are thought to personify such a perspective, as their participation is conceived and represented as a way to infuse criminal justice with an average citizen's perspective. What does this mean in practice for decisions on criminal responsibility made in lay judge trials?

50 As also indicated before, the numbers of defendants who were found to be of diminished responsibility and who (accordingly) received a sentence reduction are unfortunately not available.

The district courts in Japan's 48 prefectures have organized numerous meetings in which participants in lay judge trials exchange opinions with legal professionals, and at times also with members of the press, about their participation (on the numbers of meetings in which issues of diminished responsibility and criminal insanity were discussed; see note 2).[51]

Some lay judges indicated that they did not fully understand either the testimony or the explanation provided. That understanding came when they discussed what they had heard in court with their fellow lay judges and with the other professional judges. The following quotes are illustrative in this regard:

> At first I didn't understand at all. But during the deliberation we talked a considerable time about criminal responsibility, and while listening to the opinion of others, I came to understand.
>
> (Meeting Gifu District Court, 14–4–2015);[52] and

> When it comes to the question of what criminal responsibility is all about, rather than what was being said in court, it was through the explanation by the judge after coming back [to the deliberation room), that he so thoroughly provided, it was really because of that, that I understood the meaning of that word.
>
> (Meeting Sapporo District Court, 23–3–2016)

Some lay judges noted how helpful the judges had been in summarizing what had been said and argued, and explaining the implications of these arguments in legal terms. While many indicated that the testimony provided by forensic psychiatrists was an important point of reference, some also noted that their own, personal observations had played an important part in judging whether the defendant could be held criminally responsible. In the words of one lay judge:

> As the trial progressed and we asked the defendant questions, we somehow got the idea "he's a normal person, isn't he?" and "he's talking normally, isn't he?" But the defense steadfastly said that he in any case had a mental disturbance. That he had a disturbance they said and showed using

51 Meeting records were searched using the following terms: criminal responsibility (*sekininnōryoku*); diminished responsibility (*shinshinkōjaku*); criminal insanity (*shinshinsōshitsu*), psychiatric evaluation (*seishinkantei*). The aim of these searches was to look for any references to understandings of issues of diminished criminal responsibility or criminal insanity in connection with references to decisions made on these issues. The 19 meeting records in which such references were found were examined for commonalities and recurring themes with regard to decisions on issues of criminal responsibility. Given that questions were frequently asked to the lay judges as a group, and that some persons talked much while others stayed silent, a quantitative representation of recurring topics is of limited value. Meeting records nevertheless do give an impression of the issues of relevance for lay judges' understandings of diminished responsibility and criminal insanity, and their decisions in this regard.

52 The records of this and the following meetings can be accessed at: at: www.saibanin.courts.go.jp/ikenkoukan/index.html. Website last visited 30–8–2018.

> documentation, but the thing was that [already) it had stopped looking like he had a disturbance. (. . .) Lay judges cannot judge on the basis of documents. (. . .) [In the deliberation room) we had a discussion that was based on everybody's experience, rather than a legal point of view.
>
> (Meeting Sendai District Court, 4–7–2016)

Similarly, one lay judge noted:

> Two forensic psychiatrists provided testimony as witnesses, but if you ask whether I understood, I have to say: not so much. But, the whole crime situation was recorded on a surveillance camera, so based on that, I stated my opinion [during deliberation) that if the defendant was mentally disturbed, it wouldn't have been like that. (. . .) I looked at the defendant's movements and actions, and so on, and drew my conclusions.
>
> (Meeting Sendai District Court, 25–11–2014)

These lay judges thus more or less consciously let their own life experience and ideas concerning normal behavior prevail over specialist knowledge and reasoning. Other lay judges, however, did not. Instead, they deferred to such specialist knowledge and reasoning, often with feelings of resignation, as they were confronted with knowledge the accuracy of which they could not effectively assess or question:

> If you're told: it's this kind of illness, then it feels like you'll just have to accept that. (. . .) I suppose he [the doctor) must say those things, but even if he tells us, tells me those things, I'll hardly understand, and so I have no other option than to judge whether I should believe him or not believe him.
>
> (Meeting Saitama District Court, 13–7–2015); and

> It was the psychiatrist who wrote that evaluation, so I thought: that's the way it is. I couldn't help but wonder who had hired him and where, but there's no room to doubt that, and even if you do have doubts, there's nothing to be done.
>
> (Meeting Ashikawa District Court, 24–3–2015)

Besides the issue of knowledge that lay judges felt they could not question or dispute, there was also the issue of legal principles. Different lay judges indicated that they did not subscribe to the idea that a mental disturbance could or should affect a person's criminal responsibility and the punishment accordingly meted out. While their presence and contributions are, as we have seen, intended to infuse criminal proceedings with an average citizen's perspective, these lay judges found that the room to include their citizens' perspective was, of course, limited by legal principles and precedent – much like the following lay judges:

> The legal professionals find that people who suffer from a mental disturbance should be saved, that it's necessary to help them, to not put them in prison, but to cure their illness. The biggest issue for me was that that is a point of view different from the point of view held by ordinary citizens.
>
> (Meeting Yokohama District Court, 26–5–22); and

> During the deliberation the chief judge told us that this was also a trial where the parties disputed the sentence in relation to mental issues. I suppose the chief judge had accurately assessed that, but as far as I was concerned, that wasn't really the point. If you settle things on the basis of mental issues, victims' feelings will not be satisfied, and I thought that things can't be settled in terms of mental things or a mental disorder. To me that seemed like an excuse [nige], but (. . .) until the very end the chief judge told us to take into consideration that there also was that kind of disturbance.
>
> (Meeting Tokyo District Court, 3–6–2016)

The meetings did not allow for an assessment of the exact role of legal precedent in lay judges' decisions on defendants' criminal responsibility, although different jurors did mention that during deliberations they had made use of the Evaluation Manual (Meeting Tokyo District Court, 3–6–2016). These meetings did however bring into focus the role of legal precedent in sentencing decisions in cases involving diminished criminal responsibility. It was especially in connection with these decisions that the limitations on lay judges' freedom to decide became apparent. Rather than being presented with the range of sentences the relevant legal statutes provide for, lay judges were presented with the range of sentences normally imposed in similar cases. Using a database of cases and sentencing decisions, judges would essentially show the going rates for cases such as the one they were assigned to. This is however an issue that will be further addressed in Chapter 6.

The picture that emerges from these meetings, then, is one of lay judges who struggle to understand the legal concepts they are expected to apply. With help from their fellow (lay) judges on this they try to make sense of the concepts of criminal insanity and diminished responsibility. In applying these concepts some relied at least in part on their own conceptions of mental sanity and "normal" behavior, while others felt they had no choice but to go along with forensic psychiatrists' testimony. Similarly, they had little choice but to go along with judges' instructions to take mental health issues into consideration, in spite of their own reservations. Guided by their fellow lay and professional judges they did their best to position themselves within existing legal frameworks to the extent that their contribution did not translate into decisions breaking with existing trends. Even the case of Kazuhiro O., in spite of all the uproar it caused, can ultimately be said to have been in line with the increased importance of social defense, which has characterized Japanese criminal justice since the late 1990s.

## Concluding discussion: psychiatrists, (lay) judges and the act of finding criminal responsibility

Throughout Japanese history criminal courts have treated acts committed by those perceived to be mentally disturbed differently. Typically, a lenient legal judgment – lenient in terms of less or no punishment – went hand in hand with measures aimed at restricting the movements of mentally disturbed persons, in order to keep society safe from such persons. This chapter has showed how societal understandings of mental disturbances have developed throughout especially the post–World War II period, translating into shifting legal understandings of acts of mentally disturbed persons. In line with the shift from the idea that one cannot understand the mental state behind such acts (*fukachiron*) to the idea that one can (*kachiron*), judges have in the past decades been striving to understand defendants' actions in these defendants' own subjective terms, allowing for the Court's understanding of even the most deluded motives. Remarkable here is the attention given to psychological issues, without necessarily grounding this attention in "formal" psychiatric insights or speech acts (cf. Dreyfus & Rabinow, 1983: 48). The post–World War II period is thus characterized by a trend of increasing responsibilization of persons with mental disturbances, leading to ever smaller numbers of persons found criminally insane and of diminished responsibility in court, and more and more mentally disturbed persons being sent to prison to get their just dessert. The standardization of psychiatrists' evaluation, catering to legally relevant criteria, has further contributed to this process of responsibilization and increased retributivism.

The virtual disappearance of defendants found criminally insane or of diminished responsibility is however also tied with concerns of social defense. Keeping the history of the legal treatment of mentally disturbed persons in mind, one can in fact say that concerns of social defense are an ever recurring theme. While the mentally disturbed offender has become increasingly considered as a person who can be held responsible, societal concerns about dangerous mentally disturbed persons from whom society should be protected have in especially recent years been growing again. The conceptions of the responsible and at least partially rational mentally disturbed person accordingly exists side by side with the conception of the mentally disturbed person as a potentially dangerous being who cannot be trusted to not behave (rather than act) in dangerous ways. In this sense, in allowing for seemingly incompatible images of actors and penal philosophies (retributivism and social defense) Japanese criminal justice shows its overdetermined character (cf. Garland, 1990: 280–281).

The 2005 introduction of the Medical Treatment and Observation Act (MTOA) has not translated into clearly higher numbers or percentages of suspects not prosecuted by reason of criminal insanity. Prosecutors are not diverting more suspects away from regular trials to be dealt with through MTOA procedures. Neither verdicts nor statistics suggest that the introduction of the lay judge system has changed existing decision making practices or norms regarding criminal responsibility. Mentally disturbed persons by and large remain the responsible actors they have become in the post–World War II period. Nevertheless: every year a few hundred persons who would have been placed in the care and under the supervision of medical doctors and staff, are now, on the basis of the MTOA, in addition subject to the assessments of criminal justice professionals, who have a say in when they can be released.

Criminal insanity and diminished criminal responsibility are legal, normative concepts that are nevertheless grounded in forensic psychiatric expertise – psychiatrists' factual determinations. These are offered in very peculiar circumstances, as psychiatrists are asked to present their findings on the basis of unproven past events and alleged behavior, as well as a manual that allows for a diagnosis that legal professionals can make easy use of. Psychiatrists' contribution thus very much takes place on legal terms and conditions – especially those of investigators. Nevertheless, juridified as psychiatrists' contribution thus is, at the pre-trial stage this contribution is decisive, as prosecutors by and large follow psychiatrists' lead.

Much as in the pre-trial stage, the legal reasoning on which in MTOA hearings decisions on criminal insanity are based remains hidden, as both types of procedure take place behind closed doors. It is only in regular criminal trials, where claims regarding criminal insanity are typically rejected, that the reasoning behind decisions on criminal insanity as well as diminished responsibility become clear. Given the fact that the reasoning processes in these different procedures cannot be compared, it is also not possible to assess whether there might in fact be two standards of criminal responsibility. What is clear, however, is that the conclusions drawn at the pre-trial stage do not allow for any predictions, while the conclusions of both MTOA hearings and public trials are by and large foregone – regardless of the common sense, citizens' perspective that lay judges bring to the table in the latter procedure.

Meeting records show lay judges who rely on their knowledge of how things normally work, how a "normal person" talks in court or behaves when caught on camera. The records thus do show lay judges looking for clues in defendants' demeanor and speech (cf. Valverde, 2009: 83). But at the same time, they also show lay judges who see no other choice but to submit to the authority of forensic psychiatrists, judges, legal principles and jurisprudence. While thus based on hybrid forms of knowledge made up of common sense, life experience and legal principles and jurisprudence, the latter were very much represented as dominant, inescapable and overruling.

When it comes to the question of whether these decisions convey the impressions that, given the rules, the decision follows from the facts of the case (cf. Luhman, 1991: 1430) such impression management is clear in the formal trial phase, while in the pre-trial phase and in MTOL hearings, it is not. What is also clear is that in current Japanese criminal justice the conclusion of criminal insanity is found only "off stage" in procedures that do not require a public explanation. Once such a public explanation is part of the decision making process, that is, "on stage", courts virtually always find the defendant responsible. Thus courts are relieved from the task, a difficult one in times of penal populism, to publicly explain why certain offenders should not be punished for their acts.

While criminally insane defendants have thus virtually disappeared from regular trials, prisons have been more and more acknowledging the mental disturbances of their inmates. We do not know how many of the defendants who stand trial each year have a mental disturbance. We do know, however, that mentally disturbed persons represent about 1.8% of the total number of persons arrested for penal code offenses. We also know that of the 20,467 persons sent to prison in 2016, 14.3% (2,992 persons) were diagnosed with a mental disturbance, compared to 3.7% (708 persons) in 1992 (Ministry of Justice, 1993, 2017). These percentages, which according to different sources are in fact much higher, suggest that once arrested, mentally disturbed persons have a relatively high chance of being incarcerated (Tashima Yoshiaki/Ministry of Health, Labour and Welfare, 2008: 6). Mentally disturbed persons in Japan have for a long time been subject to measures of segregation and surveillance. The White Paper percentages, combined with the introduction of the MTOA suggest that the net of forcible institutionalization, regardless of whether that institution is a prison or a mental hospital, has in recent years widened again.

Parallel with the responsibilization of mentally disturbed persons, policy makers have in recent years however also become sensitized to the fact that considerable percentages of Japan's inmates have some form of mental disturbance, and to the implications of this fact for both prison life and policies aimed at preventing recidivism. Of course those on the floor had long been aware of this problem, which cannot be considered detached from the trend toward increased responsibilization addressed in this chapter (Sato, 2011). In any case: a growing awareness of these implications has contributed to changing policies at the criminal justice "entrance", and efforts to support offenders and divert them away from trials, or in any case from prisons. Chapter 3 will address this "support at the entrance" (*iriguchishien*) and the role that another legal outsider, the social worker, plays in this regard.

## References

Dando, Shigemitsu (1970). System of discretionary prosecution in Japan. *American Journal of Comparative Law* 18: 518–531.

Dreyfus, Hubert L. and Paul Rabinow (1983). *Michel Foucault: beyond structuralism and hermeneutics*. Chicago: University of Chicago Press.

Fujino, Yayoi (2005). Wagakuni ni okeru seishinshōgaisha shōgun no rekishiteki hensen: hōseido wo chūshin ni. *Niigata Seiriku Daigaku Kiyo*: 201–215.

Garland, David (1990). *Punishment and modern society: a study in social theory*. Oxford: Oxford University Press.

Hayashi, Mitsuko (2013). Sekinin nōryoku handan to seishin kantei: saikōsai Heisei 20 nen 4 gatsu 25 nichi hanketsu wo keiki toshite. *Rikkyo Hogako* 87: 286–246.

Hirata, Toyoaki (2009). Kiso mae kan'i kantei ni okeru sekinin nōryoku hyōka, in Nakatani Youji (ed.), *Sekinin Nouryoku no Genzai*. Tokyo: Kongo Shuppan: 87–104.

Ichinose, Masaki (2008). 'Seishin iryō to shokuhokōi no shiseigaku: satsujin kōi wo megutte' hōkoku (kokusai shinpojiamu seishin iryō to shokuhōkōi no seishigaku: satsujin kōi wo megutte). *Shiseigaku Kenkyu* 9: 346–342.

Japan Federation of Bar Associations (JFBA) (2012). *Hattatsushōgai no aru hikokunin ni yoru jisshi shisatsujiken no Ōsakachisaihanketsu ni kansuru kaichōdanwa*. Available at: www.nichibenren.or.jp/activity/document/statement/year/2012/120810_3.html. Website last visited 30 August 2018.

Johnson, David T. (2002). *The Japanese way of justice: prosecuting crime in Japan*. Oxford: Oxford University Press.

Kanai, Naomi (2010). *Jinken no shiten kara mita keihō 39 jyō no datōsei: shokuhō seishin shōgaisha no sekinin nōryoku to shogū wo meguru kōsatsu*. Available at: https://m-repo.lib.meiji.ac.jp/dspace/handle/10291/14982. Website last visited 30 August 2018.

Konishi, Yoshiro and Junya Hokama (2011). *Iryōkansatsuhō ni kansuru ichikōsatsu: Okinawaken no jirei nimo furete*. Available at: http://okinawa-repo.lib.u-ryukyu.ac.jp:8080/handle/okinawa/9601. Website last visited 30 August 2018.

Kudo, Toshiaki (2016). *Kan'i kantei no mondaiten*. Available at: www.kms.ac.jp/~hsc/kugoh/kantei/kantei_11.htm. Website last visited 30 August 2018.

Legal Research and Training Institute (ed.) (2009). *Nankai na hōritsugainen to saiban'in saiban*. Tokyo: Hōsōkai.

Luhmann, N. (1991). Operational closure and structural coupling: the differentiation of the legal system. *Cardozo Law Review* 13: 1419–1441.

Maeda, (2000). Sekinin nōryoku no handan to 'kihanteki hyōka'. *Sandaihōgaku* 34(3): 263–264.

Ministry of Health, Labor rand Welfare (MHLW), Japan (2006). *Shōgaisha no jiritsu to shakaisanka wo mezashite*. Available at: www.mhlw.go.jp/bunya/shougaihoken/idea01/. Website last visited 30 August 2018.

Ministry of Justice (MOJ) (annual). *White paper on crime*. Available at: http://hakusyo1.moj.go.jp/en/nendo_nfm.html. Website last visited 30 August 2018.

Miyoshi, Mikio (2008). *Shinshinsōshitsushanado iryōkansatsuhō go 2nen no genjō to kadai ni tsuite*. *Hanrei Taimuzu* 1261: 25–35.

Nakatani, Yōji (2000). Psychiatry and the law in Japan: history and current topics. *International Journal of Law and Psychiatry* 23(5): 589–604.

Nakatani, Yōji (2001). Seishinkantei no igi to jissai. *Nichii Zasshi* 125(9).

Nakatani, Yōji (2007). Hō to seishin igaku. *Psychiatria et neurologia Japonica* 109(9): 882–886.

Nakatani, Yōji (2009a). Saikō kensatsuchō ni yoru seishin kanteishorei ni kansuru shiken. *Psychiatria et neurologia Japonica* 111(11): 1363–1368.

Nakatani, Yōji (2009b). Sekininmunōryoku seido no shōrai, in Nakatani Youji (ed.), *Sekinin Nōryoku no Genzai*. Tokyo: Kongo Shuppan: 9–24.

National Institute of Mental Health (2011). *Wagakuni no seishin fukushi 2011 nendo*, 20. Available at: www.ncnp.go.jp/nimh/information03.html. Website last visited 30 August 2018.

Okada, Takayuki et al. (2012). Saibaninsaibanka no Keijiseishinkantei ha dō aru beki ka. *Seishiniryō/Psychiatry* 66: 9–27.

Okae (2008). *Keijisekinin nōryoku handan no aratana dōkou*. Available at: www.kansatuhou.net/04_ronten/04_01_keijisekinin_nouryoku.html.Websitelastvisited 30 August 2018.

Okae (2013). *Tōgō shichōshō no sekinin nōryoku naze tsumiga karuku narunoka*. Tokyo: dZero.

Ogata, Ayumi (2013). Hattatsushōgaisha no keijisekinin nōryoku to ryōkeihandan: Osaka kōsai Heisei 25 nen 2 gatsu 26 nichi hanketsu wo tansho to shite. *Chukyo Lawyer* 19: 1–26.

Onuki, Takamichi and Matsuki Hiroto (2003). Hankō dōki no kōsei to seiin kategorīka jissen. *Hanzaishakaigaku Kenkyū* 28: 68–81.
Ozawa, Tatsuya (2009). Kanteinin oyobi saibankan no keijisekinin nōryoku handan ni kakawaru yōin no kenkyū: saibansho tō wo tōshite jisshi shita zenkoku 50 jirei no kankei kiroku no bunseki yori. *Hō to Seishiniryō* 24: 37–40.
Satō, Makoto (2011). Keijishisetsu no seishinkairyō. *Waseda daigaku shakai anzen seisaku kenkyūjo kiyō* 4: 201–221.
Study Group on the Evaluation of the Criminal Responsibility of Persons Who Harmed Another Person (Study Group) (2009). *Keijisekininnōryoku ni kansuru seishinkantei sakusei no tebiki.* Available at: www.ncnp.go.jp/nimh/shihou/tebiki40_100108.pdf. Website last visited 30 August 2018.
Takimoto, Shigeko (2010). *Keiji shihō seishin kantei no kenkyū.* Available at: www.osipp.osaka-u.ac.jp/archives/DP/2010/DP2010J003.pdf. Website last visited 30 August 2018.
Tashima, Yoshiaki/Ministry of Health, Labour and Welfare (2008). *Kōseirōdōkagakukenkyū, tsumi wo okashita shōgaisha no chiiki seikatsu shien ni kansuru kenkyū, hōkoku.* Available at: www.airinkai.or.jp/kenkyu_pdf/2008/2008_1/h19/01_tashima.pdf. Website last visited 30 August 2018.
Tokyo Bengoshikai (2013). *Sekininnōryoku wo arasou keijibengo.* Tokyo: Gendaijinbunsha.
Valverde, M. (2009). *Law's dream of a common knowledge.* Princeton: Princeton University Press.
Yamagami, Akira (1997). Seishin kantei oyobi shihōseishinigaku no kongo. Seishin Kantei (special issue, Yamagami, A. (ed.)) *Kokoro no Kagaku* 75: 96–99.
Yamagami, Akira (1999). Seishin kantei: sono rekishiteki hensen to shokadai. *Seishinigaku* 41(10): 1030–1042.
Yamauchi, Tadamitsu (2001). Kisomaekantei. *Nichi'i Zasshi* 125(9): 1394.
Yoshikawa, Kazuo (2009). Wagakuni no sekinin nōryoku hantei no yukue, in Nakatani Youji (ed.), *Sekinin Nōryoku no Genzai.* Tokyo: Kongo Shuppan: 65–86.

### *Verdicts:*

Daishin'in, Keishū 10, verdict of 3 December 1931.
Daishin'in, Keishū 12, verdict of 30 November 1933.
Fukuoka High Court Heisei 23 (u) 122, verdict of 18 October 2011.
Osaka District Court, Heisei 18 (wa) 6978, verdict of 26 May 2008.
Osaka District Court, Heisei 21 (wa) 6154, verdict of 31 October 2011.
Osaka District Court, Heisei 23 (wa) no. 6063, verdict of 30 July 2012.
Osaka High Court, Heisei 24 (u), no. 1159, verdict of 26 February 2013.
Osaka High Court, Heisei 25 (a) 729, verdict of 25 May 2015.
Tokyo High Court, Heisei 20 (u) 1097, verdict of 25 May 2009.
Supreme Court Second Petty Bench, Heisei 18 (a) 876, verdict of 25 April 2008.
Supreme Court, Shōwa 45 (a) 1310, verdict of 4 April 1973.
Supreme Court Shōwa 58 (a) 753, verdict of 13 September 1983.
Supreme Court Third Petty Bench Shōwa 58 (a) 1761, verdict of 3 July 1984.

# 3 Support at the entrance

## Introduction

Until 4 September 2000, things were looking good for Jōji Yamamoto. Aged 38, he was a rising star within the Democratic Party of Japan and a member of the House of Representatives. But on that day in September he was arrested on suspicion of fraud. For a number of years Yamamoto had been claiming a government-paid salary for a fictitious secretary. For this act as well as the fraud he committed to cover his tracks Yamamoto was charged, convicted, and sentenced to 18 months in prison.

Most prisoners in Japan are required to perform prison labor. Yamamoto's task was that of seeing after the physical care of a number of prisoners who, because of their intellectual disabilities, were not fully able to do so themselves. Yamamoto quickly discovered that in fact many of his fellow inmates suffered from various mental, intellectual and physical disabilities and disturbances, and that many of them were in addition elderly repeat offenders who had left prison many times only to come back again, as they typically had no one they could turn to for help, and no place to go.

Yamamoto's days in prison, and especially his task of taking care of some of these offenders made him painfully aware of the problem of mentally disturbed inmates in ill-equipped prisons. His prison days in fact made such an impression on him that he decided to write a book on his experiences. This book, Yamamoto's prison memoirs (2003), provided an enormous stimulus for debates on the treatment of persons such as those described in Yamamoto's book, and on ways to prevent them from repeatedly coming back to prison. These debates ultimately translated into policy changes and a new role for another legal outsider contributing to legal decision making processes: the social worker.[1] This chapter zooms in on their role in diverting offenders away from trial or at least from prison.

1 The Japanese word used most frequently is that of *shakai fukushishi*, which literally translates as "social welfare worker", but that is in any case used to refer to certified social workers. These social workers, who all passed a national exam, "provide counseling, advise, guide and other services with social work knowledge and skills for those who are physically or mentally disabled and cannot lead a daily life due to environmental reasons". As part of this

Social workers play their new role as part of a new, combined effort by prosecutors and lawyers to provide support for repeat offenders, who, because of a lack of perspectives and social connections, their economic situation, a mental disturbance and so on, would simply keep reoffending, and returning to prison. This support is provided at the criminal justice "entrance" (*iriguchishien*), at the stages of investigation and at trial, as opposed to support provided at the exit (*deguchishien*) – that is: upon leaving prison. The role of social workers and the support at the entrance they help provide are worth examining as they have emerged after years in which Japanese style *penal populism* had been dominating criminal justice policy making. As also outlined in Chapter 1, since the early 2000s Japanese criminal justice policy has become increasingly harsh as politicians aimed to give the Japanese people the policies that these people in their perception wanted, under the influence also of the lobbying and input from victims' rights organizations (cf. Pratt, 2007; Miyazawa, 2008a). The question is therefore whether social workers' new role and support at entrance represent a shift, a Japanese criminal justice policy and practice turn toward rehabilitation and away from punitivism. Studying social workers' role and support at the entrance is accordingly important when trying to make sense of such policy and practice. In 2008 Setsuo Miyazawa raised the question of whether penal populism in Japan could be expected to decline in the foreseeable future. His answer: no (2008b: 132). One question that this chapter will accordingly address is whether support at the entrance highlights the beginning of such a decline.

One could of course argue that this new policy, by aiming to divert and support rather than punish, is already of symbolic significance. The significance of support at the entrance in terms of actual criminal justice *practice* however cannot be answered without examining how in practice social workers contribute to the legal decision making process – a question which of course touches on the central theme of this book. As this chapter will show, social workers bring their own perspective to the table, a perspective that is focused on the welfare of their client. They have no interest in retribution or crime prevention per se, but rather in bringing about a situation that would allow their client to lead a stable life, of which one could in hindsight say: no crime was committed. Their perspective is thus obviously very different from that of prosecutors or judges, who concern themselves with dispensing justice, protecting the social order and preventing the offender from committing more crimes. There is accordingly a tension between social workers' aims and the aims of these two criminal justice insiders. How is this tension in practice resolved?

In addressing this question – by looking into social workers' role in criminal justice decision making practices – this chapter too examines the role of a

---

general job description social workers work to support, among others, elderly and disabled people and those who need support due to economic reasons. They in addition "support the improvement of community welfare" through volunteering groups' networks (Japanese Association of Certified Social Workers, 2018).

"non-juridical element". On the role of such elements Foucault has noted that "what is so odd about modern criminal justice is that, although it has taken on so many extra-juridical elements, it has done so not in order to define them juridically and to gradually to integrate them into the actual power to punish: on the contrary, it has done so (. . .) in order to stop this operation being simply a legal punishment; in order to exculpate the judge from being purely and simply he who punishes" so as to allow for the criminal to be treated (1978: 22). Foucault here referred to the fact that judges' decisions on punishment are not just act-based, but also on treatment oriented understandings of the actor. While act-based punishment is here qualified as juridical, punishment based on considerations regarding the actor are qualified as anthropological or psychological (cf. Foucault, 1981/2000: 462–463). Of course, Foucault's observations concern a Western context – although it is not always clear which Western context. The question is here nevertheless an important one. Are social workers, whose main concern is that of the practical consequences of any legal decision, in fact exculpating Japanese judges and other legal professionals involved in the process, for that matter, from being those who "simply" impose legal punishment?

This chapter addresses these practice and policy questions on the basis of the relevant laws and policy documents, notably the Act on the Promotion of the Prevention of Crime, etc. (Act no. 104, 2016, hereafter: Crime Prevention Act) and the Plan to Promote Crime Prevention (Cabinet Crime Committee, 2017), which together define the legal and policy framework in which support at the entrance is now formally embedded. The chapter is however also based on social workers' and legal professionals' accounts in their professional and other fora, such as the journal *Keiji Bengo*, a journal for criminal defense lawyers that contains many personal accounts of especially lawyers and social workers with regard to support at the entrance. The chapter is in addition informed by semi-structured interviews with public prosecutors ($n$ = 10), social workers ($n$ = 5) and criminal defense lawyers ($n$ = 5), conducted between July 2015 and January 2018 as well as correspondence with the head of the Nagasaki Community Living Settlement Support Center (*chiiki seikatsushien sentaa*) – compare also the book Introduction.

This chapter accordingly zooms in on the appearance of social workers and their contributions to legal decisions made at the criminal justice entrance, examining not only how social workers contribute to legal decision making processes, but also pursuing the policy significance of social workers entering the criminal justice stage.

## 1. The discovery of the repeat offender

In order to make sense of social workers' appearance and role on the criminal justice stage it is necessary to first look into why and how these came about. The seed for this development was planted with the discovery of the repeat offender – and that is where we will start.

Yamamoto's book played an important part in (further) raising awareness and stimulating debate on the plight of mentally handicapped, elderly repeat offenders, among social workers, legal professionals and the general public alike (Matsutomo, 2014: 167; Kobayashi, 2016: 70; *Asahi Shimbun*, 2004). The impact of this book and the debate it sparked were further amplified, however, by some events that occurred after its publication, such as the case of Kyuemon F.

According to newspaper and police reports Kyuemon (74) had arrived by train in the town of Shimonoseki, located in the southwestern part of the main island Honshū on the evening of Friday 6 January 2006. He had lain down on one of the benches inside the station, as he had done in the station he had traveled from. Here, however, one of the employees of the railway station found him and told him to leave. He had been hungry and had become irritable because of it. To get rid of the tension that had been building up inside him, he set fire to the wooden station. The fire he caused burnt the station to the ground; no one got hurt. Kyuemon made no attempt to flee, and when the same railway station employee approached him in a parking lot 350 meters away from the station he quickly admitted to having set the fire. Kyuemon was homeless and had no family or friends to turn to. He had just been released from prison one week before the fire. The money he had earned through his prison labor, about 20,000 yen (around 150 Euro), was all gone. Kyuemon wanted to return to prison, where he had already spent more than 50 years of his life (*Asahi Shimbun*, 2006a, 2000b; Okada, 2010). During the investigation that followed, Kyuemon was psychiatrically evaluated, and found to be "slightly retarded" (*karui seishin no okure*), but not so as to affect his criminal responsibility – much like had happened in a previous court case. He was found guilty and sentenced to 10 years in prison (*Asahi Shimbun*, 2006c).

This highly publicized case served to further highlight the problem of repeat offenders with a mental disability, of persons without a social safety net who, once released from prison, find that there is little for them in the outside world. Even though there are few offenders who set fire to a station to return to prison, Kyuemon's case nevertheless brought into focus an all too common problem, highlighted by Yamamoto, practitioners and researchers alike (Kimura & Sawaki, 2013; Satō, 2011).

Other cases involving suspects with mental disabilities furthermore brought into focus a different problem, namely the vulnerability of such suspects in criminal investigations. There was for example the case of a man with a mental disability charged with a robbery in the city of Utsunomiya in 2004, who, as it later turned out, had simply answered every police question with "yes, yes", because in the past that had always resulted in the police letting him go (Tsujikawa, 2014: 240). Similarly, statements made by an arson suspect with a mental disability in the city of Kaizuka in 2009 turned out to be the result of that suspect going along with investigators' suggestive line of questioning. Both cases served to raise both Prosecutors' and lawyers' awareness of the problems surrounding suspects with mental disabilities, not only in terms of recidivism but also in terms of the risk of wrongful convictions (Committee for Review of the State of the Prosecutors Office, 2011a; Tsujikawa, 2014: 240).

Before getting into the various initiatives, measures and reforms that the different criminal justice players undertook in response to Yamamoto's book and cases such as the ones highlighted here, it is fruitful to first establish more clearly the extent and the roots of the problem of the mentally disturbed repeat offender, that these initiatives and measures (etc.) were and are being meant to address.

### *1.1. Numbers of mentally disturbed offenders in the criminal justice chain*

For the period 1992–2016 crime statistics show a rise in crime in which mentally disturbed offenders are involved.[2] The number of assaults committed by mentally disturbed persons, for example, has between 1992 and 2016 more than quadrupled. For the crimes of robbery, extortion and theft the numbers have also risen drastically. Overall, the number of crimes committed by mentally disturbed persons has in this period more than doubled (from 1,740 in 1992 to 4,084 in 2016), while the percentage of the total of general penal code offenses has gone up from 0.6% to 1.8%. This rise in crimes committed by mentally disturbed persons went also hand in hand with a steep rise in the numbers and percentages of mentally disturbed persons sent to prison. As shown in Graph 3.1, the influx of inmates with a mental disturbance has risen to 14.3% of the total influx in 2016.

The available statistics thus suggest that once a crime committed by a mentally disturbed person is reported and a suspect is apprehended, chances are high that this suspect will also be punished and go to prison. To further illustrate: overall arrest rates for general penal code offenses have between 1992 and 2016 translated into a 9% incarceration rate. That is, in 2016 there were 22,6376 (100%) persons arrested for general penal code offenses (excluding traffic offenses), while the influx of new inmates incarcerated for this category of offenses was 20,467 (9%). As noted earlier, mentally disturbed persons constitute around 1.8% of the total number of persons arrested for general penal code offenses = 4,084 (100%) persons in 2016. The total number of mentally disturbed persons incarcerated for general penal code offenses in the same year was 2,922 (71%).[3]

---

2 During this period, registration practices remained constant, while the period between 1952 and 1991 is characterized by different registration practices, rendering a statistical representation of long term trends in crimes committed by mentally disturbed persons and their influx in prison problematic.

Mentally disturbed persons are in the 1992–2016 statistics defined as "persons suffering from a mental disturbance such as integration function syndrome (previously known as schizophrenia), acute poisoning or addiction as a result of psychoactive substances, a mental disability, a mental illness or another mental disturbance (. . .), as well as persons suspected of suffering from such a mental disturbance" (Ministry of Justice, 2017).

3 In the statistics on mentally disturbed inmates, mentally disturbed persons are defined as "persons who within a correctional institution were diagnosed as having a mental disability, a personality disorder, a neurotic disorder or another mental disturbance, including a mental

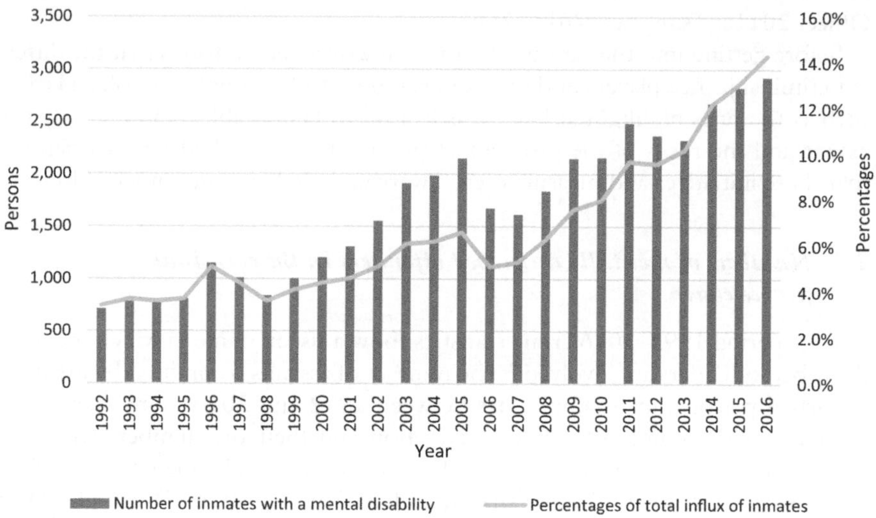


*Graph 3.1* Inmates with a mental disturbance: numbers and percentages of yearly influx of inmates

Source: (Correction Bureau Statistics, 1992–2014; MOJ White Papers on Crime, 1992–2017).

Of course, the numbers of persons arrested do not directly translate in an influx of offenders in the same year. It is also not clear whether the criteria used to apply the label "mentally disturbed offender"/"suspected mentally disturbed offender" at the arrest stage are identical to the criteria used for new inmates (see the definitions used at both stages provided in notes 2 and 3). These numbers and percentages accordingly need to be treated with caution (Correction Bureau Statistics, 1992–2014; Ministry of Justice, 1992–2017).[4]

Crime statistics in the period 1992–2016 furthermore show that the numbers of murders and acts of arson have remained stable. As such acts normally do not go unreported, they are generally a good indicator of crime trends and developments. These statistics accordingly suggest that the actual number of incidents involving mentally disturbed persons has not gone up. In other words: the rise in crimes committed by mentally disturbed persons and the corresponding influx of mentally disturbed persons in prison may very well be the result of an increased awareness on the part of criminal justice officials of the possibility that

or behavioral disturbance caused by the use of psychoactive substances, integration function syndrome and mood disorders" (Ministry of Justice, 2017).

4 Estimates of the total percentage of inmates with a mental disturbance in addition vary between 1.5% and 22%, further highlighting the problem of definitions (TashimaYoshikai/ Ministry of Health, Labour and Welfare, 2008: 6).

an offender may have a mental disorder. This increased awareness has then led to more offenders and more inmates being registered as such.

Nevertheless, this increase is also likely to be at least partly caused by increased numbers of offenders with a mental disturbance being found criminally responsible in court, resulting from the changed ideas about criminal responsibility discussed in the previous chapter. The general increase in crime committed by elderly offenders may in this regard also play a part (cf. also Sugie, 2017).[5]

But while these percentages point to the relatively high percentages of mentally disturbed offenders in the prison population, the problem that Yamamoto's book highlighted was especially that these were *repeat* offenders – mentally disturbed and often elderly offenders caught in a cycle of committing a typically petty crime, going to prison only to reoffend upon release and being sent back to prison again (hereafter: the repeat cycle).

### *1.2. Factors that keep the repeat cycle going*

Different factors contribute to keeping this repeat cycle going. First of all, prosecution and sentencing practices play a part. Foote has famously characterized Japanese criminal justice as a system of "benevolent paternalism" with a focus on "reformation and reintegration into society through lenient sanctions tailored to the offender's particular circumstances" that allows prosecutors considerable discretion in gathering and using information on the offense and particularly also the offender (1992: 317).

Given this approach, the existence of a group of repeat offenders caught in the earlier described repeat cycle would seem surprising. Indeed, as also explained in Chapter 1, prosecutors dispose of the majority of all penal code offenses (56.5% in 2016) by suspending offenders' prosecution, in spite of enough evidence to indict (Ministry of Justice, 2017). They do so on the basis of considerations that very much include offenders' circumstances. Such considerations are however normally reserved for *first* offenders. Against recidivists and repeat offenders harsh sentences are, in line with Japanese law, routinely demanded and imposed, regardless of how trivial the repeat offense may be.[6]

5 Sato, a former prison director also draws a connection between interpretations of the concept of criminal responsibility and the problem of mentally disturbed offenders in prison, stating: "with regard to the principle of criminal responsibility as defined in (Criminal Code) Article 39 there has been a historical development, and lately this principle is being hotly debated. That debate is focused on the (offender's) mental state at the time of the crime, but from the perspective of someone working in a correctional institution, it is extremely hard to understand that what happens after a person is being incarcerated is hardly being considered. Mentally disturbed persons who are forced to live a daily life behind bars exhibit severe symptoms of mental illness" (2011: 203).

6 In accordance with Criminal Code (CC) Article 57, repeat offenses may be punished by a sentence that is twice the usual maximum length. The qualification "repeat offense" applies when the offense is committed by a person within five years of having served a prison sentence (CC art. 56).

Thus, it may happen that the prosecution demands a five year prison sentence against a 67 year old woman for pickpocketing a used envelope worth about 1 Euro cent (≈ 2 Yen), because she "has been repeatedly pickpocketing, and a severe sentence is necessary for the sake of social defense". This woman was a homeless repeat offender without family or a job, who had been released from prison for a similar offense five months earlier. The Court ultimately imposed a sentence of three years (Hamai, 2009: 120–123; *Asahi Shimbun*, 2006d; Ruihans hōgaishamondaishuzaihan, 2013: 8). The question is, of course, how this woman fared when she, at 70, left prison. This we unfortunately do not know.

We do however know that there are many offenders like her, for whom breaking the repeat cycle is difficult. Not just because of criminal justice practices, but also – as was the case with this offender – because of the difficulty of finding or keeping a job and not having anyone to turn to for help. Of course not all repeat offenders are homeless people without any income. Many do receive an allowance, but find that it's too small to live on – or find themselves unable to not spend this allowance in a few days. In addition, many are unable to independently find the right place to go to in order to receive help (Izumaru, 2017;[7] Ruihansh ōgaishamondaishuzaihan, 2013).

## 2. Addressing the problem of repeat offenders

In order to address the problem of mentally disturbed persons caught in the repeat cycle different criminal justice players have each undertaken various activities. In 2006, in reaction to the Utsunomiya case, lawyers from the Osaka Legal Bar Association put together a manual for lawyers to use if they suspected that their client had a mental disturbance. Lawyers were for example urged to be extra attentive of written interrogation statements and the possibility that these contained statements that were not in line with how their client expressed him or herself. In 2011 the Japan Federation of Bar Associations has also created a leaflet to alert lawyers of the high percentages of inmates with mental disturbances and the possibility that their client might also have a disturbance. The leaflet contained a list of behaviors that might be indicative of a disturbance, but also stated that lawyers can do much more than dispute criminal responsibility: they can bring their client into contact with social services, aiming for a suspended prosecution or sentence (JFBA, 2011). Lawyers can do so in various ways, but one often used way is that of contacting one of the Community Living Settlement Support Centers (*chiiki seikatsushien sentaa*) set up by the Ministry of Health, Labor and Welfare. The first Center was set up in Nagasaki in 2009, and as of 2013 every prefecture has its Center.

These Centers were initially set up to arrange support for those leaving a correctional institution – especially mentally disturbed and elderly persons without a place to go. This constitutes the so-called support at the exit (*deguchishien*).

7 Personal correspondence with Takeshi Izumaru, head of the Nagasaki Community Living Settlement Support Center

The centers aim to connect the former convicts with the institutions that can give them the help they need, by for example arranging a place in a halfway house and signing a person up for the necessary social services. They do so at the request of the probation office that coordinates convicts' return to society.

Those working at the Centers realized however that providing support at the exit was not enough. Taking the Nagasaki Center as an example: in spite of its formal focus on providing support at the exit, from the very beginning defense lawyers contacted the Center to help provide their elderly, mentally disturbed repeat offender clients with support. At the Center the feeling was that in order to break the repeat cycle it was indeed necessary to intervene before these offenders might receive another prison sentence. So the Center, like other Centers would in later years also do, started helping to organize support at both the investigation and trial stages: "at the entrance" (Izumaru, 2014: 25; Izumaru 2017).

More concretely, different Centers have set up Committees consisting of social workers, clinical psychologists, psychiatrists and others with experience in counseling persons with mental disturbances. At the request of either a lawyer or a public prosecutor these Committees investigate a suspect's need for support. Findings are communicated to prosecutors or lawyers at the investigation stage, or to the Court, when one of the parties, typically the lawyer, presents the committee findings at trial (Izumaru, 2014: 26).

Lawyers often approach a Center to refer them to an organization providing social services – as they do with the Nagasaki Center – although they also approach such organizations themselves. In such cases a lawyer may ask a social worker to accompany him or her to the detention center where a suspect or defendant is held in custody, in order to preliminarily assess that person's social welfare needs (Tsujikawa, 2017). To this end the social worker may also meet with the suspect's or defendant's family and others familiar with this person and his or her personal situation. In accordance with his or her assessment, the social worker will write up a rehabilitation support plan and will arrange support for those who will be asked to testify on matters related to the defendant's rehabilitation (Urazaki, 2016: 78 – see also later).

Prosecutors have also come to seek the opinion of social workers as well as their support for especially mentally disturbed and elderly repeat offenders. They typically do so within the context of their decision as to whether a defendant's prosecution should be suspended or not.[8] Given the generally harsh approach that repeat offenders face under Japanese law – see note 6 – Prosecutors' embrace of

8 As of 2015 prosecutors however also have the option of placing offenders, with their consent, under Protective Emergency Rehabilitation (*kōseikinkyū hogo*). Under this measure, the Probation Office can arrange the necessary measures to provide short term support – usually no longer than six months – for offenders who have no social network to support them, and who are not yet placed in a caregiving institution. The Probation Office is a Ministry of Justice organ charged with supervising and supporting the rehabilitation of former convicts and other former offenders placed under its care. This measure of Protective Emergency Rehabilitation is applied most of all to those who have served their sentence or who have been given parole from a prison sentence, and are about to be released. It is however also available for, among

"support at the entrance" represents a change of course, a "soft" approach that is all the more remarkable given the increasingly harsh criminal justice climate that, as noted earlier, has developed in Japan in the past decades. This receptiveness to a new, softer approach – that was not actually entirely new[9] – can be linked to the reforms that the Prosecutors Office has undergone in recent years. These reforms came about in response to a range of scandals that involved, among other things, prosecutorial tampering with evidence and forced confessions that had resulted in wrongful convictions.[10]

---

others, those whose prosecution was suspended. Applying this measure to the latter category of offenders is however still only done as part of a trial (Ministry of Justice, 2017).

9 "Support at the entrance" bears similarities to the so-called Yokohama approach, named after the city in which it was first implemented, in 1961, and that by 1969 had been adopted by 22 District Prosecutors' Offices. Under this approach persons between 20 and 25 years old who were suspected of certain designated penal code offenses that would normally be prosecuted would receive a suspended prosecution in view of suspects' motivation to rehabilitate and the estimation, based on an investigation of the offender's circumstances, that given proper guidance they would not reoffend. That proper guidance was provided by volunteer probation officers, on the basis of Protective Emergency Rehabilitation Law (see also note 8). Volunteer probation officers (VPOs) are "community volunteers who are appointed as part-time government officials to support the work of professional probation officers. VPOs support the work of professional probation officers by supervising and assisting offenders in the communities in which they live." I will come back to the role of VPOs below.

The Yokohama approach came about as a way to deal with the problem of recidivists for whom imprisonment did not appear to be a productive sanction. This approach however received much criticism in view of the intrusive investigation that it necessitated, in spite of the fact that no court had actually formally established the (alleged) offender's guilt. The Yokohama approach was discontinued because of a lack of funding to support the supervising probation officers, although it has also been argued that it was stopped because of its incompatibility with Criminal Procedure Law. See Yoshikai, 2015: 107–113. This approach is this similar to "support at the entrance" in its aim to divert repeat offenders from prison and prevent recidivism through other "rehabilitation means". Like with the Yokohama approach, with regard to "support at the entrance" too there are issues of compatibility with Criminal Procedure Law. I will return to these below.

10 One case that was especially damning to Prosecutors' reputation was that of Atsuko Muraki, the then head of the Equal Employment, Children and Families Bureau at the Ministry of Health, Labour and Welfare. In June 2009 Muraki was arrested on suspicion of issuing a false accreditation to a self-proclaimed organization of disabled people thereby allowing it to fraudulently make use of the postage discount system available for such organizations. She was put in solitary confinement and questioned for 20 days and subsequently detained for more than four months. In spite of the enormous pressure put upon her, Muraki was able to maintain her innocence and to not confess to a crime she had not committed – something that has been known to have happened in other cases (cases such as the "big four" referred to in Chapter 1, and the Ashikaga case referred to in chapters 2 and 5). Prosecutors nevertheless went forward with the case. The reason why this case was so damning to Prosecutors' reputation was not that they had prosecuted a person whom the Court, the Osaka District Court on 10 September 2010, found innocent. It was rather that it became apparent that they had actively tried to frame this person. Prosecutors had been leading witnesses into making statements in line with their case theory, the investigation's lead prosecutor had in addition tampered with material evidence while his superiors had conspired to cover the tracks of such tampering (Japan Times, 2011; Asahi Shimbun, 2012, 2013). This case was clearly not

Significantly, the reforms resulted in a policy in all Prosecutors Offices to record, as of October 2011, interrogations with persons suspected of having a mental disturbance "who have trouble communicating" (Supreme Public Prosecutors Office, 2012: 11).[11] They however also resulted, in 2011, in the formulating of *The Principles of Prosecution*, a short document outlining "the spirit and fundamentals of prosecution". Besides formulating some general guiding principles, this document also contains a job description that includes an official commitment to contribute to offenders' rehabilitation, "in cooperation with police and other law enforcement authorities, correctional and probation services and other relevant agencies and organizations" The new principles in addition reemphasize Prosecutors' role as representatives of the general interest (Supreme Public Prosecutors Office, 2011).

The reforms and the formulation of these principles helped to bring about the Prosecutors Office embrace of "support at the entrance". As one of the parties to the process, such an embrace was not obvious, but it was facilitated by the renewed commitment to rehabilitation and the emphasis on Prosecutors' role as a servant of the public interest, as expressed in the principles (Supreme Public Prosecutors Office, 2018; Ruihanshōgaishamondaishuzaihan, 2013: 187–199). Prosecutors' embrace of "support at the entrance" accordingly brings into focus Prosecutors' double role in Japanese criminal justice, namely as one of the two parties to the process, and as a more neutral, magistrate-like actor.

Concretely, the Prosecutors Office embrace of "support at the entrance" resulted in District Prosecutors' Offices setting up internal offices dedicated to providing such support. To this end they employ, as temporary workers, "social welfare advisers", who are in fact certified social workers. These advisers receive information from prosecutors on suspects and defendants whose prosecution may be suspended or against whom a suspended sentence may be demanded. They will receive information on the facts of the case, the suspect or defendant's criminal record, family relations, life history, present living circumstances and whether the person in question has a mental disturbance or not – etc., etc. The advisers will also ask the prosecutor for information they find relevant, and may also meet with the suspect and his family (Waseda Convention on Corrections and Probation, 2015: 30). In accordance with their findings, in order to make

about one prosecutor crossing the line, but rather indicative of a more structural problem that also included an overreliance on confessions of guilt, and that necessitated the need for better checks on Prosecutors' power (Kingston, 2011; Committee for Review of the State of the Prosecutors Office, 2011b).

11 Recent statistics suggest that Prosecutors Offices are indeed following through with this policy, as a part of which most persons suspected of diminished criminal responsibility or criminal insanity are also in principle recorded (Supreme Public Prosecutors Office, 2017). This policy is now actually also required by law, in line with the Law That Partially Revises the Code of Criminal Procedure (Act no. 54, 2016). For an outline of the law (in Japanese), see the Japan Federation of Bar Associations website: www.nichibenren.or.jp/library/ja/publication/booklet/data/keijisoshohoto_kaisei_01.pdf – last visited 22-5-2018.

the implementation of actual support possible, they will, together with the earlier mentioned Community Living Settlement Support Centers (Centers) and other social welfare organizations, make the necessary arrangements for a place to stay and the social services that are to be provided.[12]

### *2.1. Funding*

The previous paragraphs outlined the process of institutionalization of "support at the entrance". In this regard it is important to also consider the issue of funding. The Prosecutors Office formally hires social workers, though be it as temporary staff. These social workers are accordingly paid for the work they do in the context of "support at the entrance". The staff working at the Centers also do such work as part of their paid job. Other social workers however often remain unpaid. There are social workers who do not accept money from lawyers because the aim of their organization is to work in connection with lawyers, and not as their subordinates. In such a case the organization uses its own funds to compensate "traveling fees and so on". Effectively, these social workers are working for free, even if this is something they cannot just continue doing (Tamura & Takahashi, 2016: 41). But aside from those taking such a principled approach, many social workers do simply not get paid because there is no state-funded system yet to compensate them for their "support at the entrance" work, which they often do at the request of a lawyer appointed by the state (Tsujikawa, 2014: 250–251; JFBA, 2017). When social workers accompany lawyers visiting their client in custody, or when they write up a statement of opinion on the care this client should receive, or when they put together a rehabilitation support plan, they are playing their criminal justice role out of idealistic motivations.

## 3. Social workers' role in decision making processes

The social advisers at the Prosecution Office, or other social workers approached by a Center or the suspect or defendant's lawyer, will thus inform and advise prosecutors on the possibilities and prospects for support and rehabilitation. Social advisers accordingly have no formal say in the legal decisions that prosecutors make. But they do provide advice or present a proposal as to what to do with a particular suspect or defendant, meaning that they may for instance also advise a prosecutor to demand a suspended sentence (Chida, 2014: 222). Such advice and the information that social advisers provide do figure into decisions on

12 They will typically do so in close cooperation with the Rehabilitation Bureau, the local government, and other potentially relevant institutions (Yoshikai, 2015:106). "The Rehabilitation Bureau of the Ministry of Justice is responsible for the overall administration of rehabilitation services, the main aspect of which is community-based treatment to offenders. The Bureau handles planning and policy making which are then implemented by the 50 Probation Offices and eight Regional Parole Boards throughout the country" (Akashi, 2018: 9). I will come back to the topic of community-based treatment of offenders below.

prosecution and sentence demands, as well as the sentences that judges impose – much like the results of the "regular" investigation into the offender's circumstances figure into such decisions (interviews with prosecutors, 2016–18; Chida, 2014: 218). Tamano Tsujikawa, an Osaka lawyer and expert on "support at the entrance" and related issues, states in this regard:

> [the awareness of the importance of providing social welfare support) is having an effect not only in terms of suspended sentences, but also on decisions regarding the suspension of prosecution. (. . .) When it comes to whether social welfare support is turned into a condition for a suspended prosecution: this is something that lawyers are opposed to, as it would result in forced social welfare support. However, it is the public prosecutor's exclusive right to decide to prosecute or not, and it seems like in practice there are cases in which support does become a condition [for a suspended prosecution). Still, even if a prosecutor suspends prosecution under such a condition, and the suspect does not meet that condition, that person can still be prosecuted, as the prohibition against double jeopardy does not apply to the decision not to prosecute. There are in fact reports of such cases.
>
> (2017).[13]

Prosecutors may suspend prosecution and judges may suspend a sentence on the assumption that, for example, the defendant will be admitted into a social welfare institution (cf. also Doi, 2014: 69; Chida, 2014: 221; Ruihanshōgaishamondai shuzaihan, 2013: 89). Social workers will arrange the support that might allow for such a suspended prosecution or suspended sentence. To this end they will be working with either lawyers or prosecutors or, more typically, both. If the prosecutor does bring the case to court a social worker will be asked, typically by the defense, to testify about the defendants' circumstances, their views on and advice concerning the defendants' prospects for rehabilitation.

It is especially at this stage that the differences in perspective between lawyers, prosecutors and judges on one hand and social workers on the other come to light. For example: social workers will, as noted earlier, typically draw up a rehabilitation support plan that outlines things such as the defendant's personal and medical history and the means and institutions available to support the defendant's rehabilitation. If available, lawyers will normally try to have this plan submitted into evidence. They will subsequently outline the plan in court, possibly with some explanation added through the testimony of a social worker. Social workers in this plan typically make use of information gathered from those who had dealings with the defendant. In doing so they may refer to offenses that the prosecution and the Court are not aware of. Relevant as such information may be to social workers, for the Prosecution and Court it would constitute proof of the defendant's criminal tendencies, rather than information conducive to a

13 Personal correspondence with criminal defense attorney Tamano Tsujikawa.

lenient treatment. It accordingly happens that lawyers find that they cannot submit the Plan into evidence – although they will more typically ask social workers to rewrite certain parts (Tsujikawa, 2014: 249, 2016: 45).

Such differences of opinion as to what information a rehabilitation support plan should contain and what not point to a basic difference in perspective. Lawyers generally aim to secure the most lenient treatment possible for their clients. In specific connection with "support at the entrance", they will aim to show that given the support that has been arranged, their client's prospects for rehabilitation are looking good, and that therefore a prison sentence is not necessary or even is counterproductive. *Irrespective of lawyers' personal commitment*, in their arguments rehabilitation and social welfare arrangements accordingly serve as a means to an end: a lenient treatment for their client. This end is furthermore also where lawyers' active involvement ends – that is, when a prosecutor suspends their clients' prosecution or when the court hands down a verdict. For social workers, however, these legal decisions are the beginning of a typically long, bumpy process aimed at improving the quality of their clients' difficult life. (Urazaki, 2016: 81; Izumaru, 2017). That being said, not having regular run-ins with the law of course also very much helps making a person's life a little less difficult. It is from this perspective that one can understand that social workers do actually try to make their clients more aware of the difference between right and wrong, and to steer them away from law breaking behavior (Ruihanshōgaishamo ndaishuzaihan, 2013: 91–92).

Improving a suspect's or defendant's quality of life is normally not the first consideration driving judges' and Prosecutors' actions. Their decisions on to how to deal with the person under suspicion or on trial are determined by a host of different considerations on matters including criminal responsibility, general and specific prevention, victims' feelings and the extent to which the offense in question affected the social order. The most important of these are the considerations on a person's criminal responsibility. Other considerations are pursued within the limits allowed by criminal responsibility, which form the basis on which similar cases are dealt with similarly, and different cases differently (Yoshikai, 2015: 90).

As far as prosecutors are concerned this means that their decisions are guided first of all by an evaluation of the facts of the case, the criminal responsibility that the *act* implies and the retributive response that such responsibility necessitates. Accordingly, support at the entrance is normally only an option for relatively minor offenses (Yoshikai, 2015: 92, 94). Judges operate on the basis of very much the same criteria (cf. Johnson, 2002: 66). Of course, considerations on the *person* of the offender and special prevention also play a part, but formally only in a second instance (Yoshikai, 2015: 92). Still, this is not a matter of either/or: the pursuit of a person's criminal responsibility may and does go hand in hand with making plans, from the very beginning, to support this offender's rehabilitation (Chida, 2014: 221).

One difference with social workers, however, is that for prosecutors as well as judges, rehabilitation is something that stands in service of crime prevention and maintaining social order. In line with this perspective, lawyers also frame social welfare support as a way for the offender to lead a life without crime – that is: to not reoffend (JFBA, 2011; Ruihanshōgaishamondaishuzai han, 2013: 75; Yoshikai, 2015: 16). This not surprising given also that Prosecutors' formal commitment to "support at the entrance" is based on the Crime Prevention Act and the Plan to Promote Crime Prevention, enacted in 2016 and 2017, respectively (see Introduction). Support at the entrance is just one means through which the general goal of crime prevention is pursued. But in any case: here, offenders' rehabilitation is a means to an end, rather than a goal in and of itself.

Given this means-to-an-end outlook of legal professionals,[14] "support at the entrance" accordingly brings with it the risk of social welfare being put in service of criminal justice goals. The available literature and my talks and correspondence with social workers suggests that they are aware of this issue, as the following quote also illustrates:

> our goal is not to respond to lawyers' requests so as to make suspects' or defendants' sentence lighter; it is also not to respond to Prosecutors' requests so as to prevent crime. Social workers enter the environment of clients experiencing difficulties in their daily lives (. . .) with the aim of improving the quality of that life. That is what their role is essentially about. When they intervene at the criminal procedure stage too, that is essentially the role that they fulfill.
>
> (Urazaki, 2016: 81).

Nevertheless, social workers do find themselves faced with legal professionals looking for assurances, asking, for example, whether the proposed rehabilitation plan will keep the offender from committing more crimes (Tamura & Takahashi, 2016: 37).[15] It is against this background that we can understand the policy of some social workers' organizations to not accept money from lawyers for their services (see Tamura & Takahashi, 2016: 41).

## 4. Locating "support at the entrance" in criminal policy

The previous sections highlighted the growing awareness, among criminal justice professionals and the general public alike, of especially elderly, mentally disturbed

14 This is not to deny, of course, that there are many lawyers and other legal professionals who are genuinely committed to a person's rehabilitation for that person's sake, and who in fact emphasize that the goal of arranging welfare support is that of improving a person's welfare, rather than arranging welfare support with the ulterior aim of preventing crime (Tsujikawa, 2017; Osugi, 2016: 72–75)

15 Of course, when a person is put on probation (*hogo kansatsu*), as part, for example, of a suspended sentence, he or she is placed under the supervision of volunteer probation officers (VPOs) who on one hand aim to help persons to deal with the difficult circumstances they are often experiencing, but who at the same time watch over these persons to see if they stay on the right track (cf. Doi, 2014: 67–68).

repeat offenders caught in a cycle of offending, going to prison only to reoffend upon release. Yamamoto's prison memoirs and some highly publicized crimes involving mentally disturbed persons played an important part in raising such awareness, and in this way contributed to the eventual institutionalization of "support at the entrance". The Prosecutors Office reforms that allowed for a renewed, official commitment to offenders' rehabilitation also contributed to this process.

Nevertheless, the Prosecutors Office commitment to providing "support at the entrance" ultimately came about as a more general effort to reduce *recidivism* – although rehabilitation and the prevention of recidivism could be seen as two sides of the same coin. In any case, in order to understand why "support at the entrance" took the shape it did and accordingly to understand the entrance of the social worker on the criminal justice stage – that is: the stage at which decisions on suspects' and defendants' fate are taken – it is necessary to examine support at the entrance as a recidivism reduction policy embedded in more general policies and efforts aimed at reducing crime.

This general effort has been coordinated by the Cabinet Crime Committee (CCC), that was established in 2003. At that time rising crime rates were a great source of public and political concern, and so "forceful measures" were called for. As part of such measures many legal reforms were implemented that had in common that they allowed for harsher ways to deal with offenders (see generally Chapter 1). But in addition to such reforms then–Prime Minister Koizumi thus also established the CCC, charging it with the mission to build a "crime-resistant society" and to "restore Japan's status as the safest country in the world" (CCC, 2003a). The CCC has since then played an important role as a driving force of criminal policy.

In 2012 the CCC compiled a report devoted especially to recidivism. It noted that in 2006 an estimated 71% of all offenders were first offenders, while the remaining 29% were repeat offenders. Looking at the crimes committed by these two groups of offenders, however, it turned out the repeat offenders were responsible for 58% of all offenses. The CCC report noted in addition that according to the 2011 MOJ White Paper on Crime, 43% of all those arrested for general penal code offenses were repeat offenders, and that repeat offenders furthermore made up 56% of the total influx of new inmates. Considering the general CCC mission, the prevention of recidivism was thus an important issue (CCC, 2012: 1), and with its 2012 report the CCC very much put recidivism on the criminal policy map. Furthermore, special attention for repeat offenders with no social safety net, those without their own place in society, was from the very beginning part of the CCC plans (CCC, 2012: 1).[16]

16 In this regard it also important to note the passing, in 2013, of the Law Concerning the Suspension of Part of the Sentence of Those Who Committed the Offense of Possession of Drugs, etc. (Act no. 50), made possible by the Law That Revises a Part of the Criminal Code (Act no. 49). These laws, aimed at preventing recidivism among especially drug abusers by making use of suspended sentences while offering these persons specialized care, also

One of the principles on which these CCC plans have been based is that of supporting the Japanese people in securing their own safety (CCC, 2003a).[17] In specific reference to recidivism the CCC motto was that of "building a society that does not breed crime". The common thread running through the CCC plans was that of the emphasis placed on the role of the local community in preventing crime in general and recidivism in particular (CCC, 2003b). However, even though this role was emphasized as part of a new plan with great ambitions, the idea of involving citizens in preventing crime or recidivism was hardly new. In fact, Japanese citizens have for a long time been involved in the prevention of crime and the rehabilitation of offenders, as well as other goals set by the authorities, for that matter (cf. Garon, 1998). Akashi notes, for example, that in 1939 there were 14,000 volunteers who were formally recognized as "rehabilitation workers" (2018: 2). These volunteers were the precursors of today's approximately 48,000 Volunteer Probation Officers (see note 9). Crime prevention volunteering has furthermore been a fixed part of the many volunteering activities organized by neighborhood associations and the local government. As Herber notes: in 2003, 177,831 people were registered as crime prevention volunteers; by 2016 that number had (as a result of CCC policies) risen to 2,758,659 (Herber, 2018: 2; cf. also Johnson & Carol, 2000: 35–62).[18] Accordingly, the CCC plans reaffirmed the importance of a long used guiding principle of Japanese governance in general and criminal policy in particular.

In accordance with this policy the aim was and is for "the government and the people to become as one", and "(for the government) to gain a wide understanding and cooperation from the people and Regional Public Bodies, and so on" (Ministry of Justice, 2016).[19] The setting up of Community Living Settlement Support Centers, the use made of often unpaid social workers so as to arrange support for repeat offenders by placing them in local institutions run by NPOs, placing them on probation so as to be supervised by volunteer probation officers: all this is very much part of a continuing community oriented approach toward criminal policy that leans heavily on people's civic engagement.

Here, "support at the entrance" is part of a more general effort to link formal criminal justice practices with local community resources. Social workers and

illustrate the emphasis placed on rehabilitation as part of a bigger recidivism prevention effort. See generally Ota (2014).

17 This departing principle was in fact formulated in the first meeting of the CCC. Records of this and following meeting records and other materials are available (in Japanese) on the CCC website: www.kantei.go.jp/jp/singi/hanzai/ – last visited 24-4-2018.

18 Crime prevention volunteering can take many forms. The most common one however, involves volunteers patrolling their neighborhoods in small groups, wearing fluorescent jackets that typically on the back say "crime prevention patrol", looking for suspicious persons and things and urging people to be vigilant and alert to the possibility of crime. See generally Herber (2018).

19 Regional Public Bodies (*chihōkōkyō dantai*) are made up of inhabitants from a specific region, and within that region they aim to exercise public governance on the basis of their constitutionally guaranteed right for self- governance.

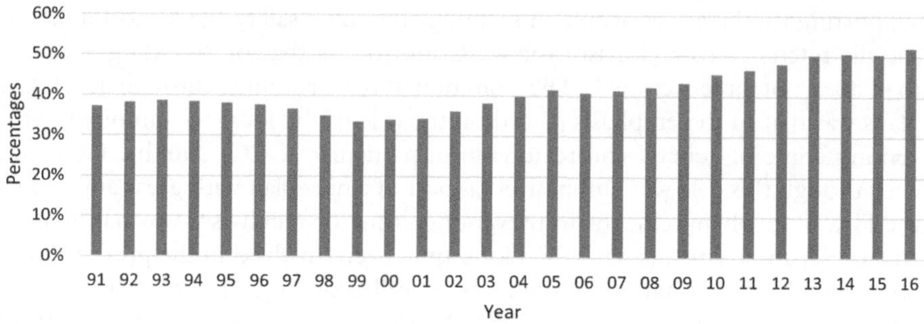


*Graph 3.2* Percentages of suspended prosecutions 1991–2016

Source: (MOJ White Papers on Crime 1992–2017).

the Community Living Settlement Support Centers play an important role in realizing that link. Given that the CCC relies on a familiar recipe – keeping in mind also the close resemblance of "support at the entrance" with the Yokohama approach of the 1960s – "support at the entrance" is indicative of the continuity in Japanese criminal policy. This type of policy continues to rely on fostering citizens' understanding of "the good cause" and their willingness to contribute in, regardless of the penal populist policy currents addressed in Chapter 1.

Prosecution practices too are indicative of not only continuity, but in fact also of an increased emphasis on diversion and rehabilitation. As Graph 3.2 shows, public prosecutors have in the past years been suspending the prosecution of more and more defendants – for both minor and serious offenses.[20] Remarkably, this trend of increasing diversion started in the year 2000, long before there was talk of "support at the entrance", and at a time when criminal justice policy was dominated by penal populist discourse and characterized by increased punitivism. In recent years prosecutors have been diverting still more offenders than they used to, on the basis of "support at the entrance" policies and social workers' input.

Percentages from the total number of general/penal code offenses for which prosecution was suspended. These are penal code offenses excluding negligent vehicular manslaughter and similar traffic related offenses. In the White Paper statistics from 2015 on the category of general penal code offenses was renamed penal code offenses, while the category of penal code offenses, that up until then referred to penal code offenses including negligent vehicular manslaughter (etc.) was replaced by the category "penal code offences/negligent vehicular manslaughter, etc". Graph generated on the basis of data from MOJ White Papers 1992–2017.

20 To give a few examples of the suspended prosecution rates in 2016: assault leading to injury (*shōgai*), 57.4%; assault (*bōkō*), 67.9%; robbery, 14.3%; extortion, 47.9%; murder (including attempted murder), 12.1%; rape, 11.9% (Ministry of Justice, 2017).

Exactly how many more offenders prosecutors are diverting on this basis is as yet unclear. National figures on other forms of "support at the entrance" – i.e. on persons who received a suspended prosecution or a suspended sentence in connection with social workers' advice and the arranged social welfare support – are as yet unavailable (Supreme Public Prosecutors Office, 2018). We do know that in 2016 prosecutors suspended the prosecution of 79,186 offenders (= 52% of all penal code offenders), 1,170 of which were placed under Protective Emergency Rehabilitation and provided with different kinds of social welfare support (Ministry of Justice, 2017). We also know that the Nagasaki Community Living Settlement Support Center has between 2012 and 2016 supported 30–40 persons per year, as part of "support at the entrance" (Izumaru, 2017). Each of Japan's 47 prefectures now has such a Community Living Settlement Support Center, but it is unclear whether these are all supporting similar numbers of persons. Given that the Nagasaki Community Living Settlement Support Center caters to a much smaller population (approximately 1.4 million people) than for example the Center in Tokyo (approximately 14 million), one could assume the numbers in Tokyo and other densely populated prefectures to be much higher. Taking into account however that Nagasaki was the first prefecture with a Community Living Settlement Support Center and that Nagasaki had already before then established welfare oriented criminal justice practices, it is also possible that the Nagasaki numbers are high for the size of its population.

In any case, the persons that through "support at the entrance" are diverted from either trial or prison often depend on the local community to help to provide these persons with the support they need. The question is how the community's involvement will develop. For a long time, citizens' willingness to become involved to help local governments achieve their goals has been a given.[21] In recent years, however, their willingness to perform demanding volunteering tasks is waning. The average age of volunteer probation officers is now of 65, a result of the fact that it has become increasingly difficult to recruit younger persons.[22]

21 To give an impression: first of all there are the already mentioned 48,000 volunteer probation officers (VPOs) who under the guidance of around 1,000 Ministry of Justice professional probation officers (PPOs) perform all sorts of activities to help former offenders – those who were released from prison, but also some of those who were given a suspended sentence or suspended prosecution – stay on the right track and reintegrate into the community. As part of their activities these VPOs for example meet with their supervisees about two to three times per month, typically at the VPO's own home. Secondly, there is the Women's Association for Rehabilitation Aid that counts 162,612 members who, among other things, visit correctional facilities, set up of exhibitions of products manufactured by inmates, supply inmates with daily goods – etc., etc. Further, there are the 4,509 volunteers who as "elderly brothers and sisters" organize sports and other recreational activities for former juvenile delinquents and the approximately 10,000 companies who have indicated the willingness to employ former convicts.

22 Not helpful in this regard was an incident, in 2009, involving a probationer setting fire to his VPO's home. Minoura, a PPO, notes however that "there have been a few harmful incidents", but also that such incidents are very few and far between (Minoura, 2018: 9)

Volunteers involved in other civic activities are getting older too.[23] This not is not surprising, however, when one considers that people involved in one form of volunteering are often also involved or have been involved in other forms of volunteering (Akashi, 2018: 4).[24] Given volunteers' important role in Japanese criminal policy, the question is what will happen when, in the next 10 years or so, the majority of these volunteers will have to stop their activities because they are getting too old. With specific reference to social workers' role in providing "support at the entrance": many play this role voluntarily. The question is how long they are able and willing to do so, and whether "support at the entrance" will suffer the same fate as "the Yokohama approach", that was discontinued in part because of a lack of funding to support the supervising probation officers, that is: a lack of funding to support the key volunteer players involved. Given the increasing population of elderly people and the accompanying increase in elderly offenders (Ministry of Justice, 2017), however, the need for support at the entrance is also likely to only increase.

## Conclusion

"Support at the entrance" and social workers entering the criminal justice stage has been a result of (1) an increased awareness of the problems surrounding mentally disturbed and often elderly repeat offenders in the criminal justice chain, (2) Prosecutors Office reforms and (3) Cabinet Crime Commission policies aimed at reducing recidivism. For prosecutors, social workers' input constitutes part of the whole of factors they consider when making their charging decision. This decision however is still formally determined first and foremost by suspects' and defendants' alleged criminal responsibility, which is in turn largely determined by the nature of the act committed. In this sense "support at the entrance" remains firmly rooted in a retributive penal philosophical outlook. Having said that, statistics show that prosecutors are prepared to suspend prosecution also for serious, violent offenses. Thus, the primacy-of-act-based criminal responsibility in Prosecutors' decision making is far from absolute. While act-based criminal responsibility is the first guiding principle, Japanese law does grant prosecutors and judges considerable discretion in reaching their conclusions concerning a suspect's or defendant's legal treatment. Social workers' input is juridified to the extent that as one of the factors that prosecutors and judges take into consideration, it is incorporated into the decision that these legal professionals ultimately take.

On one hand, different from what Foucault has argued, within Japanese criminal justice practices social workers' contributions are in fact juridically defined and integrated into the power to punish (cf. Foucault, 1978: 22). On the other

23 Hino notes, for example, that the majority of men involved in crime prevention volunteering are in their late 70s(!) (Hino, 2018: 3).

24 When participating in the crime prevention volunteering activities of three groups based in the Tokyo area, I also found that all the members I spoke with ($n$ = around 30) were also active in other fields of volunteering for the local government (see generally Herber, 2018).

hand, one can of course say that Prosecutors' and judges' decisions are of course no longer about "simply punishing", in the sense that their decisions are purely act-based – Foucault's implicit definition of juridical punishment (Foucault, 1981/2000: 462–463; 1984/2000: 388–389). They are, as this chapter has also shown, also about treating the person being investigated (!) or on trial, even if for the purpose of preventing recidivism. Here one can also wonder how simple "simply punishing" ever was. In the Tokugawa period, for example, who the person on trial was, was very relevant to determining the right amount of punishment – though be it in first instance in terms of the social status and rank of this person, although there also was an assumed connection between status and moral quality or weakness (Botsman, 2005: 59 and following; 104).

Be that as it may, incorporated though social workers' advice may be in legal decision making processes, the extent to which social workers' advice affects the actual decisions remains as yet unclear. This, then, is a consequence of the fact that social workers' contribution is incorporated in Prosecutors' and judges' discretionary judgment. Accordingly, social workers' contribution to a certain extent disappears in the "'hole in the doughnut' that is discretion, even if that hole does not exist except as an area left open by a surrounding belt of restriction" (Dworkin, 1977: 52). While judges still explain their exercise of discretion, Prosecutors' discretionary judgment mostly takes place "off stage", as they are not required to publicly explain why one suspect is granted a suspended prosecution and another is not.[25]

Still, sources show that prosecutors do suspend prosecution or demand a suspended sentence, and judges impose suspended sentences on the assumption

25 It should be noted, however, Japan has a system of Prosecution Review Commissions that may review Prosecutors' decision not to prosecute. As of May 2009 the citizens that review these decisions have been given more power than before to review Prosecutors' decision not to file charges. As Herber has noted: "under the reformed procedures a panel of 11 laypersons reviews Prosecutors' decision not to prosecute, pursuant to a victim's or a victim's proxy's complaint regarding said decision. While in the past PRCs' recommendations often went ignored, as of 21 May 2009 prosecutors can ignore the recommendations of a PRC once, but if after a second review the commission again comes to the conclusion that prosecution is appropriate, a 'forced prosecution' procedure will take place, in which a lawyer designated by the court will file a public indictment, meaning that the suspects (by then defendants) will have to stand trial" (2016: 89–90). Forced prosecutions take place only very sporadically. Since 2009 there have been forced prosecutions in nine cases, which for now have resulted in two convictions (the trial of three defendants in the so called Tokyo Electric Power Company [TEPCO] case, which concerns the criminal responsibility of three former executives of TEPCO, the power company that operated the Daiichi nuclear power plant at which a meltdown occurred in the wake of the earthquake and tsunami of 11 March 2011, is still in progress). This case is illustrative of the high public interest cases that PRCs have handled, highlighting again that a small quantity of decisions does not translate into those decisions being of minor significance. For more information on PRCs see Fukurai, 2011a, 2011b. Given that this book focuses on criminal justice practices from the stage of the pretrial investigation to the moment a verdict and sentence are handed down, it will not further address PRCs' functioning.

that the suspect or defendant will receive social welfare support, and that such support will help this person rehabilitate. This assumption is in turn based on the rehabilitation prospects typically argued by lawyers, on the basis of social workers' input. Social welfare support may however still be planned and arranged when prosecutors do after all decide to prosecute, and when judges hand down a prison sentence. Here, different goals are pursued on parallel tracks, something which again, as in Chapters 1 and 2, brings into focus the multi-dimensional character of decision making processes on punishment.

Prosecutors, judges and lawyers each have their own perspective on the legal treatment that a suspect or defendant should receive. Within that perspective social workers' input typically constitutes a means to an end: a means to assess and limit the risk of recidivism (for prosecutors and judges) and an opportunity to argue the desirability of a lenient, non-custodial sentence (for lawyers). By contrast, social workers' perspective is focused first of all on the person of the alleged offender and his or her well-being. From this perspective the first priority is to get clients the help they need so as to make their often difficult life a little less difficult. As a result of such help it is possible that one might in hindsight say that this person stayed away from crime after receiving help. At the same time, regardless of social workers' commitment to priorities different from those of the legal professionals, their input is incorporated in the arguments and decisions of the legal professionals. In this way, social workers' expertise and insights are unavoidably put to legal use. Nevertheless, their unwillingness to "play along" and give legal professionals the assurances they are looking for does imply a margin of uncertainty in the decision making of these professionals. But this of course is a familiar part of the territory of future oriented decisions, as opposed to more retribution oriented backward looking ones.

"Support at the entrance" is embedded in bigger efforts to reduce recidivism, efforts in which Japanese citizens, as volunteers, play an important part. As such, it is also very much in line with a long established line of criminal policies predicated on citizens' willingness to help the (local) government achieve its policy aims. Different from penal populist style policy, "support at the entrance", with its focus on treatment rather than punishment, involves fostering citizens' understanding rather than catering to citizens' perceived wishes. In this sense, "support at the entrance" looks like the criminal justice policy book has turned over a new page. At the same time, as it is, "support at the entrance" is a small scale practice. With an aging population and rising numbers and rates of crimes committed by elderly people, that scale may very well become much bigger.

All this does not automatically imply, however, that the pendulum is swinging back and that Japanese criminal justice is *overall* becoming (more) rehabilitation oriented. As this chapter shows, efforts are under way to deal specifically with repeat offenders in more rehabilitation (read: recidivism prevention) oriented ways. It is important to keep in mind, however, that as a result of reforms implemented since the early 2000s the Japanese criminal justice infrastructure allows for more punitive ways of dealing with offenders.

While we do now know that Prosecutors' suspending practices have not been affected by the penal populist turn, there is still much that needs to be examined in this regard. For example: pursuant to legal reforms in 2000 and 2008 crime victims' role in Japanese criminal justice was dramatically expanded. What effect, if any, has this expansion had on administration of justice practices? To that question the next chapter will turn.

## References


Akashi, Fumiko (2018). The role of volunteer probation officers in Japan: recent challenges and responses. *International Journal of Law, Crime and Justice* 54: 121–132.

*Asahi Shimbun* (2004). 'Hei no naka' no taiken, keimushochō he kataru Yamamoto Jōji moto gi'in, kaikaku ni hitoyaku, 26 May.

*Asahi Shimbun* (2006a). Shimonoseki eki, hōka de enjō 74 sai no yōgisha taiho 'kūfuku de mushakusha', 7 January.

*Asahi Shimbun* (2006b). Kurikaesareta hōka dedokoro shussho shitemo shigoto nashi miyori nashi JR Shimonoseki jiken yōgisha, 14 January.

*Asahi Shimbun* (2006c). Hikoku, ichijirushī shōgai nashi seishin kanteinin, saibansho ni hōkoku Shimonoseki eki hōka/Yamaguchi ken, 1 August.

*Asahi Shimbun* (2006d). 2 en no fūtō nusunda onna ni hanketsu, jyōshūruihansettōzai de chōeki 3 nen, 17 October.

*Asahi Shimbun* (2012). Tokusō gurumi, nintei 2 hikoku no muzaishuchō wo shirizokeru FD kaizan inpei, motobuchōra yūzai, 30 March.

*Asahi Shimbun* (2013). FD kaizan, 3 nengo no shūketsu Osaka chiken moto tokusōbuchōra jōkoku sezu, 9 October.

Botsman, D.V. (2005). *Punishment and power in the making of modern Japan*. Princeton: Princeton University Press.

Cabinet Crime Committee (hanzaikakuryōkaigi) (2003a). Available at: www.kantei.go.jp/jp/singi/hanzai/. Website last visited 30 August 2018.

Cabinet Crime Committee (hanzaikakuryōkaigi) (2003b). *Hanzai ni tsuyoi shakai no jitsugen no tame no kōdō keikaku*. Available at: www.kantei.go.jp/jp/singi/hanzai/kettei/031218keikaku.html. Website last visited 30 August 2018.

Cabinet Crime Committee (hanzaikakuryōkaigi) (2012). *Saihanbōshi ni muketa sōgō taisaku*. Available at: www.kantei.go.jp/jp/singi/hanzai/kettei/120720/honbun.pdf. Website last visited 30 August 2018.

Cabinet Crime Committee (hanzaikakuryōkaigi) (2017). *Saihanbōshi suishin keikaku*. Available at: www.kantei.go.jp/jp/singi/hanzai/kettei/171215/honbun.pdf. Website last visited 30 August 2018.

Chida, Sanae (2014). Sendai chihō kensatsuchō ni okeru jinkō shien no genjyō to kadai: keiji seisaku suishinshitsu ni okeru saihan bōshi to kōsei shien oyobi higaisha/izoku shien ni tsuite. *Waseda daigaku shakai anzen seisaku kenkyūjo kiyō* 7: 215–235.

Committee for Review of the State of the Prosecutors Office (2011a). *Meeting 11*. Available at: http://webcache.googleusercontent.com/search?q=cache:oubaeTL_0dsJ:www.moj.go.jp/content/000071941.pdf+&cd=2&hl=en&ct=clnk&gl=nl. Website last visited 30 August 2018.

Committee for Review of the State of the Prosecutors Office (2011b). *Kensatsu no saisei ni mukete kensatsu no arikata kentō kaigi teigen.* Available at: www.moj.go.jp/content/000072551.pdf. Website last visited 30 August 2018.

Correction Bureau Statistics (1992–2014). Available at: www.moj.go.jp/housei/toukei/toukei_ichiran_kousei.html. Website last visited 30 August 2018.

Doi, Masakazu (2014). Keijishihō to fukushi no renkei wo meguru konnichiteki kadai (kadaikenkyū keijishihō to fukushi no renkei no arikata: hanzai kōisha no shakai fukki shien no genjō to kadai). *Japanese Journal of Sociological Criminology* 39: 67–81.

Dworkin, Ronald M. (1977). Is Law a System of Rules?, in Ronald M. Dworking (ed.) *The Philosophy of Law*. Oxford: Oxford University Press: 38–65.

Foote, Daniel H. (1992). The benevolent paternalism of Japanese criminal justice. *California Law Review* 80: 317–390.

Foucault, M. (1978). *Discipline and punish*, trans. Alan Sheridan. New York: Vintage.

Foucault, M. (1981/2000). To punish is the most difficult thing there is, in James D. Faubion (ed.), trans. Robert Hurley, *Michel Foucault-power-essential works of Foucault*. New York: New Press Essential: 462–464.

Foucault, M. (1984/2000). What is called punishing, in James D. Faubion (ed.), trans. Robert Hurley, *Essential works of Michel Foucault*. New York: New Press Essential: 382–393.

Fukurai, Hiroshi (2011a). Japan's prosecutorial review commissions: lay oversight of the government's discretion of prosecution. *University of Pennsylvania East Asia Law Review* 6: 1–42.

Fukurai, Hiroshi (2011b). Japan's Quasi-Jury and Grand Jury systems as deliberative agents of social change: de-colonial atrategies and deliberative participatory democracy. *Chicago Kent Law Review* 86(2): 789–829.

Garon, S. (1998). *Molding Japanese minds: the state in everyday life*. Princeton, NJ: Princeton University Press.

Hamai, Kōichi (2009). *2 en de keimusho, 5 oku de shikōyūyo*. Tokyo: Kōbunsha.

Herber, Erik D. (2016). The 2011 Fukushima nuclear disaster Japanese citizens' role in the pursuit of criminal responsibility. *Zeitschrift für japanisches Recht* 42: 87–109.

Herber, Erik D. (2018). Crime prevention in Japan orchestration, representation and impact of a volunteering boom. *International Journal of Law, Crime and Justice* 54: 102–110.

Hino, Kimihiro (2018). Plus bouhan: a new community-based approach to crime prevention in Japan. *International Journal of Law, Crime and Justice* 54: 79–88.

Izumaru, Takeshi (2014). Keijishihō to fukushi no renkei ni kansuru genjō to kadai ni tsuite: Nagasakiken chiiki seikatsu teichaku sentāno 'jissen' kara mietekita mono (keijishihō to fukushi no renkei no arikata: hanzai kōisha no shakai fukki shien no genjō to kadai). *Japanese Journal of Sociological Criminology* 39: 24–36.

Izumaru, Takeshi (2017). Personal correspondence with Takeshi Izumaru, head of the Nagasaki Community Living Settlement Support Center (between 22-8-2017 and 6-10-2017).

Japanese Association of Certified Social Workers (2018). *About certified social workers*. Available at: www.jacsw.or.jp/16_FooterLinks/English.html. Website last visited 30 August 2018.

Japan Federation of Bar Associations (JFBA) (2011). *Kizuite imasuka anata no higisha/hikokunin ni shōgai ga aru ka mo shiremasen*. Available at: www.nichibenren.

or.jp/library/ja/activity/data/handicapped_person_criminal.pdf. Website last visited 30 August 2018.

Japan Federation of Bar Associations (JFBA) (2017). *Tsumi ni towareta shōgaisha tō ni taisuru shihō to fukushi no renkei hiyō ni kansuru ikensho*. Available at: www.nichibenren.or.jp/activity/document/opinion/year/2017/170825.html. Website last visited 30 August 2018.

Johnson, Elmer H. and H. Carol (2000). *Linking community and corrections in Japan*. Carbondale: SIU Press.

Johnson, David T. (2002). *The Japanese way of justice: prosecuting crime in Japan*. Oxford: Oxford University Press.

Kimura, Takao and Yukie Sawaki (2013). Kōrei/shōgaihanzaisha no shakai fukki shien shisaku no genjō to kadai. *Nihon Fukushi University Journal of Social Welfare* 128: 83–113.

Kingston, Jeffrey (2011). Justice on trial: Japanese prosecutors under fire. *The Asia-Pacific Journal* 9(10:1).

Kobayashi, Yoshiko (2016). Keiji jiken ni okeru shakai fukki shien nitsuite. *Waseda daigaku shakai anzen seisaku kenkyūjo kiyō* 9: 69–82.

Matsutomo, Ryō (2014). Tokyo Chihōkensatsuchō Shakaifukkishienshitsu ni okeru “iriguchi” shien no torikumi, in Waseda Institute of the Policy of Social Safety (ed.), Masaoki Ishiwaka. *Shihō shisutemu kara fukushi shisutemu he no daibājyon puroguramu no genjō to kadai*. Tokyo: Seibundoh: 159–184.

Ministry of Justice (MOJ) (2017). *Kōsei kinkyū hogo oyobi kōsei hogo ni okeru shakai fukki shien shisaku ni tsuite*. Available at: www.moj.go.jp/content/001236860.pdf. Website last visited 30 August 2018.

Ministry of Justice (MOJ) (annual). *White paper on crime*. Available at: http://hakusyo1.moj.go.jp/en/nendo_nfm.html. Website last visited 30 August 2018.

Minoura, Satōshi (2018). Offender rehabilitation reform in Japan: effective cooperation between professional and volunteer probation officers. *International Journal of Law, Crime and Justice* 54. 111–120.

Miyazawa, Setsuo (2008a). The politics of increasing punitiveness and the rising populism in Japanese criminal justice policy. *Punishment & Society* 10(1): 47–77.

Miyazawa, Setsuo (2008b). Will penal populism in Japan decline? (symposium: globalized penal populism and its countermeasures). *Japanese Journal of Sociological Criminology* 33: 122–136.

Osugi, Mitsuko (2016). ‘Shihō to fukushi tono renkei’ ni okeru bengoshi no tachiba: mokuteki ha, saihan bōshi dewanaku, shakai ni okeru seikatsu saiken de aru (tokushū shihō to fukushi tono renkei). *Keiji Bengo* 85: 72–77.

Ōta, Tatsuya (2014). *Kei no ichibu shikkōyūyo – hanzaishano kaizenkōsei to saihanbōshi*. Tokyo: Keiōgijukudaigaku shuppankai.

Otake, Tomoko (2011). Atsuko Muraki: fighter for justice. *Japan Times*, 1 May.

Pratt, John (2007). *Penal populism*. London: Routledge.

Okada, Tomoshi (2010). Daisan no konkyū to hanzai: hōmuresu shien no genba kara Shimonoseki hōka jiken wo kan’gaeru (hinkon to hanzai/hikō). *Japanese Journal of Sociological Criminology* 35: 21–37.

Ruihanshōgaishamondaishuzaihan (2013). *Ibasho Sagashite – Ruihan Shōgaishatachi*. Nagasaki: Nagasaki Shimbunsha.

Satō, Makoto (2011). Keijishisetsu no seishinkairyō. *Waseda daigaku shakai anzen seisaku kenkyūjo kiyō* 4: 201–221.

Sugie, Naomi F. (2017). When the elderly turn to petty crime: increasing elderly arrest rates in an aging population. *International Criminal Justice Review* 27(1): 19–39.

Supreme Public Prosecutors Office (2011). *The principles of prosecution.* Available at: www.kensatsu.go.jp/content/000128760.pdf. Website last visited 30 August 2018.

Supreme Public Prosecutors Office (2012). *Kensatsu kaikaku no shinpo jyōkyō.* Available at: http://www.kensatsu.go.jp/content/000128763.pdf. Website last visited 30 August 2018.

Supreme Public Prosecutors Office (2017). *Chiteki shōgai ni yori komyunikeishon nōryoku ni mondai ga aru higisha tō/rokuon/rokuga no jisshiritsu.* Available at: www.kensatsu.go.jp/content/001248008.pdf. Website last visited 30 August 2018.

Supreme Public Prosecutors Office (2018). Correspondence with Ms Sanae Chida, in charge of coordinating support at the entrance policy at the Supreme Public Prosecutors Office Criminal Justice Policy Promotion Chamber (*keijiseisakusuishinshitsu*).

Tamura, Mitsuko and Masako Takahashi (2016). Shakai fukushi Tamura Mitsuko san ni kiku shihō to fukushi no renkei wo dō kisukuka (tokushū shihō to fukushi tono renkei). *Keiji Bengo* 85: 36–41.

Tashima, Yoshikai and Ministry of Health, Labour and Welfare (2008). *Kōsei rōdō kagaku kenkyū: tsumi wo okashita shōgaisha no chiiki seikatsu shien ni kansuru kenkyū/hōkoku.* Available at: www.airinkai.or.jp/kenkyu_pdf/2008/2008_1/h19/01_tashima.pdf. Website last visited 30 August 2018.

Tsujikawa, Tamano (2014). Bengoshikai ni yoru tsumi ni towareta shōgai no aru hito no 'iriguchi' shien no jōkyō to kadai. *Waseda daigaku shakai anzen seisaku kenkyūjo kiyō* 7: 237–251.

Tsujikawa, Tamano (2016). Fukishiteki shien no kōchiku ni tsuite – bengoshi no shiten kara (tokushū shihō to fukushi to no renkei). *Keiji Bengo* 85: 42–54.

Tsujikawa, Tamano (2017). Personal correspondence with criminal defense attorney Tamano Tsujikawa (between 23-8-2017 and 20-9-2017).

Urazaki, Hiroyasu (2016). Tokyo TS net no katsudō: bengonin to sōsharu wākā no tsunagu chōsen (tokushū shihō to fukushi tono renkei). *Keiji Bengo* 85: 78–82.

Waseda Convention on Corrections and Probation (2015). *Kōreisha/Shōgaisha no saihanbōshi: shihō to fukushi no chōwa ni mukete.* Booklet from convention held in Tokyo, 19 November.

Yamamoto, Jōji (2003). *Gokusōki.* Tokyo: Sinchō Bunko.

Yoshikai, Taichi (2015). Kensatsukan no sotsui handan ni kansuru ichi kōsatsu: 'jinkōshien' no shikō wo fumaete. *Kokushikan Law Review* 48: 77–121.

# 4 Victim participation

## Pursuing the therapeutic potential of criminal procedure[1]

### Introduction

For years, crime victims' only role in Japanese criminal justice was that of a witness providing evidence. Beyond that, their perspectives were largely overlooked, as were their interests and needs. In line with a growing worldwide acknowledgment of victims' rights and interests in Japan two different reforms were implemented to help remedy this situation. As a part of that process the Japanese Code of Criminal Procedure (CCP) was revised, twice (in 2000 and 2008), so as to make it possible for victims to participate in both the pre-trial and trial phases of criminal proceedings. They were given the opportunity to play a role as crime victims, rather than as witnesses in service of a process focused on the defendant. Thus, these reforms created a new criminal justice role for another "outsider" – a role that was theirs if they wished to play it.

The aim of these reforms has been to better protect victims' rights and interests, as criminal justice has now officially been acknowledged to "also exist for the sake of victims". Victims' participation in "their" proceedings is in fact assumed to be helpful for their mental recovery.[2] Victims' expanded role accordingly comes with the acknowledgment of criminal proceedings as potentially therapeutic. Added to the list of criminal justice concerns such as truth finding, retribution, special and general deterrence – to name just a few – there now is the added concern for victims' recovery.

Against the background of the societal developments that led to the acknowledgment of proceedings' therapeutic dimension and victims' new role, this

1 Parts of this chapter were previously published in the *Washington International Law Journal* (2017: 27(1), 119–148): "East Asian Court Reform on Trial: Victim Participation in Japan", and the *Asian Journal of Law and Society* (2016: 3(1), 135–157): "Victim Participation in Japan: When Therapeutic Jurisprudence Meets Prosecutor Justice". Published with gracious permission of the publishers.

2 Basic Act on Crime Victims (2003); Crime Victims Basic Plan (2004). The Basic Act on Crime Victims (Act no. 161, 8 December Heisei 16) is available at http://www8.cao.go.jp/hanzai/kihon/hou.html – Cabinet Office Website (accessed 15–4–2015); the Crime Victims Basic Plan is available at http://www8.cao.go.jp/hanzai/kuwashiku/keikaku/keikaku.html – Cabinet Office. Website last visited 31–8–2018.

chapter will examine what victim participation in practice entails, the impact that this participation is having on the roles of other criminal procedure players and how they pursue or do not pursue criminal procedure's newly acknowledged therapeutic dimension.

This chapter is based on transcripts of 12 two-and-a-half-hour-long meetings organized by the Japanese Ministry of Justice ("MOJ meetings"),[3] in which legal professionals who had participated in "victim participation trials" as well as representatives of victim interest groups shared their experiences and exchanged opinions about the system to determine whether a revision of the 2008 system was necessary. This chapter is in addition based on interviews, conducted between 2011 and 2016, with 15 Japanese lawyers and 8 public prosecutors with experience in trials in which victims participated, as well as a Ministry of Justice survey conducted among 111 crime victims who had recently participated in criminal trials.[4]

## 1. Prelude to legal change

Victims' new role is closely linked to two developments addressed in Chapter 1, namely (1) the penal populist developments that since the late 1990s have led to a harsher criminal justice climate and (2) the legal reforms aimed at bringing about a legal system "that could meet the expectations of the people" and that would be more accessible to the people and reflective of their perspectives. The new victim participation is in line with that agenda. After all, when the long neglected perspectives of crime victims are being included into criminal proceedings, the perspective of another *citizen party* is added to the criminal process. The adding of this perspective signals a change in the playing field within which legal professionals go about their job, and exercise their "property rights" of the conflict (Christie, 1977). Like lay participation, victim participation has the potential for an increased democratization of criminal justice, in the sense that average citizens have a stronger say in how a case is to be handled – in line with the goals of the commission charged with reforming the Japanese legal system, the Justice System Reform Council (JSRC). The roots of victims' new role however lie in a development that long predates the JSRC, namely a growing international acknowledgment of victims' rights and interests.

When in the 1960s state-run victim compensation schemes were introduced in New Zealand and England and countries such as Finland, the Netherlands and Austria followed suit, in Japan too the issue of victim compensation became a topic of study and discussion (Ogawa, 1974). General interest in victims' rights and needs was nevertheless still very limited. This started changing, however,

3 Transcripts of these meetings can be accessed at www.moj.go.jp/keiji12_00068.html. Website last visited 31-8-2018. For ease of reference, individual meeting transcripts will be referred to by meeting number followed by the specific page number.

4 Survey Results available at www.moj.go.jp/content/000110030.pdf. Website last visisted 31-8-2018.

when in 1974 a group of terrorists bombed the Mitsubishi Heavy Metal Company building, killing 8 people and injuring another 380. Some of those injured received compensation from their insurance companies, as they had been injured on the job. There were also those however who just happened to have been passing by and were eligible only to very limited social insurance compensation. The plight of these people helped bring about a public awareness of the necessity of a compensation scheme for victims of crime leading to the adoption, in 1980, of the Crime Victim Assistance Act.[5] Under this act the families of victims killed in a crime as well as those seriously injured were entitled to (relatively limited) amounts of "consolation money" (*mimaikin*). This act was thus not aimed at *compensating* victims or their families for damages suffered, but only aimed at providing support (Abe, 2010: 970).[6]

At a 1991 a symposium held to commemorate the enactment of the Crime Victims Assistance Act it became clear, however, that the existing support mechanisms were far from sufficient. This sentiment was conveyed vividly and painfully in a speech given by a mother whose son had been killed in a drunk driving incident:

> [W]ith everything I had, I looked if there wasn't any place in Japan where they could provide me with mental support, but there wasn't. . . . In the Japan of today you can't cry out loud even if you want to. It seems to me that victims' role in today's Japan is one of having to silently endure by yourself.[7]

In addition to making those present aware of the need for more measures to support victims of crime, speeches such as these provided a direct impetus for the setting up of victim consultation bureaus that provided different kinds of counseling services, and finally the coming about, in 1998, of the National Network of Victim Support, an umbrella organization for various kinds of victim support groups set up with the support of both volunteers and the police.

5 This law, often referred to as the Crime Victim Assistance Act, is officially titled the Act Concerning the Support of Crime Victims and so on by Means of Payment of Crime Victims and so on Support Funds (Shōwa 55, 1 May) and is available at http://law.e-gov.go.jp/htmldata/S55/S55HO036.html. On this law, see also Abe, 2010: 969; Matsui, 2011: 60–61.

6 Matsui notes in this regard that the amounts of money victims or the surviving family of the victim were entitled to were typically not enough to sustain livelihood, especially when the victim had been the provider of the main source of income (Matsui, 2011: 61).

7 Statement available at http://nnvs.org/higai/history/. Website last visited 31–8–2018. Besides a shortened version of Emiko Okubo's statement this National Network for Victim Support website also provides a timeline of the different measures and laws set up in support of victims of crime. See also this National Police Agency website overview of measures taken by the Japanese police to support crime victims: www.npa.go.jp/english/kyuuyo1/Police_Support_for_Crime_Victims.pdf. Website last accessed 31–8–2018. This document also contains an overview of the development of support measures for crime victims that also includes a translation of Emiko Okubo's speech.

The sarin gas attacks carried out in 1995 by members of the Aum Shinrikyō doomsday cult in addition prompted a further increase in measures to support victims, and a still increased awareness of victims' needs and rights. The attacks in fact led to the adoption of a law created specifically to compensate victims of these attacks,[8] as well as the adoption of new National Police Agency Guidelines aimed at a better protection of victims' rights.[9]

The serial killing of two elementary schoolchildren by a 14-year-old boy in Kobe in 1997 that, as we have seen, was also a trigger for penal populist trends, again drew attention to the issue of victim support as well as the limited involvement of victims and their families in criminal and juvenile proceedings. Miyazawa has in fact argued that "the establishment of the victim participation system for criminal trials began from this point on" (2014: 78). The Kobe murder case more generally appears to mark the beginning of a period of increased media attention for crime victims and their families, as well as increased "victim activism" (Hamai & Ellis, 2006, 2008). Particularly significant in this regard was the establishment, in 2000, of the National Association of Crime Victims and Surviving Families (NAVS). This organization succeeded in generating much attention for victims' rights and was very influential not only as a result of media exposure, but also because of the fact that its head, Isao Okamura, was the former president of one of the three Tokyo bar associations and the former vice president of the Japan Federation of Bar Associations (JFBA). Both his professional stature and connections allowed Okamura to exercise considerable (political) influence and achieve results (Miyazawa, 2008: 64), allowing the NAVS to become *the* organization to speak on victims' behalf.

## 2. Visible and invisible victims

The previous sections may read like the positive story of a development that has allowed for crime victims to become visible, and for victims' rights and interests to be increasingly acknowledged and recognized. Indeed, when compared to just a few decades ago, important positive developments have taken place. It is at the same time important, however, to note that a great deal of victimization still goes unnoticed or unregistered.

Chapter 1 addressed the penal populist developments that started in the late 1990s. As we have seen, perceptions of rising crime and the perceived need for measures to address this rise provided a strong impetus for these populist

8 The Act Concerning the Payment of Benefits in Support of Victims etc. of Crimes of Aum Shinrikyō (Heisei 20, 18 June). Available at http://law.e-gov.go.jp/htmldata/H20/H20HO080.html. Website last visited 31-8-2018. See in this regard also Takano (2009).

9 These guidelines, adopted in 1996, thus aimed at police practices more mindful of victims' position and interests (in e.g. criminal investigations) as well the bringing about of (police) services to support victims of crimes, such as providing information on victim support groups and counseling services. See: www.npa.go.jp/higaisya/data/yoko.htm. Website last accessed 31-8-2018.

developments. Since then – that is, since the late 1990s – Japanese police forces have taken various measures that show an increased attentiveness to crime victims' needs, including the need to be listened to and be taken seriously.[10] These measures however compete with guiding principles that have long shaped the way in which the police operate, such as that of "the law does not interfere with families", and that of non-interference in affairs between citizens. In line with these principles, originally derived from Roman law, the police have been reluctant to intervene when a case centers on "troubles" within the family as well as other intimate relationships.[11] For a long time these principles contributed to only a small percentage of such cases entering the official crime and criminal justice statistics. Accordingly, especially crimes such as domestic violence, child abuse but also sexual offenses have for a long time remained almost invisible in these statistics.

An increasing general awareness of victims' rights as well as national and international developments more specifically contributing to an increased awareness of crimes with a domestic component, such as domestic violence and child and elderly abuse, have led to the compiling of laws aimed at preventing exactly these crimes, which were for a long time thought to hardly exist in Japan (Arai, 2013; Goodman, 2012, 2002). While these developments have thus obviously allowed for a greater awareness of crimes and their victims, they have not necessarily translated into a more accurate understanding of the scope of the problem. There are furthermore indications that despite an increased awareness of both victims' rights and the risks associated with the practice of non-intervention, police officers are still refusing to register crimes reported by victims.[12] A 2008 Ministry of

10 In addition to raising awareness among police officers of victims' rights and needs, the police have for example increased the number of female officers to deal with reports of sexual offenses and have taken different measures to prevent secondary victimization when reporting such offenses (see Makino, 2013: 59). In many prefectures the police have in addition established windows that crime victims can turn to, in order to receive information on support services and on the options available to them within criminal procedure. For a comprehensive overview of the various measures, see the link provided under footnote 6.

11 As was also the case in the earlier mentioned Okegawa stalker case and the Tochigi lynch case. Following these cases the Police Reform Council did note, in its meeting in 2000, that the police officers involved had acted on the basis of an incorrect understanding of the principle of non-intervention. Nevertheless, in doing so they thus also confirmed the continued relevance of this principle (see www.npsc.go.jp/notice/act/summary/conference/20000616_g.html. Website last visisted 31-8-2018). It should also be noted here that this principle of non-interference is also formally recognized in article 244 of the Japanese Criminal Code, that holds that (among others) theft committed against a spouse, lineal blood relative or a relative with whom they live together shall be exculpated.

12 This refusal mostly concerns reports of victimization, rather than the act of pressing charges, that creates an obligation on the part of the police to investigate, in accordance with the Rules of Investigation, articles 67 and 76. Nevertheless, the police do not always act on this obligation. See Kurosawa, 2011 on police dealings with reports of victimization, etc. For anecdotal evidence see the following online platform where people can ask legal questions to lawyers: www.bengo4.com/c_1009/c_22/c_21/bbs/%E8%A2%AB%E5%AE%B3%E5%B1%8A%E4%B8%8D%E5%8F%97%E7%90%86/. Website last visited 4-6-2018.

Justice crime victim survey furthermore illustrates the problem of people not reporting what happened to them. To give one example: only 13.3% of those who indicated having become a victim of a sexual offense had actually reported that offense to the police (Ministry of Justice, 2008)[13].

While crime victim surveys as these allow for levels of victimization to become visible, many crime victims remain, as ever, invisible in the official criminal justice statistics, either because, for various reasons, they choose not to engage with the first line of representatives of the criminal justice system, the police, or because that engagement does not translate into an officially reported offense.

## 3. Legal reforms

Even though many crime victims thus still remain invisible to the criminal justice system, societal and political awareness of victims' rights and needs has increased and translated into a range of victim focused laws and revisions of laws. Especially important here was the revision, in 2000, of CCP article 292–2 pursuant to which victims or their legal representatives now have the opportunity to make a statement regarding victims' sentiments and their opinion regarding the case. Of major significance was also the adoption of the Basic Act on Crime Victims (Act 161, 2004), followed, in the same year, by a Basic Plan that constituted a road map to give concrete shape to the aims and principles defined in the Basic Act (Cabinet Office, 2004; see also note 2). Explanations of the need for and timing of this Basic Act and Plan, as provided in this Act and Plan, are telling in the way they characterize the societal developments that ultimately led to legal change.

In its introduction the act paints a picture of Japanese society becoming less and less safe, as in spite of the government's efforts crime is on the rise. In such times of rising crime "each citizen has a bigger chance than before to become a victim of crime", and therefore: *"Precisely now* [*ima koso*], we need to take measures that take into account victims' perspectives, and we need to take the next step to bring about a society that aims to protects victims' rights and interests" (my italics). The act goes on to state that "we, who have the duty to deter crime and to bring about a society in which one can live safely and with peace of mind, need to pay attention and listen to victims of crime". While the act thus on one hand does recognize a general need for measures to ensure that crime victims' rights are respected and their needs are met, the need to act and to show solidarity with crime victims has become especially urgent now that each citizen has a bigger chance of becoming a victim themselves.

Especially relevant here is that as part of such solidarity it was noted that victims should be "appropriately involved" in procedures concerning matters of criminal justice related to the harm suffered. The need for such involvement was recognized

13 "Sexual offences" refers to (attempted) rape, indecent assault, unpleasant sexual acts (such as groping and sexual harassment) that are not all necessarily punishable by law (Ministry of Justice, 2008: 15) Survey available at www.moj.go.jp/content/000010429.pdf.

not just in terms of victims' rights, but also on the basis of the assumption that such involvement would be conducive to victims' recovery. Accordingly, victims' participation in criminal trials was envisioned to be not just about the inherent justice of such participation, but also about the therapeutic effects of participating. All in all the 2004 Basic Plan thus emphatically added the dimension of victims' interests to the traditional criminal justice agenda, noting that "criminal justice also exists for the sake of victims". In doing so it explicitly deviated from the conceptualization of Japanese criminal justice as formulated in 1990 by the Supreme Court, according to which criminal justice is aimed at maintaining public and state order, and not about restoring any harm suffered by crime victims, although it did recognize that this might nonetheless happen as a secondary effect of the public interest driven administration of justice (Supreme Court Third Petty Bench, 1990).[14] In the end, society's rediscovery of crime victims and the 2004 Basic Plan's reconceptualization of criminal justice translated into the following reforms:

A The revised CCP provisions regarding Victims' Statement of Opinion (VSO). As of 2000 CCP article 292–2 provides victims or their legal representatives with the opportunity to make a statement regarding victims' sentiments and their opinion regarding the case. However, considering the situation at the hearing as well as other circumstances the court may find that making a VSO is not appropriate, and order the victim or the victim's representative to submit a written VSO or prohibit the making of such a statement altogether. If a written statement is submitted the presiding judge may then read the statement out loud or explain its content – if doing so is deemed to be appropriate (CCP 292–2 (7).

B The revisions of CCP regarding victims' participation in criminal justice, the "victim participation system", that came into effect in 2008 (CCP Article 316–33). This system is available for the following serious offenses: (*a*) intentional crimes that resulted in the death of a person, (*b*) bodily injury or death through negligent conduct in breach of one's duty of diligence or in the driving of an automobile, (*c*) indecent assault and rape, (*d*) arrest and confinement and (*e*) kidnapping and human trafficking (Saeki, 2010: 151–152).

Under this system victims may do the following five things:

1 Attend the trial (meaning that they can sit with the public prosecutor) as well as the inspections and questioning of witnesses carried out in preparation of the trial (CCP 316–34);
2 Express their opinion to the prosecutor concerning the prosecutor's use of authority, in which case the prosecutor, if necessary, will have to explain the reason for using or not using this authority (CCP 316–35);

14 Shūmin no. 159, p. 161. This Supreme Court ruling is accessible at: www.courts.go.jp/app/files/hanrei_jp/645/062645_hanrei.pdf. Website last accessed 31–8–2018.

3 Question witnesses in court, when there is a dispute concerning the credibility of witnesses' statement about (mitigating) circumstances (or lack thereof). They may therefore not ask any questions concerning "the facts of the crime" (CCP 316–36);
4 Ask questions, when doing so is necessary to prepare for their statement[15] (CCP 316–37);
5 Make a statement about the facts of the case as well as the application of the law, within the limits of the charges as specified by the public prosecutor (CCP 316–38). Different from the VSO, this statement cannot be considered in sentencing, and it also does not have any evidentiary value (CCP 316–38(4)). It can be seen as similar to the concluding speech made by the prosecutor, in which he or she, after the examination of evidence is finished, presents his/her view on the facts and the application of the law, followed by the demanding of a sentence in accordance with this view (CCP 293).

Important to note here is that victims *may* do these things. Victims' engagement in these acts 1–5 is subject to various conditions, such as judges' approval for participation, which is dependent on the characteristics of the case at hand. In any case, now that the background and content of the reforms have been clarified, let us examine first of all the extent to which victims have been making use of the new possibilities that the reforms have provided for.

## 4. Victim participation in practice

As can be seen in Graph 4.1, in the first 10 years after the introduction of the Victim Statement of Opinion (VSO) in 2000, the number of victims making such a statement (CCP 292–2) gradually rose, peaking at 1,198 in 2010 and remaining relatively constant since then. While the very fact that victims make these statements and participate is of course significant in and of itself, it is also important to note that the number of cases in which VSOs are made and in which victims participate typically represents a small or very small portion of the total number of cases tried. Graph 4.2., which provides an overview of the extent to which victims have made use of the various options available to them under the victim participation system (CCP Article 316–33), shows a similar pattern, and comparable overall numbers of participants.[16]

There are various reasons for these small numbers. Victims have mentioned in this regard the mental strain of participating, as well as practical concerns such as

15 This concerns both the already mentioned VSO in accordance with CCP 292–2, as well as a statement on the finding of facts and the application of the law in accordance with CCP 316–38 (as mentioned under (5).

16 Given that in one case several victims may participate and that statistical overviews only provide the total number of participants for each offense per year, it is not possible to accurately represent participation percentages for different offenses. The vehicular negligence resulting in injury or death, different forms of sexual assault, assault and murder have in any case drawn the largest numbers of victim participants (Supreme Court Criminal Justice statistics 2009–2017).

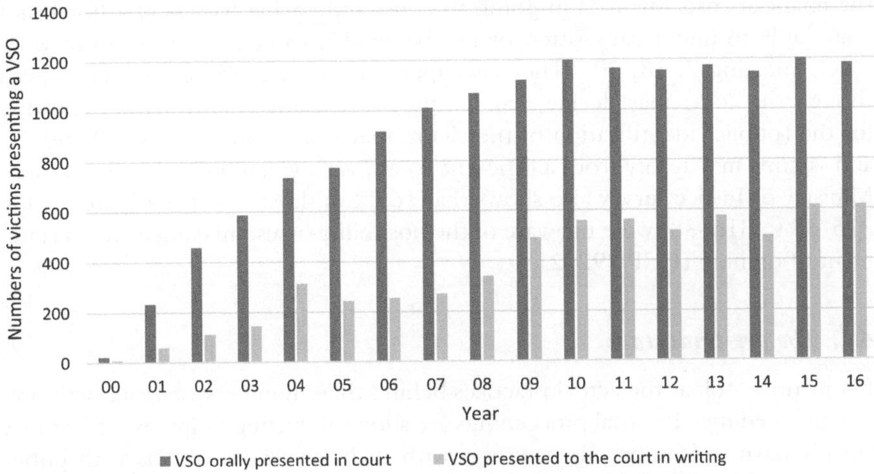


*Graph 4.1* Number of victims presenting an oral or written VSO 2000–2016

Source: Graph generated using data from the 2001–2017 MOJ White Papers on Crime. These numbers represent the combined total of victims who presented their VSO in Summary Courts, District Courts and High Courts.

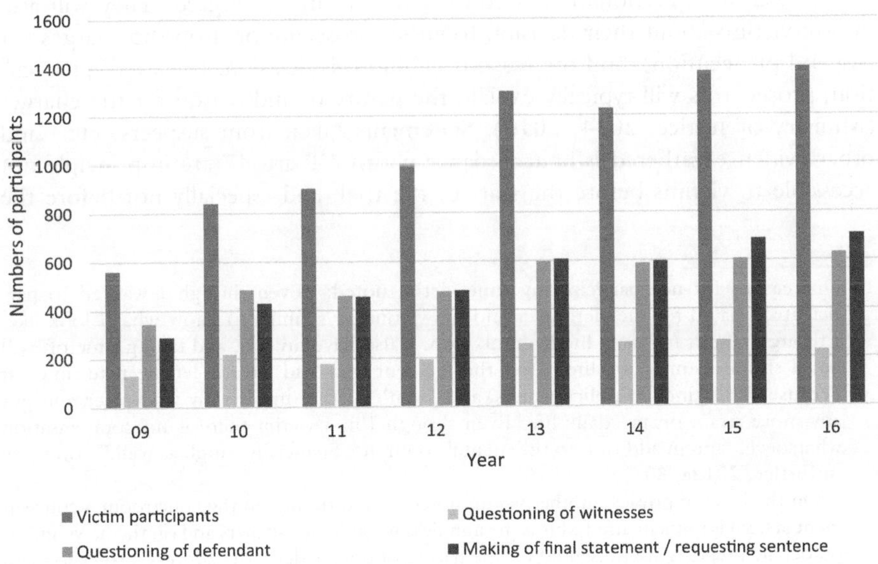


*Graph 4.2* Number of victim participants and acts performed in court as part of the Victim Participation System 2009–2016 (VPS – CCP 316–33 to 316–38)

Source: Graph generated using data from the 2001–2017 MOJ White Papers on Crime. The number of victim participants represents the combined total of victims who were given permission to participate in one way or another in first regular hearings in Summary and District Courts.

the financial costs involved in going to court and having to stay at a hotel, not being able to find a baby sitter, or not being able to take a day off from work (MOJ meeting 7: 18, 30). They also appear to involve privacy concerns, even though the court may decide that during court hearings information allowing for the (public) identification of the victim may not be divulged (CCP 290–2), and victims may testify from a different room, via a video link.[17] Finally, a 2012 Ministry of Justice survey also shows that 16.7% of those who participated (CCP 316–33 to 316–38) were unaware of the possibility of also making a victim statement of opinion (CCP 292–2).

## 4.1. *The pre-trial stage*

Let us now look at the actual practices behind these numbers, starting with pre-trial proceedings. Pre-trial proceedings are a logical starting point, as victims may already have had numerous meetings with their lawyers as well as with public prosecutors handling their case before the actual beginning of the trial (VSF, 2013: 119). As will become clear, victims' participation in pre-trial proceedings in fact forms the basis of their role in the actual trial proceedings. Zooming in on pre-trial proceedings is therefore necessary in order to paint a complete picture of victim participation in practice.

Prosecutors will typically provide information about the criminal procedure and answer any questions that victims may have in this regard. They will also inform victims about their decision to either prosecute or drop the charges (or suspend prosecution), and the reasons behind this decision. In case of prosecution, prosecutors will typically explain the nature of and reason for the charges (Ministry of Justice, 2014, 2015). Statements taken from suspects (etc.) and other evidence gathered is in accordance with CCP art. 47 are in principle not accessible to victims before the start of the trial, and especially not before the

---

17 On reasons for not participating, one victim noted: "Even though I wanted to participate, I hated for the victimizer and the victimizer's family to know what I look like. I thought about my daily life from now on. I also have my job, and taking time off will put a strain on my daily life. After the incident they had already let me take time off because of all kinds of police things, and I can't further burden my workplace and put any more strain on my daily life. Even though I'm a victim there is no compensation whatsoever, and in addition to the mental strain, it's financially tough as well." (Ministry of Justice, 2012a: 30).

On the issue of privacy another victim noted: "even though in the courtroom a concealment system is implemented, this is meaningless when in newspapers and on the news and so on detailed reports are presented on the nature of the incident, the address, profession and the age of the victim. People who live on the countryside can immediately tell who the victim is, and victims will feel ashamed. I would like care to be taken to conceal (the identity of the victim) not just in the courtroom, but also in other contexts." (Ministry of Justice, 2012a: 27). See in this regard also VSF (2013), recounting the experiences of bereaved family members in two cases of robbery homicide. In one of these family members had after the crime felt compelled to hide from the media in a neighboring town and were deeply concerned that participation in criminal proceedings would again spark media attention. (Ministry of Justice, 2012a: 115–116, 128).

decision to prosecute a defendant is made. To compensate for this circumstance prosecutors are said to often communicate the most important points of the evidence they aim to present in court.

In the case of lay judge trials the limited availability of evidence before trial is related also to the fact that prior to the first trial session a so-called pre-trial conference procedure is held. In this procedure the public prosecutor and defense lawyer gather in front of a judge to establish (among other things) which issues they will dispute at the trial, and which pieces of evidence they will select to do so. The aim of this procedure is to reduce the burden on lay jurors who will not have the time to work their way through numerous or voluminous dossiers, and to allow for a speedier trial by focusing on issues and evidence that are truly central to the case at hand (Supreme Court of Japan, 2008). As a result, however, evidence that has not been agreed upon will not be accessible to victims or their lawyers. Victims are thus, to their great dissatisfaction, excluded from procedures that very much shape the course of the trial they will be participating in. The following remark expressed by this bereaved family member is illustrative in this regard:

> We would like to see with our own eyes which will be the points of dispute, and we want to know, also for the sake of formulating our own opinion, if decisions regarding facts to be demonstrated, evidence that will be presented and trial dates are made in a correct way. (. . .) If for the sake of jury trials there really must be a pre-trial conference procedure, I'd like for us, who have suffered harm and who wish to know the truth, to be involved. To know the procedure is meaningful.
>
> (NAVS, 2012: 5)

This bereaved family member, speaking on behalf of the NAVS, thus expressed the importance of access to information about her case. This statement also reveals a commitment to substantive truth finding that may at times be hard to reconcile with pre-trial proceedings, and with rules of evidence in more general terms, as illustrated by the following quote:

> When it comes to evidence that has not been admitted, we would on the contrary want to examine that beforehand. The [defendant's] lawyer has seen it and so has the defendant. But if the victim cannot see that [evidence] s/he will be handicapped when asking questions. (. . .) What did the defendant say in his/her statements before the police and the public prosecutor? Suppose this was not admitted [into evidence}, and now the defendant has said something different in court. As there was a change in the statements made, we would like to ask questions about that. But when we cannot see what was not admitted, our in-court examination will very much become toothless.
>
> (Victim's lawyer, MOJ meeting 11: 7)

In other words: even when evidence is not admitted, victims and their lawyers should have the opportunity to ask about such evidence in court(!). From this experienced lawyer's perspective, procedural rules are thus something that handicaps victims and their lawyers when seeking the substantive truth of their case. As will become clear, however, procedural rules do not necessarily prevent victims from seeking their substantive truth.

Prosecutors may nevertheless also temporarily deny victims access to evidence that has in fact been selected and that will be introduced in court. This may happen, for example, when the knowledge obtained by examining this evidence might later affect victims' testimony in court (VSF, 2013: 155; MOJ meeting 10: 5).[18] As a result victims may be very much in the dark concerning "their" case and may be forced to go through different channels to get the information they seek:

> The prosecutor that was initially handling the case was extremely unforthcoming when it came to the disclosing of evidence. We told him/her[19] that [access} was also necessary for the sake of making a closing statement (. . .) and tried to persuade him/her in different ways, but nothing was disclosed. Because of that there was no other way than to go through the victim support centre and ask a police officer who had been involved in the investigation about the course of events. But later on, when another prosecutor took over, the records were immediately made available.
>
> (VSF, 2013: 147)

This example points to the difficulties that victims may encounter when trying to get access to relevant information. It also illustrates, however, how Prosecutors' individual case assessment and more generally the Prosecutors Office case by case policy may affect the way in which victims fare under the new system. Illustrative in this regard is the following comment of a bereaved family member with a much more positive experience:

> I was early on given information [by the prosecutor), and because of that had time to talk things over with my lawyer and family. Because I thoroughly

18 This example thus points to the tensions between unprejudiced testimony and truth finding on one hand, and victims' rights to access to information about matters that they are deeply concerned about. Pursuant to the Victim Protection Act (2000/2014) art. 3 victims may be given permission to consult trial records (including evidence presented) while the trial is in progress, if doing so is necessary for the filing of a civil claim or if they have another legitimate reason to do so. Such permission will depend on the nature of the crime, the trial situation as well as "other circumstances", while the views of the prosecutor, lawyer and defendant are also taken into account. "Victim Protection Act" is a shorthand reference to the Act Concerning Measures Connected to Criminal Procedure Aimed at Protecting the Legal Interests of Victims of Crime and so on (Heisei 12, 19 May, no. 75) and is available at http://law.e-gov.go.jp/htmldata/H12/H12HO075.html. Website last visited 31-8-2018).

19 From the Japanese it is not clear if this public prosecutor was a woman or a man.

> read the contents prior to the trial, I could prepare myself for the day [of trial], and could face the trial with conviction, and thanks to that my fears towards the trial became less.
>
> (NAVS, 2012: 2)

Information does not however flow just in one direction toward the participating victim. Victims may after all express their views on the charges brought against the defendant, as well the facts. These views do not necessarily coincide with those of the public prosecutor, an issue I will come back to below. Victims may in addition express wishes concerning questions to be asked and matters to be shown. Here too victims and prosecutors may have different opinions about what is important to ask and be shown. Victims and their families may for example be very concerned about protecting the honor of the victim, and request the prosecutor to reserve time for questions aimed at this purpose (VSF, 2013: 179). Bereaved family members may in addition, for example, ask the prosecutor or their lawyer that pictures of the victim be shown during the questioning of witnesses – in support of their argument concerning victims' feelings, but also as a means to show what kind of person the victim was, beyond, say, "male company employee" (VSF, 2013: 195).

Victims will also have meetings with public prosecutors as well as their lawyers (if they have obtained one) to determine a "division of labor". During such meetings they will determine, for example, which family member will ask the defendant which questions and whether the prosecutor or rather the victim should in their statement refer to this or that fact, in order to maximize impact on judges and jury (VSF, 2013: 213). These meetings will typically also be about preparing (in accordance with CCP 191–3) for victims' testimony in court – doing what is called a "witness test" (*shōnin tesuto*). During such tests prosecutors, lawyers and their witnesses will establish and practice both questions to be asked as well as the answers to those questions, and witnesses will familiarize themselves with the role expected of them. Preparatory meetings thus tend to be frequent and intense, lasting for hours, with witness tests being repeated four-to-five times before the start of the trial (VSF, 2013: 169; 210–211).

An examination of pre-trial proceedings thus brings into focus how victims may or may not be given the information they seek, and how this results from victims being excluded from pre-trial conference procedures on one hand, and the decisions of individual prosecutors on the other. In view of their control over the information that victims but also – as we have seen – lawyers dispose of, prosecutors as ever shape the conditions for these participants' involvement in and contribution to proceedings. Zooming in on pre-trial proceedings accordingly brings into focus the dependent position of crime victims. It also reveals, however, how such involvement may affect Prosecutors' own contribution. During the pre-trial stage victims are in any case getting prepared for the role expected from them.

### *4.2. Court proceedings*

Victim participation in Japan is not limited to the sentencing stage, but is also incorporated in fact finding processes, as also becomes clear when looking at the different options available to victims under the victim participation system. When it comes to what is at stake, criminal trials in Japan are typically about confirming guilt and determining the appropriate sentence. Given that this is the case, what does victims' role entail? More specifically: given the typical lack of dispute about defendants' guilt or innocence, what role, if any, do victims play in fact finding processes, given that they do take part in these processes?

Besides their testimony as a witness, victims contribute to fact finding processes through their statement of opinion (Victim Statement of Opinion, VSO) as well as their questions and "closing statements". Even though the victim's statement of opinion concerns victims' sentiments and their opinion regarding the case, inevitably victims will base themselves on the facts of the case, as they conceive them. One victims' lawyer states in this regard "without making presumptions about facts victims could only say: 'how vexing, how sad, what a shame', and nothing else" (VSF, 2013: 191). This conception will typically, but not necessarily be in line with the facts as presented by the public prosecutor. It may and does happen that victims argue facts different from those argued by the public prosecutor, as well as the defense. Where the public prosecutor will necessarily restrict him or herself to what can be convincingly proven on the basis of the evidence available, victims at times go beyond that and argue facts that would fit a different charge – by arguing, for example, the defendant is guilty of murder rather than manslaughter (VSF, 2013: 184–191). In doing so victims may base themselves not only on the evidence presented in court, but at times also on evidence that was not actually admitted (JFBA, 2012b: 2). Judges may and do intervene and interrupt the victim when this happens. JFBA surveys do however suggest that this – victims who make statements, provide opinions but also ask questions in reference to evidence not admitted – is a recurring problem (JFBA, 2012a; MOJ meeting 3: 4). While some victims thus argue facts that would fit a different charge, they may also demand a punishment different from the one demanded by the public prosecutor. Some victims in fact not only demand a punishment heavier than what would "normally" be demanded or imposed, but one that actually goes beyond the legal maximum (JFBA, 2012b: 2). One lawyer states in this regard:

> Especially in lay juror trials people's feelings of having been victimized are extremely strong, so that the death penalty (. . .) is demanded by victims even in cases in which there would from a legal or professional point of view not be any possibility for the death penalty [to be imposed], and so the courtroom, where from our point of view [things] should be judged in a calm manner, becomes a very emotional place.
>
> (MOJ meeting 4: 5)

While victims' statements of opinion do not have evidentiary value in terms of fact finding, they may nevertheless be referred to when determining appropriate punishment. This ambiguity, where an opinion not necessarily based on the evidence may still impact the sentence imposed, causes some lawyers to feel that victims' opinion has a distorting effect on both fact finding and sentencing procedures (JFBA, 2012b: 3). In any case: with victims' new role a different voice arguing a different, typically more incriminating truth is introduced in court.

Victims' contributions are not just about further incriminating the defendant, however. They also tend to present perspectives and information not necessarily relevant to the outcome of the case in terms of guilt, innocence or punishment, but nevertheless relevant in terms of the ways in which the events and the persons involved, notably a deceased victim, are represented in court. Bereaved family members may present – or ask the prosecutor to present – information as well as pictures, or ask questions about the person of the deceased victim and (e.g.) his or her hobbies and personality. By doing so more substance is given to what may be a rather "flat character" type representations of the victim in court (VSF, 2013: 195). The information presented may also serve to protect the honor of a deceased victim, whose reputation may be at risk of becoming tarnished by a defendant's testimony (VSF, 2013: 179). Victims' participation thus allows for the finding of facts that otherwise might not have been found. In this sense, victims' participation allows for an enriching of the facts found and the truth constructed in court.

Many family members however also often take a framed portrait of the deceased with them to court. They do so not just to show a picture of the victim, but also to allow that victim to be present at the proceedings. According to NAVS Secretary General Masato Takahashi, who as a lawyer has represented many victims, bereaved family members all want to bring such a portrait with them. According to Takahashi they will want to show the victim who their killer is: "this is the criminal who killed you, you know. You'd like to give him a piece of your mind, wouldn't you?" (MOJ meeting 7: 24). Here the showing of a portrait of the victim would thus seem to be a way to confront the (alleged!) victimizer with his or her victim.[20] This practice of holding on to portraits of the deceased along with victims' statements and questions have translated into increasingly emotionally charged courtrooms.

### *4.2.1. Effects of victim participation on lawyers and defendants*

Victims' presence and voice and "the emotionally charged courtroom" also have an effect on other participants' contributions to fact finding practices, notably defendants' contribution to facts "favoring" the defense, as illustrated by the following quote from the JFBA statement on the victim participation system:

> There are many defendants who cannot say what they should say in response to the prosecutor's arguments, as they are overwhelmed by the gravity of the

20 Incidentally, while holding on to such a portrait is allowed when sitting in one of the spectator's seats, this is not allowed when entering the area ("the bar") where the prosecutor, lawyer and defendant sit. MOJ meeting 7: 24).

> consequences of the offense. Especially when it comes to important points of dispute such as victims' fault, whether [the defendant's actions] constituted self-defense or not and the existence of negligence, the more tragic the consequences [of the offense], the more difficult, psychologically, it becomes to raise issues such as these. This is the situation in which defendants find themselves.
>
> (JFBA, 2012b: 2)

The 2012 JFBA survey too reveals how defendants feel constrained by victims' presence, while essentially the same point is made in the following quote telling of lawyers' experiences in trials in which victims participate: "Especially in cases where the defendant admits guilt and victims question the defendant, this defendant will become extremely nervous, and it will be difficult for him/her to say anything in his/her own favor" (Nakajima, 2012: 5).

Lawyers themselves furthermore indicate that they are hesitant to refer to any victim's fault, and some indicate that they refrain from asking the victim potentially significant questions, as (e.g.) "it is pointless to argue with a victim" and doing so might lead to a higher sentence for their client (Nakajima, 2012: 5; communication with JFBA lawyers ($n$ = 24), 2011–2017).

One could in this regard argue, as victims' lawyers in fact have done, that victims' presence in court – as well as bereaved family members holding on to a portrait of the victim – has made it harder for the defense to tell lies to make defendants look less guilty and to blame the victim (MOJ meeting 7: 26). When taken seriously, these defense lawyers' statements can be understood in terms of victims' (increased) presence and the emotional impact thereof on defendants – something which in turn connects to the increasingly emotionally charged courtroom. Defendants' inhibition to speak can also be connected with new expectations and standards concerning appropriate behavior for defendants, connected with a new concern for victims' well-being. These will be further addressed below.

The foregoing shows the various ways in which victims participate in and contribute to courtroom procedures. It shows how participating victims may introduce a version of the truth independent from that argued by the defense and prosecution, although their contribution is more typically in line with the prosecution's argument. This section also brought into focus how victims may provide a contribution to fact finding that goes beyond the strictly legally relevant facts (i.e. not necessarily relevant for considerations about guilt, innocence or sentencing). Through victims' participation and the fact that within the courtroom opportunities have been created to present such information, an extra layer is added to the significance of fact finding practices in court, as such facts become more than the strictly legally relevant facts.

Beyond the function of, for example, protecting the honor of the victim that presenting such facts may have, the time and space allotted to the presenting of these facts also signifies that doing so is in fact of value. As such, victims' presenting of information beyond the "legally relevant facts" contributes to courtroom practices as *signifying practices* that communicate the intrinsic value of victims' presenting their perspective on their case (cf. Garland, 1990: 252). It is in this sense, as practices that communicate the value and importance of victims' perspective, that courtroom procedures are imbued with "added significance" when victims are given the time and space to present their truth.

Victim participation is not just about victims being given the time and space to contribute to proceedings in terms of information, however. The meaning of participation has been explicitly conceived in terms of the possibly therapeutic benefits that participation might bring. The next section will address these benefits, or lack thereof, as conceived by the different trial participants. It will in addition address the consequences of participants' "therapeutic focus" for the ways in which the defendant and his or her acts are judged.

## 5. Victim participation as therapeutic or traumatizing

The earlier mentioned the 2004 Basic Plan explicitly identified the supporting of crime victims' recovery as a criminal justice goal. As a consequence, Japanese criminal justice has become officially and explicitly therapeutically oriented. Accordingly, the new system of victim participation provides an opportunity to study "therapeutic jurisprudence in practice" within a Japanese context.

Therapeutic jurisprudence is the "study of the role of the law as a therapeutic agent. It focuses on the law's impact on emotional life and on psychological well-being" (Wexler, 2000: 1). As such, "therapeutic jurisprudence is not a theory, but a way of looking at the law" (Wemmers, 2017: 116). Whether criminal justice procedures can in fact have therapeutic effects is something that will depend on one's understanding of the word "therapeutic". Some link the therapeutic potential of criminal justice to (e.g.) respect for and recognition of victims, victims' satisfaction, empowerment, "moving on" and closure (Wexler, 2000; Wemmers, 2008). Others have however pointed out that such understandings of the word "therapeutic" do not necessarily correspond to those in the psychological literature and have questioned whether court proceedings actually have any therapeutic potential (Van Stokkom, 2011; Pemberton & Reynaers, 2011; Arrigo, 2004; Roderick & Krumholz, 2006).

Here I will not attempt to address the question of whether victim participation in Japan is or is not therapeutic. Aside from the question of the "right" or, for research purposes, operationable understanding of the word the word "therapeutic": doing so would in any case require relevant data on victims' experiences that are as yet not available. Instead, then, this section will first of all address the therapeutic dimensions of victim participation as conceived, referred to and invoked by participating victims, those speaking (or claiming to speak) on their behalf, as well as the other courtroom participants: prosecutors, judges and lawyers.

Trials play an especially important part when it comes to the realization of this newly defined therapeutic goal of criminal justice. Both victims and legal professionals, especially victims' lawyers, have frequently referred to the importance of the opportunity to state what one wants to say and ask what one wants to ask. Doing so was said to provide victims with a sense of satisfaction, a feeling of accomplishment and of being liberated. Regardless of the defendant's response, without this – so it was said – victims cannot move forward. Speaking out was in fact presented as something that constitutes an indispensable first step for victims to leave what has happened behind them (MOJ meetings 3: 5, 28; 6: 2; 10: 2; Ministry of Justice (2012a, 2012b), Aichi Bar Association (2009).

Similarly, the Aichi Bar Association survey refers to victim(s) who "felt they could recover" as they had been able to convey their suffering to the defendant (2009). Conversely, being denied the opportunity to speak out was presented as something that may cause victims to be unable to "move forward toward recovery" – something that may "hinder victims' mental recovery" and that in fact may lead to a lifelong trauma.[21]

Significantly, victims' mental well-being here has become a rhetorical device used to persuade other courtroom participants – notably the judge – of the desirability of letting victims perform the acts they wish to perform. The phrasing of a statement submitted to the court by a victim's lawyer is telling in this regard. This statement was submitted after the presiding judge had announced that he would read a bereaved family member's statement in court, rather than allowing this family member to read it herself:

> If she is not allowed to make her statement, I fear that for the rest of her life she will not be able to organize her feelings. (. . .) Her not conveying the facts might result in a verdict in which only the murder victim's honor will be stained. If that happens she will believe that she was not able to do anything for her mother and her heart will probably suffer a deep wound that she will bear for the rest of her life.
>
> (VSF, 2013: 171)

Participating in trial proceedings was often also portrayed, however, as something that could result in "secondary victimization". For example: one judge feared for the "secondary victimization" that allowing a young girl to participate as a victim in trial proceedings might lead to (MOJ meeting 5: 5), while one victim's lawyer argued that the "irrelevant questions" that his client was asked by curious lay jurors "unfortunately led to secondary victimization" (VSF, 2013: 163). The general conditions under which participation takes place too were discussed as a source of potential secondary victimization (Ministry of Justice, 2012b: 1–2).

---

21 MOJ meeting 6: 2; VSF, 2013: 171, 173. The fact that victims cannot participate in the pre-trial conference procedure and are at that stage being denied the opportunity to speak out has similarly been referred to (by victims' representatives) as something that brings with it "the risk of hindering victims' mental recovery". VSF, 2013: 173). Participating in this procedure is also argued to be important as doing so will allow victims to understand and accept why (e.g.) certain pieces of evidence were excluded, and others were not and it is, according to one lawyer specialized in representing victims, "precisely (that) understanding which is *the right medicine* for recovery" (MOJ meeting 8: 31 – my italics).

Victims' experiences were and are thus discussed – by victims, victims' support organizations, lawyers, prosecutors and judges – in terms of the benefits of such participation for "victims' recovery" and "victims' mental health". Or conversely, they were discussed in terms of the trauma, damage and secondary victimization that either the limiting of victims' participation or such participation itself might lead to.

However, what "mental recovery" or "secondary victimization" entailed, remains unclear as in the sources cited these terms were used without any definition or specification,[22] much less a reference to psychological, psychiatric or any other disciplinary discourse. Discussions and statements were rather based on implicit "commonsense" assumptions and knowledge. Assumptions concerning on one hand the therapeutic benefits of matters such as speaking out, saying what one wants to say and accordingly being able to move forward, and on the other hand the traumatic, "victimizing" effects of jurors' "irrelevant questions", etc. The assumed therapeutic effects here thus appear to be based on victim satisfaction, resulting from victims being able – "empowered" – to do "what they want". The idea of being able to move forward only after having said what one wanted to say furthermore implies that doing so provides a form of closure.

As such, these conceptions are in line with those of the therapeutic jurisprudence sources referred to earlier. Here too it is not clear to what extent such commonsense conceptions correspond with "specialist" psychiatric knowledge in this regard. Especially significant here, however, is that in the various fora and sources examined those speaking on victims' behalf discussed victims' "therapeutic wants and needs" in generalized terms. Victims were thus represented as a rather monolithic group of people who share the same wishes, notably severe punishment for the sake of victims' recovery.[23] The idea of all victims sharing the wishes for harsh punishment is however inconsistent with findings about the diversity in victims' needs and wishes in other (non-Japanese) contexts (cf. Lens, Pemberton & Bogaerts, 2013; David & Choi, 2009; Partnership for Safety and Justice, 2011; Maruna & King, 2004.

22 In the 2004 Basic Plan, however, secondary victimization is defined and used to stand for "new mental injury" (1), while in documents of the Japan Legal Help Centre (year of publication not provided) secondary victimization is defined as "mental injury" (Japan Legal Help Centre website www.houterasu.or.jp/cont/100180048.pdf. Website last visited 31–8–2018). It is of course possible that, for example, the speakers at the MOJ meetings were familiar with these definitions. Nonetheless, specified they were not.

23 As indicated earlier, NAVS representatives have played an important part in raising awareness of victims' position within criminal justice as well as the lobby that led to the formal expansion of victims' role within criminal justice. As such, the NAVS voice is an influential one. The NAVS regularly issues statements on victims' behalf, containing phrases such as the following: "Victims want victimizers to receive strict punishment, and this is also *necessary for victims' recovery*. If an unjustly light punishment is meted out, (. . .) victims' retributive feelings will be severely hurt, and they will be disadvantaged" (my italics). Statement (2002) available at: www.navs.jp/report/1/opinion2/opinion2-3.html. Website last visited 31–8–2018.

## 6. Consequences of a therapeutic focus

As shown, the possible therapeutic benefits of participation thus related most of all to victims' own contribution to court proceedings. Conversely, the potentially traumatizing and damaging aspects of participation were portrayed as resulting from the (in-)action of the other participants. This, then, led and leads to an evaluation of other courtroom participants' actions in terms of their potentially traumatizing or damaging character.

Judges, for example, should "take care that jurors do not hurt victims" by asking irrelevant questions, and it appears that they in fact also do, by limiting the number of questions a juror could ask to just one question, when this is thought to be necessary (MOJ meeting 7: 20–21; VSF, 2013: 161). It was however especially the defendant, who was and is perceived to present a risk of secondary victimization.

The possibility of "defendants' verbal attacks" in court, and the secondary victimization these could lead to have been presented by the Japan Federation of Bar Associations (JFBA) as a reason to call for a revision of the existing participation system (JFBA, 2012a). While this argument could be viewed with suspicion in view of the JFBA's earlier opposition to the system the JFBA was not alone in its concern for secondary victimization because of defendants' verbal attacks (JFBA, 2007; Hōmuinkaichōsashitsu, 2007: 5).

Within this context of a general concern for victims' well-being, then, defendants' statements and demeanor were presented as a potential source of victimization and suffering. Thus, victims are said to have been "further tormented" by defendants' (partial) denial of the facts, or have undergone "further mental anguish" because of defendants' lack of cooperation (VSF, 2013: 131, 233).

Verdicts more generally show that defendants' behavior is scrutinized as a potential source of victim's suffering. The following quote from a verdict in a case of professional negligence resulting in injury or death is instructive in this regard:

> The defendant not only (. . .) has not shown any consideration for the bereaved family members of the victims, [his] words and deeds in court have caused them irritation and have further hurt their feelings. [His] attitude and these words and deeds can be thought of as inconsiderate. They suggest not only a serious lacking of any self-awareness on the defendant's part concerning his (. . .) responsibility, but it is [accordingly] also hard to detect an attitude of serious remorse.[24] The defendant's criminal tendencies are deeply rooted.
>
> (Saitama District Court, 2006: Heisei 18 (wa) 1701)

This quote thus shows (1) a concern for the impact of the defendant's in-court behavior on the participating victims. In this context (2), the absence of appropriately considerate behavior vis-à-vis these victims is presented as something that

24 The defendant had however written letters of apology to the victims, had visited the houses of those victims who let him in and had given these victims goods and money as tokens of consolation (as is customary).

adds to the defendant's blameworthiness.[25] This quote in addition shows (3) how a defendant's demeanor toward the victim constitutes another criterion on the basis of which the quality of his remorse is measured and the criminality of his character assessed. The evaluating of defendants' behavior toward the victim thus provides an opportunity to show concern for this victim's well-being, while also helping to assess the defendant's potential for rehabilitation. The following quote from a verdict in another victim participation case is also illustrative in this regard:

> The defendant has (. . .) not taken any effective measure to compensate [the victims]. On the contrary, the defendant has in this court done and said things that have to be seen as irritating for the victims, and in his final statement too, the defendant has not expressed any sentiment of mourning. (. . .) It accordingly has to be said that his attitude of reflection on his own responsibility was extremely insufficient, and when one takes these factors into account (. . .) one has to say that the defendant's criminal responsibility is grave.
>
> (Kobe District Court, 2002: Heisei 13 (wa) 636)

This verdict too shows a concern for victims' feelings in connection with the defendant's in-court behavior, and how the defendant's behavior vis-à-vis the victims adds to his criminal responsibility. This behavior is represented as symptomizing the defendant's failure to reflect on his own responsibility – evidence, in turn, of a relative lack of rehabilitative potential.[26]

Here, it is important to realize that irrespective of victims' in-court participation, public prosecutors and judges have generally taken victim-suspect/defendant relationships into consideration. They have mostly done so, however, in relation to suspects' or defendants' eligibility for lenient dispositions. In making decisions concerning (the suspension of) prosecution and sentencing, prosecutors and judges have thus generally taken into account whether the suspect or defendant has made efforts to compensate the victim, or achieve a settlement, etc. (Kawaai, 2011: 188–189). Significantly, the verdicts quoted from here suggest that a defendant's failure to show the expected demeanor vis-à-vis the victim not only makes the defendant ineligible for a lenient treatment, but in fact adds to this defendant's criminal responsibility. Concern for victims' well-being in any case constitutes an amplified opportunity to focus on the person of the offender

25 To what extent such reference to defendants' failure to act considerately toward the victim also translates into higher sentences remains unclear – I will come back to this matter below.

26 The evidence provided here is of course anecdotal. Many more examples of verdicts exhibiting the same line of reasoning however, can be found on www.courts.go.jp, Website last visited 31–8–2018. Furthermore, while a remorseful attitude may, as indicated earlier, contribute to a lower sentence, it may thus also hinder the defendant as any statement in his or her own defense may be construed as evidence of a less than truly remorseful attitude and lack of rehabilitative potential (personal communication with public prosecutors, 2012–2017 (n = 7); Kawaai, 2011: 195 and references provided there.

and his or her lack of rehabilitative potential. Here, the concern for victims' well-being is accordingly put in service of the "traditional" way of judging offenders[27].[28] Victim participation in this way affects the traditional courtroom script, in that defendants are more than before pressured – "in their best interest" – to show remorse and display their rehabilitative potential, rather than trying to argue in their own favor.

The impact of victim participation goes further, however, than an alteration or reinforcement of traditional courtroom scripts. Even if participating victims do not constitute a new party to the two party process, they do constitute a new numerical and physical presence in court – one that literally sides with the prosecution, as participating victims are given a seat next to them. Victims' numerical presence is especially felt when there are multiple victims making statements and asking questions, leaving the defense's argument relatively underrepresented, as is illustrated by the following quote from one defense lawyer, reporting on lawyers' experiences with the victim participation system:

> While the defendant will most of the time will be one person and there will be one or two lawyers present, on the victims' side there may be a line-up of many persons: the participating victim[s], the prosecutor[s], victims' lawyers and so on. (. . .) These persons then present a statement of opinion, they cross-examine witnesses, and they question the defendant. They in addition

27 Victims' participation appears to provide more than an opportunity to judge the defendant's character. Victims' participation and presence in court are also explicitly conceived in terms of their potential to bring about or deepen defendants' remorse. Thus a MOJ/Prosecutors Office pamphlet with information for participating victims states: "Providing the defendant with the opportunity to directly hear about victims' and family members' (. . .) feelings is something that is also useful to deepen the defendant's remorse" (Ministry of Justice, 2015: 31). Pamphlet available at: www.moj.go.jp/content/000121888.pdf. Website last visited 31–8–2018. Similarly, in victims' lawyers' perception, hearing directly from the victims does indeed deepen defendants' remorse (Aichi Bar Association (2009). The Aichi Bar Association survey also notes that much can be expected from advising the participating victims to ask questions that "will prompt the defendant's remorse, and that will have an educational effect." Victims' participation is thus explicitly represented as something that could invoke or strengthen defendants' remorse and accordingly help defendants take the first step on the road to reform and rehabilitation. The idea of the courtroom as a place for remorse is not new, however. Long before the participating victim entered the picture, trials have been represented as opportunities for defendants to acknowledge what they have done and (re-) commit to a non-deviant lifestyle (see e.g. Wagatsuma and Rosett (1986); Peters (1992). Nevertheless, by explicitly conceiving of participating victims' contribution in terms of their potential to invoke remorse, victims are assigned a role within the "courtroom as a place for remorse". Doing so implies that victim participation is here again looked at as a means to bring about a "traditional" trial goal.

28 Interestingly, in the 2004 Basic Plan the therapeutic benefits of participation actually coincide with victims' role in service of criminal proceedings: "when it comes to the process leading to a solution (of the criminal case): by contributing to this (process) victims feel that they could fulfill their *responsibility* (. . .), and this has aspects that are conducive to victims' (. . .) mental recovery" (my italics).

> present (. . .) what we call the victim's closing statement. These repeated actions by participating victims and the factual impact this has on those judging [the case] (. . .), this has led to a change in the structure of proceedings.
> (MOJ meeting 3: 4, 16)

As an example, one JFBA survey mentions a case in which the statements of five bereaved family members, taken during the pre-trial investigation, were read out loud. These five family members also made a Victim Statement of Opinion. Four family members in addition delivered a final statement requesting the death penalty, making a total of 14 statements. And so "the words (. . .) 'death penalty' were uttered in court countless times" (JFBA, 2012b)

This JFBA survey thus portrays a situation in which lawyers and defendants are outnumbered by a prosecution that is joined by participating victims, who together argue both defendant's guilt and participants' feelings of victimization over and over again. It is also in light of such circumstances, then, that lawyers' remarks about the "increasingly emotional courtroom" can be understood, as well as observations concerning defendants who become overwhelmed and unable to speak up on their own behalf. In this regard it is also important to consider the risk that defendants who do speak up run a risk, in terms of being seen to act inappropriately vis-à-vis the victim and the negative perceptions concerning their "criminal character" that this may lead to – as we have seen.

Much like the concern for victims' well-being, it is also hard to assess to what extent victims' increased presence and the "changed structure of proceedings" impact the outcome of those proceedings. Would fewer or no VSOs have resulted in a lower sentence, or a non-guilty verdict? Both lawyers who have represented victims and those who represented defendants in victim participation trials have in any case referred to cases in which "harsher than usual" punishment was both demanded and meted out (JFBA, 2012b; VSF, 2013: 218). Such anecdotal observations, then, do provoke a key question, namely: does victim participation indeed result in harsher sentences?

## 7. Victim participation, lay judges and sentencing

Given the large number of factors that affect the sentence meted out and the difficulty of comparing "like cases", the impact of victim participation on sentencing decisions is difficult to assess. This difficulty also becomes apparent in research on this topic. Based on an extensive review of such research and a range of experiments involving mock trials and mock jurors, Masahiko Saeki (2016) finds that one cannot conclude that victim participation and VSI do not have an impact, but that it is nevertheless difficult to determine the exact nature and extent of that impact. Saeki's findings suggest that the impact of victims' contributions may not so much lie in the length of the sentence meted out, but that these may rather affect decisions as to whether a sentence should be suspended or not (328). Saeki also finds that victims' wishes and feelings regarding punishment may have an impact on sentencing decisions, even if this impact is limited (331).

Important and meaningful as this research is, however, it has been focused on information that can be gleaned from verdicts and *experimental* settings. To gain a better understanding of participating victims' impact on judges sentencing decisions it is fruitful to take a look at what they themselves have said in connection with this issue. It is also useful to again turn to the records of meetings organized by district courts all over Japan, in which especially lay judges exchanged opinions about their experiences (on these meetings see also the Introduction of this book and Chapter 1). About 30% of the trials in which victims participate are lay judge trials (Ministry of Justice, 2017). The meetings however present the opportunity to look into the reasoning that went into the sentences meted out, beyond their formal justification in the final verdict.

As also noted earlier, the meetings were led by a judge who had also taken part in one of the trials in which the jurors had participated and in which other judges, prosecutors and lawyers who had participated were also present. In some meetings members of the press were also present and given the opportunity to ask questions. The topic of sentencing in connection with victim participation came up when lay judges in whose trial a victim had participated were asked to say something on that – "anything at all".[29]

There were lay judges who indicated that they thought it was important to take note of victims' opinions and feelings, while also noting how difficult it had been to listen to victims' testimony, and how it had emotionally affected them. In the words of one lay judge, following up on another:

> Bottom line: I also think that that [hearing victims' opinion] is necessary. When the victim had been listening, you would hear her sobbing and so on, and then also when she testified, this extremely strong resolve or something like hatred came to the forefront – that's the impression I got. It was very hard to see that, but, as it is something to take into account, it's better to have it [victim's testimony].
>
> (Tachikawa District Court, 13–1–2015)

But at the same time lay judges also expressed doubts about what do with victims' testimony, much like this lay judge:

> In the words of the victim you could feel the hatred toward the victimizer, and I thought that [such testimony] was necessary, but when

29 Meeting records were searched using the terms "victim participation" (*higaisha sanka*) and "sentencing"/"sentence" (*ryōkei*) – a search the produced 30 hits – as well as the terms "sentencing" and victim (*higaisha*) – 342 hits. The records of the meetings in which these terms were used were examined for references to any connection between victim participation and sentencing. References to these issues were found in 21 meetings. These references were in turn searched for themes and commonalities. Lay judges' statements on the issue of sentencing in connection with Meeting records (in Japanese) are accessible at www.saibanin.courts.go.jp/ikenkoukan/index.html. Website last visited 31–8–2018.

> I actually heard his story, it was difficult. (. . .) How should you take into account what the victim says? I thought that that was something extremely difficult.
>
> (Tachikawa District Court, 13–1–2015)

In connection with this point some also expressed reservations about the system, and whether an assessment of victims' feelings should actually be one of the purposes of a criminal trial. But while the importance of hearing from the victim was a recurring theme in the meetings, what that meant for the impact of victims' contributions on the sentence meted out remained unclear. Several lay judges indicated that they had looked at victims' feelings as one of the many different pieces of information they had taken into account when taking a fair sentencing decision. Some believed that victims' contributions had had an effect on the sentence, while others believed they had not. Some had the impression that decisions went victims' way, while others felt that in legal decision making more weight is given to the defendant's rehabilitation than to victims' feeling on how that defendant should be punished.

Many lay judges in any case seemed concerned about the defendant and his or her future, while also thinking about victims' interest:

> We all had this feeling that we wanted the defendant to rehabilitate, and when deciding on the sentence we thought about how he would atone for his crime and we thought about the victim and so on, and so we spent one week single-mindedly focused on that.
>
> (Chiba District Court, 29–9–2015)

Another lay judge remarked:

> Looking at the victims and how they suffered I felt all kinds of emotions. Like, this was unforgiveable after all. Still, I thought that he [the defendant] was surely standing there because he had made a mistake in his life. And as I thought that he must have been an ordinary person and wondered why he had messed up his life, I was all the time watching him wishing he would rehabilitate.
>
> (Yokohama District Court, 18–5–2016)

In their focus on defendants' future, some lay judges also remarked how they felt constrained by the jurisprudential framework within which they had to make their decision:

> When it comes to citizens' emotions and my personal emotions, well, it's better not to go to prison for that long, and you think: "just go get a job as quick as you can, you hear". But because you have to take other cases and legal precedent into account, there's nothing to be done.
>
> (Tokyo District Court, 23–4–2015)

Meeting records thus do not show lay judges to be vindictive in their decisions. Nor do they show lay judges to be easily swayed by emotional appeals. Some in fact expressed their resentment regarding "meaningless expressions of emotion", as the following quote also illustrates:

> When the victim's lawyer appeared he became really pretty emotional you know, crying in court, so that we all took our distance. Was there any sense to his coming to court? That's what we, lay judges, talked about afterward. Given that he had especially come to court, it would have been better if he had talked some sense.
>
> (Tokyo District Court, 14–3–2016)

Lay judges' accounts do illustrate how they wrestled with the emotions that victims' statements and testimony provoked, and how, if at all, such emotions should relate to their sentencing decisions. The picture that emerges from these meetings is in any case mixed. In accordance with lay judges' impressions and observations it is possible that sentencing decisions would one time go the defendant's way, and another time the victim's way. While recognizing the importance of hearing from the victim, the question of whether and how to incorporate victims' perspective was not easily answered, although the lay judges in these meeting in any case generally did take this perspective into consideration when making their decision.

## Conclusion

This chapter has identified characteristics of the functioning of the new CCP provisions for victim participation against the background of changing societal and legal understandings of victims' rights and their role in criminal justice. It has in addition examined the practical implementation and impact of victims' expanded criminal justice role.

As of 2000 victims can present a VSO in any case, as long as the judge gives his or her permission. Participation in other ways is – under the 2008 victim participation system – still only available for a limited number and type of cases, meaning that victims do more than just providing testimony in only a small percentage of all cases. It is significant that crime victims now have various opportunities to participate in Japanese criminal justice, and that the number of victim participants has grown each year since the introduction of the system. Still, the vast majority of victims choose not to participate, meaning that crime victims are still not regular criminal justice players.

When it comes to those who do participate: their involvement starts long before the beginning of actual trial proceedings, when victims, their lawyers and prosecutors meet to provide and exchange information, victims prepare for their questions, statements and testimony and a division of "court room labor" is decided upon. In court victims may present different perspectives on the evidence, the facts the defendant is accused of and the charges that are accordingly brought against him or her. Victims may here present a truth in line with that of one of the parties, typically the prosecution, as well as their own truth, thus adding a new voice to fact-finding procedures.

The expression of this voice and time and place that Japanese law now provides for such expression communicate the intrinsic value of victims' presenting their truth, regardless of whether this truth coincides with that presented by one of the two parties (defense and prosecution) and regardless of case outcomes. Nevertheless, victims' contribution comes about in close connection and cooperation with the public prosecutor. Victims and their lawyers in addition physically join the side of the prosecution in court. As victims and prosecutors thus become courtroom allies, victims' voice is also one that lends support to the prosecution's argument, strengthening the prosecutor's position within a criminal justice process characterized by a conviction rate of around 98%.

The reformed CCP introduces a therapeutic perspective that is never clearly circumscribed or defined. In practice this perspective in any case involves a commonsense concern for victims' well-being as well as commonsense assumptions held by courtroom participants about the beneficial effect – beneficial for victims' recovery – of speaking out, asking and saying what one wants to say. Such understandings are in line with (criticized) therapeutic jurisprudence understandings of the subject. Aside from the question of whether such understandings correspond to those in the specialist psychiatric literature on the subject, they in any case come about in reference to rather implausibly monolithic representations of "what victims want and need".

In view of the Japanese conviction rates, court proceedings can *for practical purposes* be said to be about deciding on the right sentence rather than deciding innocence or guilt. Within these procedures defendants are expected to play the role of the remorseful criminal who, based on a full acknowledgment of the error of his or her ways, might still be rehabilitated. Victims' presence and (repetitive) contributions here add to the character of court proceedings as a way to confront the defendant with his or her crime and impress upon him or her the seriousness of this crime.

As a consequence of the adopted therapeutic perspective, defendants' in court behavior vis-à-vis the victim – behavior that contains the perceived risk of "secondary victimization" – becomes one more criterion on the basis of which defendants' character and their prospects of rehabilitation are evaluated. It is in view of especially the combination of a therapeutic concern for victims' well-being on one hand and the emphasis on remorse and rehabilitation on the other, that victims' in-court presence and participation affect the defendant and defense's "liberty to speak". Similarly, it is because of the combination of therapeutic and "traditional" rehabilitation oriented concerns that victims' participation provides expanded opportunities to judge defendants' character. It is, in addition, because of such concern for defendants' rehabilitation, that victims are looked at to elicit defendants' remorse, and to thereby play a role in service of traditional criminal justice goals.

At the same time, the attention paid to defendants' in court behavior and the attention paid to victims' wants and needs: these are part of a rhetorical criminal justice script to which victims' role has been added. In terms of *signifying practices* that communicate the importance of these issues through the attention they are being given, this rewritten script is important. Its impact in terms of criminal justice decisions however remains as yet unclear. Existing mock trial based research and the transcripts of meetings in which lay judges exchange experiences and views do not allow for clear conclusions as to how victim participation impacts sentencing practices – or fact finding practices, for that matter. These two, fact finding and sentencing practices, will be further addressed in the following two chapters.

## References

Abe, Chizuko (2010). Higaishasankaseido ni kansuru ikkōsatsu: higaishasanka no konkyo/higaishasanka no mokuteki/higaisha no hōteki chii. *Dōshisha Hōgaku* 62: 963–1084.

Aichi Bar Association (2009). *Higaishasankaseido no jisshijōkyō*. Available at: www.aiben.jp/page/library/kaihou/2110_01.html. Website last visited 30 August 2018.

Arai, Meiko (2013). *Deconstructing domesutikku baiorensu: through the voices of foremothers and forefathers of the domestic violence movement in Japan*. Dissertaion, University of Hawai'i at Manoa.

Arrigo, Bruce A. (2004). The ethics of therapeutic jurisprudence: a critical and theoretical enquiry of law, psychology and crime. *Psychiatry, Psychology and Law* 11: 23–43.

Cabinet Office (2004). *Hanzaihigaisha nado kihonkeikaku*. Available at: http://www8.cao.go.jp/hanzai/kuwashiku/keikaku/keikaku.html. Website last visited 30 August 2018.

Christie, Nils (1977). Conflicts as property. *British Journal of Criminology* 17: 1–15.

David, Roman and Susanne Y.P. Choi (2009). Getting even or getting equal? retributive desires and transitional justice. *Political Psychology* 30: 161–192.

Garland, David (1990). *Punishment and modern society: a study in social theory*. Oxford: Oxford University Press.

Goodman, Roger (2002). Child abuse in Japan: 'discovery' and the development of policy. *Family and Social Policy in Japan: Anthropological Approaches* 131–155.

Goodman, Roger (2012). The 'discovery' and 'rediscovery' of child abuse (jidō gyakutai) in Japan, in Roger Goodman, Yuki Imoto and Tuukka Hannu Ilmari Toivonen (eds.), *A sociology of Japanese youth: from returnees to NEETs*. Vol. 83. London: Routledge: 103–122.

Hamai, Kōichi and Tom Ellis (2006). Crime and criminal justice in modern Japan: from re-integrative shaming to popular punitivism. *International Journal of the Sociology of Law* 34: 157–178.

Hamai, Kōichi and Tom Ellis (2008). Japanese criminal justice: was reintegrative shaming a chimera?" *Punishment & Society* 10: 25–46.

Hōmuinkaichōsashitsu (2007). *Hanzaihigaisha nado no keijisanka*. Available at: www.sangiin.go.jp/japanese/annai/chousa/rippou_chousa/backnumber/2007pdf/20070420017.pdf. Website last visited 30 August 2018.

Japan Federation of Bar Associations (JFBA) (2007). *Hanzai higaisha nado ga keijisaiban ni chokusetsu kanyo suru koto no dekiru higaisha sanka seido ni hantai suru ikensho*. Available at: www.nichibenren.or.jp/library/ja/opinion/report/data/070501.pdf. Website last visited 30 August 2018.

Japan Federation of Bar Associations (JFBA) (2012a). *Genkō no higaishasankaseido no minaoshi ni kansuru ikensho*. Available at: www.moj.go.jp/content/000109468.pdf. Website last visited 30 August 2018.

Japan Federation of Bar Associations (JFBA) (2012b). Untitled unpublished survey on victim participation, material distributed at Ministry of Justice *Heisei 19nen Kaisei Keijisoshōhōnado ni Kansuru Ikenkōkankai*. Meeting Minutes available at: www.moj.go.jp/keiji1/keiji12_00068.html. Website last visited 30 August 2018.

Japan Legal Help Centre (year of publication not provided). *HanzaihSigaisha shien Q&A*. Available at: www.houterasu.or.jp/cont/100180048.pdf. Website last visited 30 August 2018.

Kawaai, Masayuki (2011). Hikokunin no hanseitaido nado to ryokei, in Osaka Keijijitsumukenkyūkai (ed.), *Ryōkei Jitsumu Taikei* 3: 172–215. Tokyo: Hanrei Taimuzusha.

Kurosawa, Mutsumi (2011). The abuse of the so-called right to press charges and the legal theoretical response. *Hōritsu ronsō*: 267–273.

Lens, Kim M., Anthony Pemberton and Stefan Bogaerts (2013). Heterogeneity in victim participation: a new perspective on delivering a victim impact statement. *European Journal of Criminology* 10: 479–495.

Maruna, Shadd and Anna King (2004). Public opinion and community penalties, in A. Bottoms and S. Rex et al. (eds.), *Alternatives to prison: options for an insecure society*. Portland: Willan Publishing: 83–112.

Matsui, Shigeru (2011). Justice for the accused or justice for victims: the protection of victims' rights in Japan. *Asian-Pacific Law & Policy Journal* 13: 54–95.

Ministry of Justice (MOJ) (2008). *Dai3kai hanzaihigaijittai (ansū) chōsa kekka gaiyō*. Available at: www.moj.go.jp/content/000010429.pdf. Website last visited 30 August 2018.

Ministry of Justice (MOJ) (annual). *White paper on crime*. Available at: http://hakusyo1.moj.go.jp/jp/61/nfm/mokuji.html. Website last visited 30 August 2018.

Ministry of Justice (MOJ) (2014). *Hanzaihigaisha no katagata he*. Available at: www.moj.go.jp/keiji1/keiji_keiji11.html. Website last visited 30 August 2018.

Ministry of Justice (MOJ) (2015). *Hanzaihigaisha no katagata he*. Available at: www.moj.go.jp/content/000121888.pdf. Website last visited 30 August 2018.

Miyazawa, Setsuo (2008). The politics of increasing punitiveness and the rising populism in Japanese criminal justice policy. *Punishment & Society* 10: 47–77.

Miyazawa, Setsuo (2014). Citizen participation in criminal trials in Japan: the saiban-in system and victim participation in Japan in international perspectives. *International Journal of Law, Crime and Justice* 42: 71–82.

Nakajima, Hiroshi (2012). *Keijisoshō ni okeru higaishasankaseido no jisshōteki kenkyū: kaiseihō no "3nengo no minaoshi" ni mukete*. Available at: http://ir.kagoshima-u.ac.jp/bitstream/10232/14705/1/21530067seika.pdf. Website last visited 30 August 2018.

National Association of Crime Victims and Surviving Families (NAVS) (2002). *Ikensho*. Available at: www.navs.jp/report/1/opinion2/opinion2-3.html. Website last visited 30 August 2018.

National Association of Crime Victims and Surviving Families (NAVS) (2012). *Higaisha sanka seido no 3nengo no minaoshi ni kansuru ikensho*. Available at: www.moj.go.jp/content/000102446.pdf. Website last visited 30 August 2018.

Ogawa, Tarō (1974). Hanzai ni yoru higaisha no kyūsaiseido: eibei hōkei wo chūshin ni. *Jurisuto* 575: 42–49.

Partnership for Safety and Justice (2011). *Victim advocates call on public safety commission to consider diversity of victims' needs.* Available at: www.safetyandjustice.org/spotlight/victim-advocates-call-public-safety-commission-consider-diversity-victims%E2%80%99-needs. Website last visited 30 August 2018.

Pemberton, Anthony and Sandra Reynaers (2011). *The controversial nature of victim participation: therapeutic benefits in victim impact statements.* Available at: http://papers.ssrn.com/sol3/papers.cfm?abstract_id=1745923. Website last visited 30 August 2018.

Peters, Antonie (1992). Some comparative observations on the criminal justice process in Holland and Japan. *Journal of the Japan-Netherlands Institute* 4: 247–294.

Roderick, Dennis and Susan T. Krumholz (2006). Much ado about nothing: a critical examination of therapeutic jurisprudence. *Southern New England Roundtable Symposium Law Journal* 1: 201–223.

Saeki, Masahiko (2010). Victim participation in criminal trials in Japan. *International Journal of Law, Crime and Justice* 38: 149–165.

Saeki, Masahiko (2016). *Hanzaihigaisha no shihōsanka to ryōkei.* Tokyo: University of Tokyo Press.

Supreme Court of Japan (2008). *Kōhanmae seiritetsuduki ni tsuite.* Available at: www.courts.go.jp/vcms_lf/20903007.pdf. Website last visited 30 August 2018.

Takano, Mao (2009). Aum shinrikyō hanzaihigaisha nado wo kyūsai suru tame no kyūfukin no shikyū ni kansuru hōritsu – terorizumu to tatakau wagakuni no shisei wo akiraka ni. *Keisatsu Kōron* 64: 42–45.

Van Stokkom, Bas (2011). Victims' needs, well-being and 'closure': is revenge therapeutic?, in E. Erez and M. Kilchling et al. (eds.), *Therapeutic jurisprudence and victim participation in justice: international perspectives.* Durham: Carolina Academic Press: 207–228.

Victim Support Forum (VSF) (ed.) (2013). *Keesusutadi higaishasankaseido.* Tokyo: Hōreishuppan.

Wagatsuma, Hiroshi and Arthur Rosett (1986). The implications of apology: law and culture in Japan and the United States. *Law and Society Review* 20: 461–498.

Wemmers, Jo-Anne M. (2008). Victim participation and therapeutic jurisprudence. *Victims and Offenders* 3: 165–191.

Wemmers, Jo-Anne M. (2017). *Victimology: a Canadian perspective.* Toronto: University of Toronto Press.

Wexler, David (2000). Therapeutic jurisprudence: an overview. *Thomas M. Cooley Law Review* 17: 125–134.

### *Verdicts:*

Supreme Court Third Petty Bench, Heisei 2, Hanji no. 1380: 94. Verdict of 2.2.1990.

# 5 The science in criminal justice fact finding

## Introduction

On 12 May 1990 a four-year old girl disappeared from the parking lot of a pachinko parlor in the town of Ashikaga, on Japan's main island Honshu. She was found dead the next day near the Watarase River, about 500 meters from the parking lot. On 1 December the police brought in Toshikazu Sugaya (45), a former kindergarten bus driver, for voluntary questioning.

They did so as the DNA test that they had carried out, using material retrieved from the garbage that Sugaya had thrown out, showed a match with DNA material found on the girl's clothing. The police confronted Sugaya with the results of the DNA test and pressured him to confess to taking and murdering the girl, which, after 13 hours of questioning, hair pulling, kicking in the shins and pounding on tables, he did. Sugaya was thereupon formally arrested and later prosecuted (JFBA, 2011: 13; Satō, 2010: 80).[1]

During the investigation and throughout the first trial hearings, Sugaya stuck to his confession, but upon being transferred to a different detention facility he started writing letters to his family in which he professed his innocence. During the tenth trial hearing Sugaya withdrew his confession and started claiming his innocence.[2] On 7 July 1993 the Utsunomiya District Court nevertheless found Sugaya guilty and sentenced him to an indefinite prison sentence.[3] Sugaya's con-

1 Sugaya in fact also confessed to two other similar cases that had happened in the same area in 1979 and 1984. As investigators however did not have any evidence against him besides his statements, prosecution for these cases was dropped in view of insufficient suspicion (Sato, 2010: 80). Significantly, Sugaya only spoke to a lawyer after his confession. This lawyer asked him if he had done the things he was being accused of. As Sugaya told him that he was and that he had in fact already confessed guilt, Sugaya's lawyer did not inform him of his right to remain silent. Having also heard beforehand in the media about the result of the DNA test, Sugaya's lawyer was already convinced of his client's guilt. Sugaya at a later point explained that his lawyer's assumption of guilt made it impossible to confide in him, or the second lawyer that later joined the defense, for that matter. Even after Sugaya withdrew his confession, his lawyers were not convinced that this initial confession was false (JFBA, 2011: 23; Sato, 2010: 80).

2 Sugaya had already once before, during the sixth trial hearing, recanted only to again confess during the seventh trial hearing (Sato, 2010: 80).

3 This indefinite sentence, *muki chōeki* in Japanese, is sometimes translated as a "life sentence". This is in fact also one of the translations provided by the authoritative Kenkyusha

fession, but especially also the results of the DNA tests played an important part in the coming about of this guilty verdict, as well as the upholding of this verdict on appeal to the High Court.

Sugaya's later lawyers subsequently had a university professor perform a second DNA test that showed that Sugaya's DNA did *not* match the DNA material found at the crime scene, and requested the Supreme Court to order a new DNA test. This request was in 2000 denied. Finally, however, following Sugaya's lawyers' relentless efforts to have the case reopened, the Tokyo High court ordered a new DNA test that showed that Sugaya's DNA did indeed not match the DNA found on the victim, in direct contradiction of the results of the initial DNA test, the accuracy of which was limited by the testing technique at the time. It however became clear that human error had also played a part in the coming about of the initial faulty DNA evidence (Satō, 2013: 107; Wada, 2011: 101). In 2010, 17 years after its initial verdict, the Utsunomiya District Court found Toshikazu Sugaya innocent (JFBA, 2011: 10; Sasamori, 2010).

The Ashikaga case is significant here because of some of the Japanese criminal justice characteristics it brings into focus, such as investigators' relentless pursuit of a confession of guilt and the hurdles that have to be overcome before a retrial is granted. This case is also especially significant here because of how it highlights the role of scientific evidence in both bringing about Sugaya's conviction as well as his release. This case accordingly draws our attention to the fallibility of scientific evidence and the person involved in its production on one hand, and the potential of scientific evidence to demonstrate the faultiness of the defendant's own statements on the other.

Both points are significant, given that the role of scientific evidence and especially DNA testing in criminal justice has over the past years become increasingly important. The Ashikaga case raises questions that are worth pursuing in more general terms, beyond this single case – questions about the extent to which science and scientific experts may be changing Japanese criminal justice, but also about scientists' role as experts with knowledge that lay and professional judges, prosecutors and lawyers, who are typically scientific laymen and -women, somehow have to incorporate in their arguments and decision making. How do they go about doing so?

In order to bring the relevant questions and their significance more sharply into focus it is necessary to very briefly zoom in on the more general criminal justice context within which scientists and scientific evidence are now assuming their role. As also explained in Chapter 1, Japanese criminal justice has long been characterized by the importance attached to statements, and in particular

Japanese-English dictionary (5th edition). Criminal Code (CC) article 28 however stipulates that "when a person sentenced to imprisonment with or without work evinces signs of substantial reformation, the person may be paroled by a disposition of a government agency after that person has served one-third of the definite term sentenced or 10 years in the case of a life imprisonment" (literally: *mukikei* = an indefinite prison term). Formally, Sugaya was thus eligible for parole after 10 years of his sentence.

confession statements considered to be "the king of evidence". Confessions of guilt – especially: *remorseful* confessions of guilt – have in addition played an important role in assessing and arguing a defendant's rehabilitative potential, constituting a prerequisite for a lenient sentence. Such statements were typically introduced into evidence in the form of written statements, taken and recorded during the pre-trial investigation. As a result of the introduction of the lay judge system in 2009 lengthy dossiers with written statements of defendants and witnesses have become less practical: lay judges cannot be expected to read through all the statements, as judges used to do – typically in their own working chambers. The lay judge system has accordingly necessitated a shift toward more oral, in court testimony.

But now, statements, written or oral, are getting more competition from DNA and other natural science-based evidence. The number of cases in which for example DNA testing was used as a part of the criminal investigation has in recent years exploded, going from 22 in 1992 to 299,805 in 2016 (NPA White Paper on Police, 2017).[4] This trend is significant for Japanese criminal justice practices in general, but it is particularly so for lay judge trials. The 2014 NPA White Paper on Police in fact notes in this regard: "with the introduction of the lay judge system, more emphasis is being placed on *objective* evidence that is conducive to appropriately forming the convictions of lay judges at trial" (2014: 19 – my emphasis).

The NPA here connects the importance of "objective evidence" to the recognition that other evidence has its shortcomings, as made clear by a range of wrongful convictions, one of which was that of Toshikazu Sugaya (NPA, 2016: 86). In these wrongful conviction cases false confession statements often played an important part (Foote, 1992; Kingston, 2011). The growing importance given to scientific evidence is accordingly part of a formal recognition, induced in part by the Ashikaga case, that criminal investigators should not rely too much on interrogations, but rather on "objective evidence" gathered through different methods, notably DNA testing (NPA White Paper on Police, 2010, 2016). One question that this chapter will therefore address is whether the increased importance of scientific evidence and scientists' role does indeed translate into less emphasis on confessions of guilt, and to what extent scientists are accordingly changing the character of Japanese criminal proceedings.

This is something that depends, of course, on how the legal professionals make use of the information and insights presented by the scientific experts. These experts are not only called upon to perform DNA tests or gather forensic evidence, they are also needed to introduce their findings in court, especially in lay judge trials, now that oral testimony has gained importance over dossiers in writing. When they do so, these experts need to translate their findings into explanations that the lay and professional judges, as well as lawyers and prosecutors, for that matter, can understand.

4 For reference: in 2016 996,120 Criminal Code crimes were registered, translating into 73,060 prosecutions and 79,186 suspended prosecutions (NPA White Paper on Police, 2017).

We have already seen, in Chapter 2, that forensic psychiatrists' assessments of a defendant's state of mind is incorporated in a legal assessment of this person's criminal responsibility. A person's ability to distinguish right from wrong and to act accordingly, the Japanese law criterion for criminal responsibility, is in the end determined on the basis of legal normative grounds. Of course, criminal responsibility is a legal concept, a label for legal experts to apply. Formally, their judgment is informed but not determined by forensic psychiatrists' conclusions. In practice psychiatrists' conclusions typically carry much weight during the pre-trial investigation (off stage), while during the public trial phase (on stage), this impact is not easily predicted. Still, assessments of criminal responsibility in court are often based on psychiatrists' diverging professional opinions. Such divergence allows the professionals room to negotiate the impact of psychiatrists' scientific contributions.

DNA evidence and other natural science-based evidence are, as this chapter will also show, assumed to allow for more clear-cut, objective conclusions that leave little room for discussion or normative reinterpretation. What does that mean for legal fact finding? How do the legal experts, who, as has been pointed out, may very well be technically illiterate, go about handling evidence whose methods or substance content they may very well not fully grasp (cf. Jasanoff, 1995: 5)? These are questions that are central when thinking about the contributions of non-legal professionals and knowledge to Japanese criminal justice, as one group of outsiders is charged with making decisions on the basis of ever growing contributions of other outsiders.

Beyond the specific local context of Japanese criminal justice, these questions also speak to more theoretical socio-legal debates on the role of scientific knowledge within legal processes. Of course, such debates do not necessarily allow for a neat divorce from the local context of procedures, characteristic of a specific legal system. Fact finding procedures within an accusatorial legal environment are obviously different from those in a more inquisitorial environment. Thus, findings based on for example US contexts do not necessarily hold true for a Japanese one. Nevertheless, "cross jurisdictional" debates are relevant in the sense that they bring into focus theoretical questions on the role of science in criminal justice.

As also discussed earlier, from a Luhmannian perspective all science is "merely opinion", in the sense that courts claim the prerogative to determine what constitutes a reliable area of knowledge and who is an actual scientific expert and who is not. Facts need to be legally constituted: "legal facts are made to fit the legal framework; they have to facilitate as much as possible the deductive use of legal norms. They have to support the presentation of legal validity by conveying the impressions that, given the rules, the decision follows from the facts of the case. They have to be certified facts". (Luhmann, 1991: 1430; cf. also Van Krieken, 2004: 7–8). From a Foucauldian perspective, however, modern criminal justice functions and justifies itself by perpetually referring to something "other than itself" (Foucault, 1978: 22). This perspective thus highlights how sources of extra-legal knowledge are constantly redefining the ways in which legal professionals go about their jobs, as the assertion of guilt has been turned into "a strange scientifico-juridical complex" (19). Foucault's claims refer especially to the fact that the framework of penal judgment has come to incorporate judgments concerning the offender, how his or her actions can be explained and what legal treatment he or she accordingly should get (cf. Dreyfus & Rabinow, 1983: 148–149). They are accordingly less about more "simply" establishing, judging whether the defendant did or did not commit the crime. Nevertheless, with the enormous increase in DNA testing in recent years again an extra-legal source of knowledge is embedding itself in legal judgment. Foucault's observations remain relevant, as they alert us to the possibility that scientific evidence, such as DNA evidence, is in new ways redefining the way legal professionals go about their job.

Besides these two, the Luhmannian and Foucauldian perspective, there are of course other views on the role of scientific knowledge in legal decision making. In reference to especially US and Canadian legal contexts Valverde, for example, highlights that inquiries into the truth of immoral doings are about the pursuit of clues-driven knowledge, which is "a hybrid of science, commonsense, and the kind of partly intuitive and partly archival knowledge exemplified by the nonmedically trained hoarder of heterogeneous knowledges Sherlock Holmes". (2009: 133). In line with Valverde's argument, Chapter 2 already brought into focus exactly that hybridity of the knowledge that informs decisions on criminal responsibility. It however also showed the dominance, at least at the trial stage, of jurisprudence and common sense based insights. The psychology of the defendant here received much attention, without necessarily being grounded in "formal" psychiatric insights. Factors facilitating this approach are not only the fact that (1) criminal responsibility involves an assessment emphatically qualified as *juridical*, but also (2) the fact that, as already mentioned, different forensic psychiatrists often come to different conclusions regarding the same defendant, rendering their conclusions negotiable.

Contributions on the basis of what are perceived to be more "hard" scientific insights, which are more readily assumed to be not or less person dependent, may allow the "hard scientists" to play a role in legal decision making that is quite different from that of the forensic psychiatrist. In addressing this role, this chapter is informed by and informs the abovementioned perspectives, in addition to a more general sociology of scientific knowledge perspective that stresses the social factors that go into the production of scientific knowledge (Jasanoff, 1995: 52). The latter approach does not presume scientific claims and expertise "to exist unproblematically in a world that is independent of the day-to-day workings of the law", but rather assumes these to be very much contingent on particular, localized circumstances – counterintuitive as this may seem, especially when it comes to DNA evidence (cf. Jasanoff, 1995: xiv; Mercer, 2002).

In March 2013 the Legal Research and Training Institute (LRTI), the Supreme Court run institute where all Japanese legal professionals are trained, published a document "on the nature of scientific evidence and the criminal trials making use of it", for all involved in legal practice. The document is based on analyses of the relevant jurisprudence and written in cooperation with the Secretariat of the Supreme Court, judges and legal scholars (2013: 1). Besides establishing the ways in which scientific evidence is generally handled in Japanese courts, the document also aims to establish how courts *should* handle such evidence (2013: 4). Given its authors, this document constitutes an important source of reference for especially Japanese judges, who are all career judges expected to judge cases in similar ways (Science Portal, 2016). Accordingly it is also a reference source for other legal professionals aiming to convince these judges. It is worthwhile, therefore, to examine how the LRTI document answers the above questions. Besides examining this formal line on scientific evidence, as expressed in the LRTI document, this chapter will however also look at how in practice, in concrete cases, scientific experts' contributions are incorporated in the criminal justice decisions ultimately taken, so as to make sense of the expanding role of scientific evidence and scientific experts within Japanese criminal justice and its impact on "traditional", statements-focused criminal justice practices. The LRTI document addresses scientific evidence in general, but focuses especially on DNA evidence. This chapter follows that approach.

## 1. The science in scientific evidence

Before getting into this role it is necessary to determine what these terms, scientific evidence and scientific expert, stand for. Legal scholar Honjō writes in this regard that in *general* terms, the role of expert opinion is to compensate for judges' lack of knowledge with regard to a specific area of expertise by calling upon the help of an expert, when such knowledge is necessary. Different from witnesses, who are called upon to testify about facts that they have in one way or another experienced, experts are called upon to offer their expert knowledge. That is why, different from witnesses, these experts are in principle assumed to be interchangeable. In general terms, experts are those with knowledge and experience in a specific area of expertise. This expertise is called upon in relation to "matters that judges are not thought to generally acquire through normal daily life as a member of society, and that are not amenable to understanding on the basis of general principles of experience" (2017: 3–4). Such expertise can concern both scientific and non-scientific facts such as the way people normally prepare their fermented soybeans in Ibaraki prefecture or how the local sake is brewed in the small town of Kamo, Niigata. Scientific expertise is accordingly just one example of the expertise that courts may call upon. The question then is, what does *scientific* expertise entail? In order to answer this question it is necessary to first of all determine what, from a formal legal standpoint, *scientific* evidence stands for – as it is this kind of evidence that scientific experts offer.

The LRTI document does not provide one unequivocal definition of scientific evidence. Rather, spread out through the document it provides explanations that clarify, among other things, how scientific evidence is produced, understood and how the courts determine its admissibility and reliability. Together, these explanations clarify what constitutes "reliable scientific evidence".

The document notes first of all that scientific evidence is produced on the basis of forensic science – that is: science employed in service of the law. Forensic science is based on traditional natural sciences such as biology, chemistry and physics; it is a broad field in which various disciplines are synthesized. For example, DNA tests conducted on material found at a crime scene require medical as well as biology based insights in order to establish a match with the DNA of the defendant. When it comes to the likelihood that the DNA profile found could also be linked to other persons, statistical insights come into play. The results of analyses conducted within this interdisciplinary field are introduced in criminal trials as "scientific evidence" (*kagakutekishōko*) (2013: 2–3). Straightforward as this all may sound, it is important to note that this explanation contains an implicit acknowledgment that forensic science is a particular kind of science. It is not concerned with "getting the facts right" and finding a truth that is out there for that truth's sake. Its concern is rather to get the facts right as an "adjunct to its transcendent objective", as Jasanoff puts it, which in this case is that of determining the guilt or innocence of the person on trial (cf. Jasanoff, 1995: 10).

As scientific evidence, it is represented as clearly distinguishable from other forms of evidence, notably statements. The LRTI document explanation on this issue is worth quoting at length here. Scientific evidence refers to

> a definite amount of evidence material that has been analyzed on the basis of scientific principles. Accordingly, given that there is material to work with, it is highly objective when compared with regular statements that are based on people's memory, in the sense that the material (. . .) exists independently from the will of those involved in the case. In addition, since the process of collecting from the material a certain amount of information is also based on a given set of scientific principles and methods, it is unlikely to reflect any intentions of the person who gathered the evidence. In that sense too one can say that it is highly objective. If it is gathered by means of the appropriate method, one can generally say that it is objective in nature and also certain in terms of content. This is an important characteristic when compared to statements given as evidence, that have an uncertain character in the sense that cognition, memory and description at each stage allow for the possibility of mistakes.

The document goes on to note that "because of scientific evidence it is possible to avoid the tendency to rely too much on confession statements obtained during the criminal investigation, and to relatively reduce the reliance on the statements (. . .) on the identity of the criminal given by victims and witnesses and so on" (2013: 5–6).

The LRTI document here does more than explaining the nature of scientific evidence. It *qualifies* such evidence, highlighting its superiority vis-à-vis statements. This superiority is here directly tied to the notion that evidence produced on the basis of scientific methods is not dependent on fallible human beings.

Characteristic for the scientific method is after all its quality of reproducibility, depending on impersonal agents that are assumed to be more reliable exactly because they are impersonal, and accordingly less vulnerable to human error or subjectivity (cf. Jasanoff, 2006: 330). It is by virtue of such superiority that it harbors the potential to change one characteristic of Japanese criminal justice, namely its overreliance on confession statements.

Clear-cut as the distinction between scientific evidence on one hand, and statements on the other may here seem, the document also notes that there are cases in which the distinction between scientific and common sense based elements of a piece of evidence is actually not necessarily clear. Furthermore, as if to reconfirm that the times they are a-changing not just yet, the document continues to state that

> it is necessary to affirm that it is not the case that "common sense" = "unscientific" = "of low reliability". When it comes to the evidentiary value of facts and the reliability of ordinary statements that are based on people's memory and so on, we basically judge (matters) on the basis of unscientific common sense.
>
> (2013: 8)

This addition makes sense, of course, given that any qualification of common sense as unreliable would implicitly also render judges' own judging practices unreliable. Interestingly, in light also of the emphasis on the fallibility of human cognition and the risks of subjectivity, no explanation is offered as to why commonsense judgment is reliable. The reasoning rather seems to be that given that judges base their judgment on common sense, commonsense reasoning and judging are beyond the reach of questions of reliability.

Be that as it may – I will come back to the issue of judges' common sense based judgment below – the distinction between scientific and other forms of evidence is apparently not necessarily all too clear after all. To further complicate matters, the document notes that "the *scientific nature of scientific evidence varies in terms of both content and degree*" (my italics), while acknowledging the relativity of today's scientific truths that tomorrow may be proven false (2013: 7, 11).

Here the LRTI document thus assumes a sociology of knowledge-like perspective, as it acknowledges that the validity of scientific knowledge is in any case contingent on "local time", and that different times come with different scientific understandings of reality. One might here expect that this relativist understanding of scientific truth would also make the legal judgments that are based upon them relative, thereby threatening their authority. This is in fact a problem that the earlier mentioned Ashikaga case presents. In that case the authority of the DNA evidence that was produced on the basis of techniques that were new at the time weighed heavily in the decision that condemned Toshikazu Sugaya to spending 17 years of his life in prison. Ultimately, evidence based on different DNA testing techniques showed that the initial authoritative match was in fact not a match. What lessons, if any, could be drawn from this example of the relativity of today's scientific truths?

The Ashikaga case prompted some soul searching among the police, the bar and Prosecutors' office and the compiling of reports on where, respectively, the investigation, defense and prosecution had gone wrong (NPA, 2010; JFBA, 2011; Supreme Prosecutors' Office, 2010). No such report was written, however, on behalf of the courts. The LRTI document was however the closest thing to such a report, as it was published not long after the Ashikaga case, on behalf of a Supreme Court run institution and especially since it dealt with an issue that was central to the Ashikaga case: the evaluation of scientific evidence, notably DNA evidence (cf. Satō, 2013; Tokunaga, 2013).[5]

The LRTI document does indeed mention the Ashikaga case, but not as a case in which something had gone wrong, but rather as a case with "elements to be attentive to" (2013: 13). The document's stance on the implications of ever advancing science for the legitimacy of legal decisions, in connection also with the reopening of old cases, is however worth quoting at length here.

> Under our legal system, that has no time limits when it comes to the reopening of a case, it can happen that a court case is reviewed on the basis of the science of one or several decades later (. . .) It is impossible to categorically deny the possibility that because of science progressing with the passing of that kind of time, the conclusion regarding scientific evidence that was up until then thought of as "true", will be regarded as "false". Accordingly, it is conceivable that the reliability of scientific evidence that formed the basis of a judgment of guilt is negated as a result of the later progress of science.

How should this be thought of from the perspective of the legitimacy of trials (*saiban no seitōsei*)? According to the LRTI document it is thought that the legitimacy of fact finding in trials is supported by the fact that it is based on reasons that were thought of as rational in light of "wholesome societal common sense" (*kenzen na shakaijōshiki*), on the basis of evidence and insights that had become clear at the time of the trial. Accordingly,

> it is important to examine evidence while making the most of the insights available at the time. When it comes to scientific evidence based on science

5 The Asahi national newspaper in addition reported on 24 April 2010 that "in response to the fact that in the Ashikaga case, in which in a retrial (the defendant's) innocence was established, too much confidence placed in the result of a DNA test – a factor that contributed to an erroneous judgment – the Supreme Court's Legal Research and Training Institute decided to start a research with the theme "how to treat scientific evidence in criminal trials" (*Asahi Shimbun*, 2010). The Yomiuri national newspaper reportedly published a similar article. Even though the LRTI report itself does not mention the Ashikaga case as the trigger for the writing of the report, these newspaper articles very much suggest that indeed it was (cf. also Sato, 2013: 107).

> that is still developing, in case one cannot categorically confirm the reliability and accuracy of elements that have still not been cleared up, even if one can tentatively confirm the reliability and accuracy of what has at that point been achieved by correctly discerning that, it is necessary to carefully examine the evidence as evidence with that kinds of limitations (. . .) And so if this kind of careful examination has been done, the legitimacy of the trial itself will not directly be negated, even of the reliability of the scientific evidence that formed the basis of a guilty verdict is later on denied as a result of the progress of science. It is also with this type of situation in mind, that retrial procedures have been established.
>
> (2013: 9–10)

In other words, as long as judges carefully separate the elements that science in development has cleared from those it has not, the legitimacy of trials is unassailable, regardless of any conflicting insights that may later develop. That legitimacy accordingly hinges on judges' careful examination and discernment of the extent to which evidence based on science in progress can be relied on. Given that one could argue that all science is in constant progress, as the LRTI report also acknowledges, judges are also constantly engaged in such careful examination and discernment.

The report thus reaffirms that the validity of scientific evidence does not speak for itself. Considering the problem of science in progress as well as the earlier mentioned notion that the scientific nature of scientific evidence varies in terms of both content and degree, it is clear that it is judges who are called upon to distinguish the more from the lesser scientific truth, and to say what at any given point in time constitutes "reliable scientific evidence". Thus, the question of what such evidence entails remains.

### *1.1. "Reliable scientific evidence" in practice*

"Reliable scientific evidence", so it turns out, does not allow for a clear, a priori watertight definition. What it is depends to an important extent on what courts have in the past *made* of it – to an important extent it depends, in other words, on juridical precedent and convention. It is therefore necessary to take a brief look at how in practice courts have answered the reliable scientific evidence question.

When it comes to scientific evidence Japanese criminal courts have in practice distinguished four different types[6]:

> Type 1. The understanding is that empirically these tests and evaluations have a certain significance, even though there are unclarified aspects concerning

---

6 This categorization, used in the JRTI document, is in line with the categories distinguished by legal scholar Makoto Mitsui (2004: 263). The overview of the categories presented here is based mostly on that presented in the LRTI document.

the scientific nature of the material and techniques used for testing and evaluation, Tests are often conducted by persons with a certain training; their specialized experience gives their judgment the appearance of accuracy. At the same time, however, the scientific basis of that judgment is not necessarily clear. An important reason why the results from these types of tests are understood to have a certain significance, however, is that "the basic methodology and thinking underlying the tests correspond with the empirical things that people naturally master through their lives in society" (LRTI, 2013: 11). Judges are advised to be aware of the fact that the expertise provided is experience based, and accordingly be careful in evaluating such evidence (2013: 12). Graphology and dog sniff tests are examples of this type.[7] Interestingly, in confirming the evidentiary value of graphologist's expert opinion the Supreme Court admitted that in traditional graphology the methodology depends to a large extent on experience and feeling (*kan*), and had its limitations. It however at the same time held that "it is obvious that one cannot say that the expert's judgment is merely subjective, given that it is backed up by his or her experience, and the accumulation of such experience up until then". And so even if graphology's methodology has its limitations, that does not by itself negate the value of the graphologist's judgment, as long as this judgment is based on extensive experience (Supreme Court 21 February 1966, Second petty bench 1965 (a) no. 238).

Type 2. This type is based on comparisons between the shape and form of original material such as finger- and footprints, hairs, CCTV footage and so on, with other contrasting material. The understanding is that the principles underlying this type are clear, but that depending on the method used it may be necessary to carefully consider the reliability of the method in question. As long as the person performing the tests and the methods used are appropriate, "it is ok to think that one can obtain a certain rational test result" (LRTI, 2013: 12). In addition, given that this type is about comparing forms and shapes non-specialists too can consider and evaluate the reliability of evidence on this point. Nevertheless, there is the risk of subjective judgment entering morphological comparisons and essentially relying on judgments of experience.

Type 3. For tests and assessments of this type use is made of scientific insights and techniques. The understanding is accordingly that the reliability of this type of scientific evidence is supported precisely by those insights and techniques. Still, the understanding is that one cannot always categorically say whether a scientific insight is established or not, and doubts may have been expressed about the accuracy of specific concrete methods. Here too, the

7 The LRTI document first classifies graphology as partly type 1, then as type 2 scientific evidence, and later on again as type 1 (LRTI, 2013: 11, 12, 26). In line with this toward type 1 leaning assessment, I have also categorized it as such.

courts' understanding is that when it comes to the reliability of tests, cautious consideration is necessary. The results of polygraph tests are an example of this type. The Supreme Court in 1968 confirmed the evidentiary value of such tests, even if as of 2006 these are no longer used in Japan.

Type 4. The basic principles underlying the tests of this type are understood to be scientifically sound. Having said that, in terms of the reliability of the testing methods a distinction is made between cases in which the testing method in question can and cannot be said to be established, when for example the number of times a new method has been applied is still small. An example of such a non-established method is the MCT118 DNA testing method used in the Ashikaga case (LRTI, 2013: 13–14). When it comes to assessing the accuracy of the scientific principles and insights that lie at the foundation of tests, the guiding principle is no longer to look for "a general scientific acceptance", as was once the case.[8] The scholarly legal literature emphasizes the importance of setting high hurdles of evidentiary value and relevance for scientific evidence, in view of "the authority of science" and the risk of undue influence on (lay) judges that comes with such authority (2013: 24–25; cf. also Tsujiwaki, 2010: 440–441). The LRTI report however emphasizes that the hurdles of evidentiary value and relevance can also be taken on the basis of judges' actual judgment (*jisshitsu handan*) of the reliability and evidentiary value of evidence (25).

If there is anything that stands out when looking at these four categories, it is that for each type of scientific evidence judges are called upon to carefully evaluate the methodology, insights and principles that lie at the foundation of the results and depending on the type, as well as those results themselves. These four types thus again highlight that ***whatever "reliable scientific evidence" is depends on judges' assessment***. The LRTI report and the courts' understanding of scientific evidence, on the basis of which the four types of scientific evidence have been distinguished, do emphasize the importance of caution and careful judgment. Still the LRTI report reads as a confident confirmation of judges' ability to do what is demanded from them, as illustrated also by the trust in judges' ability to determine the reliability and evidentiary value of scientific evidence on the basis of their "substantive judgment" (*jisshitsu no handan*) of such evidence. I will come back to this issue below.

The four types outlined above, based as they are on actual legal practice, provide an impression of how judges go about separating reliable from unreliable scientific evidence. The report however wrestles with the question of the general

8 This guiding principle had come about under the influence of US legal doctrine on this issue, notably the *Frye* standard. This standard came about following a case decided by the District Court of Columbia Court of Appeals, which in 1923 refused to admit based on an early version of the polygraph test, noting that "the thing from which the deduction is made must be sufficiently established to have gained general acceptance in the particular field in which it belongs." (quoted in Bernstein, 2001: 388).

guiding principles that could be said to underlie that legal practice. While referring to literature that does identify such principles, such as the requirement that the scientific principles underlying the evidence are accurate and that the method in question is scientifically trusted, it notes that courts in practice ***do not necessarily abide by these principles.***[9]

It furthermore becomes clear that within legal practice judges have not found it very useful (*jitsueki ni toboshii*) to make clear distinctions between admissibility, reliability and probative value when evaluating and judging scientific evidence, the reasoning being that in judges' actual judgment the point is not really if a piece of evidence is rejected because it is inadmissible or because it is unreliable. Such distinctions are not that relevant given that judges are blessed with the ability to judge a piece of evidence for what it is worth, given that when judges did use (admitted) a piece of evidence "they have been sufficiently able to address its probative value on the basis of their thorough review and consideration, and their careful approach" (27).[10]

Against the background of such confidence in judges' abilities, it makes sense that judges have in practice also not really felt the need to think of admissibility requirements that clearly distinguished scientific evidence from other evidence:

> If there is any doubt when it comes to using (something) as evidence that would constitute a basis for fact finding, the difference between judging something to be unreliable or as something that is inadmissible is only relative. Because the person judging the admissibility is the fact finding judge him or herself (. . .), the necessity of making the entrance for the admissibility of evidence smaller has from the perspective of the scientific reliability of scientific evidence not really been felt.
>
> (22)

Labeling evidence as scientific, admissible or reliable or not, has from a practice based point of view not been all that relevant, given that judges have for themselves been able to carefully evaluate the probative value of that evidence.

It is also not surprising that "with regard to the evidence that was an issue in the various legal judgments previously discussed there is considerable difference in what 'scientific' stands for".

---

9 Importantly the document refers in this regard specifically to the reasoning of the Supreme Court in confirming the admissibility of MCT118DNA testing. The Supreme Court has in this regard noted that the Court can "of course" make use of the results of such testing, without any substantive engagement with the question of why this is "of course" the case (LRTI, 2013: 27 and references provided there).

10 An example of a lack of distinction between conceptual categories with regard to a different form of evidence is when judges determine the voluntariness and accordingly the admissibility of a confession by evaluating the reliability of that confession in terms of its content (cf. Foote, 1991: 458–459).

Obviously there is much in the way of jurisprudence and legal doctrine that judges can refer to when making their decisions. With regard to admissibility and relevance courts do require theoretical accuracy and scientifically reliable methods. Importantly, however, "it is not clear in what form and to what extent they do" (LRTI, 2013: 27–28).[11]

This section departed from the assumption that in order to determine what "reliable scientific evidence" entails, it is necessary to look at how the courts have given substance to this concept. All in all, however, it turns out that on the basis of findings from the LRTI document, an authoritative Supreme Court document devoted to the issue of scientific evidence, it is still not possible to clearly define or describe what "reliable scientific evidence" in practice means. As much as scientific evidence is hailed for its objectivity and superiority vis-à-vis human cognition, etc., whatever scientific evidence in practice entails – that is: how it is defined – will depend on the specifics of the evidence and especially the judges in question.

11 Having reached the conclusion that in practice much is unclear with regard to scientific methods, in terms of what it stands for and what the courts require from it, the LRTI document goes on to address US discussions on the admissibility of scientific evidence, given their relevance as a point of reference. It also notes however that in the US such discussions have centered on whether certain evidence may be presented in and to the court, while in Japan the discussion is rather focused on the question of whether a piece of scientific evidence should be allowed to be used as material on the basis of which the decision to find someone guilty is based. Furthermore, the discussion on rules of evidence with regard to scientific evidence in the United States applies to both civil and criminal trials, while in Japan the discussion is focused only on the requirements regarding scientific evidence in criminal trials. Given that those charged with carrying out the forensic investigation "have a tradition of approaching evidence in criminal trials with a careful attitude, while being aware of the (requirements regarding) the suitability of evidence in criminal trials . . . it is necessary to acknowledge the reality that at least with regard to expert opinion provided by public institutions of expertise, the probability of junk science being introduced in criminal courts is quite low, when compared with the United States" (33). Nevertheless, the verdict handed down in the famous *Daubert* case is highlighted as a point of reference on issues of reliability and probative value, while keeping in mind the differences between the Japanese lay judge system and the US jury system (Daubert v. Merrell Dow Pharmaceuticals, Inc, 509 U.S. 579, 1993). As noted by Jasanoff (1995), the majority opinion in this case posited four criteria in order to determine the relevance and validity of proposed testimony that referred to peer review and general acceptance on one hand and error rates and whether the theory or technique underlying the evidence has been tested and is falsifiable on the other. And so, "the Court managed to weave into this rehearsal both the view of the philosopher Karl Popper that science progresses through clear falsifications of erroneous claims and the view of constructivist sociologists of science that knowledge accumulates through negotiation and consensus among members of the scientific community." Jasanoff further notes that "*Daubert*'s fine disregard for a philosophically coherent decision rule on admissibility may exemplify the common law's genius for muddling through on the basis of experience rather than logic" (1995: 63). In this sense, as a recommended point of reference for Japanese legal professionals, *Daubert* too highlights the difficulty of defining a coherent approach of "scientific evidence".

### *1.2. Advice on handling scientific evidence*

That having been said, the LRTI document does outline a range of factors with regard to the handling of scientific evidence for legal professionals to consider, based in part on the relevant scholarly literature. In doing so it not only refers to US discussions on scientific evidence, and the differences with the United States to consider in this regard (see note 11). It also highlights the importance of disclosing evidence to the defense, so as to provide the defense with the opportunity to question and verify the reliability and scientific nature of that evidence, by for example providing data to ascertain the extent to which the results of a given test can be reproduced (45). It provides a list of reliability criteria, among which the extent to which the principles and standards on which a test is based can be trusted, but also whether the person performing the tests has the necessary skills and qualifications (56). It in addition addresses issues of storage, purity and the amount of material used for tests – etc., etc.

Grounded in the literature and extensive as the consideration of various relevant factors may be, this food for thought for practitioners also points to the complexity of handling "scientific evidence" in criminal trials, and especially the problem of logical coherence and consistency.

The LRTI document for example highlights that much like lay judges, professional judges are no scientific experts, and that judges need to respect experts' judgment (33, 55). In fact, judges may find themselves ***having little choice but to go along with experts' opinion*** – with regard to the question of whether a specific testing method is established or not, or whether an analysis is theoretically sound, for example (54–55). The document at the same time however emphasizes judges' ability and privilege to draw their own conclusions in a "substantive judgment" on the reliability and evidentiary value of scientific evidence. It is furthermore up to the professional judges to provide lay judges with explanations on experts' testimony and to prevent them from being overly impressed by scientific evidence, as the professional judges are after all more aware of the specific characteristics of scientific evidence (25; 34–36; 133).

In evaluating and judging (scientific) evidence the distinctions between admissibility, reliability and probative value have in practice not been considered all that useful, as an evaluation of the probative value of a piece of evidence determines its admissibility or reliability. Nevertheless, in lay judge trials professional judges are the ones who distinguish admissible from inadmissible evidence, while professional and lay judges together evaluate the reliability and probative value (23). Judges are urged to exercise caution in the evaluation of DNA evidence and to be generally alert to the danger of being overly impressed by scientific evidence. The document however at the same time holds that it is possible to find a person guilty on the basis of DNA evidence only (26–27; 40; 122–123; 138) – etc., etc.

All in all the LRTI document provides a wealth of information, criteria and viewpoints that may not categorically mutually exclude each other, but that also do not allow for unequivocal rules and principles regarding the handling of scientific evidence in criminal trials. Especially relevant here are the contradictory depictions of judges who on one hand have no choice but to go along with scientific experts' explanations but who are on the other hand fully able to assess the reliability of such explanations and the evidence for which these explanations are relevant. How come judges would have this ability remains unexplained and unclear.[12]

At this point it is important to also note the absence of any reflection on instances in which judges did go wrong, in spite of their careful assessment. As we have seen, not only has Toshikazu Sugaya spent 17 years in prison on the basis, to an important extent, of judges' evaluation of the DNA evidence presented in this (Ashikaga) case, there has also been one case in which the same DNA testing method was used, in which the defendant, Michitoshi Kuma was actually executed.[13] The lack of reference to mistakes or the possibility thereof is in line with the idea that as long as judges carefully assess evidence on the basis of knowledge and insights available at the time, the legitimacy of criminal trials is not compromised.

One can find a similar line of reasoning also among members of the bench. Former judge Kunio Harada has for example stated in this regard: "I feel that if one can say that the correct procedure has been followed and that court hearings have been exhaustive, even if that results in a judgment that goes against the truth, one cannot say anything else than that that was unavoidable. (. . .) Verdicts should be pronounced with self-confidence. However, one should not lose a sense of modesty, as the possibility of being mistaken is constantly there. Depending on the case I used to say, when informing just convicted defendants of their right to appeal: 'You're denying (the charges). On the basis of an investigation of all the evidence that needed to be investigated, this is the verdict

12 In addressing Supreme Court jurisprudence on scientific evidence the LRTI document criticized the Supreme Court for its lack of explanation as to why it was appropriate for the court in first instance to have judged an MCTT118DNA type DNA test to be reliable and therefore useable as evidence. It qualifies this explanation as a "matter of course explanation" (*mochiron kaishaku*): it goes without saying that the court in first instance was right (27). In assuming that it goes without saying that judges are able to assess the probative value, and accordingly the reliability of scientific evidence, however, the LRTI does exactly what it criticized the Supreme Court for.

13 On 8 September 2006 the Supreme Court's second petty bench rejected Michitoshi Kuma's appeal, confirming the verdicts of the High Court that, like the District Court had done before, found him guilty of the murder of two girls in 1992. The results of the DNA tests in this case were obtained using the same method as that used in the Ashikaga case, results that later on were proven to be incorrect. In the IIzuka case however there was possibility to conduct new DNA tests, as there no DNA samples had been kept. Mr. Kuma has up until his execution in 2008 always maintained his innocence. Mrs. Kuma has filed request to the Fukuoka District and High Courts to have the case reopened. Both requests were denied; a request to the Supreme Court is currently pending (Japan Innocence & Death Penalty Information Center, 2018). The Ashikaga case is different from this case in the sense that it became clear that the DNA results were tainted by the mistakes made by the scientists conducting the tests. The fact that these mistakes went unnoticed in both the original trial and on appeal is however illustrative for judges' inability to thoroughly check whether complex scientific procedures, such as those that are part of DNA testing, were followed.

that came out. Nonetheless, perhaps this conclusion is wrong, and things are as you say they are. If that's the case, please, by all means, appeal'" (Harada, 2012: 18–19).

The LRTI document's reasoning and Harada's statement have a few things in common. One is an explicit characterization of legal truths as conditional truths. Another is the element of unavoidability: judges do what they can, and accordingly – assuming that everybody followed procedure and exercised due caution – a decision comes out. Court hearings and an investigation of the available evidence naturally *result in* a judgment. This way of presenting what judges do allows for the possibility of courts who may be wrong but are not to be blamed, and for the possibility of never having to say sorry. Judges' self-proclaimed or ascribed carefulness in handling scientific knowledge, the always preliminary character of that knowledge and the following of the correct procedure thus serve an important role in the self-legitimizing discourse that the LRTI document presents.

## 2. Science and scientists in court

The previous sections have examined, on the basis of especially the LRTI document, how judges have gone about defining "reliable scientific evidence" and what rules and principles they have employed to do so. This examination brought into focus the importance of individual judges' evaluation of scientific evidence in each particular case. Up until now, scientific and scientists' expertise have only been addressed from the perspective of a judge and what he or she makes of such expertise. There is more to scientific expertise in court, however, than judges' definitional practices. Focusing on DNA evidence: when presented or employed in court, scientific expertise on this issue becomes embedded in (1) a very specific procedural context. In Japan, that context is that of what is formally an adversary criminal process. The persons offering scientific expertise in court, notably on DNA testing, are in addition persons working within (2) a particular institutional context. DNA testing and other forensic tests and investigations are in Japan carried out almost exclusively by the National Research Institute of Police Science or a prefectural scientific research institution. Remaining individual experts tend to be affiliated with prestigious universities. Finally, DNA expertise and results are tied up with (3) local reporting and interpretation practices. These three dimensions are essential to take into account when trying to make sense of the role of scientific experts and expertise in Japanese criminal courts. This section focuses especially on DNA related expertise, as it would be beyond the scope of this chapter to attempt to address each relevant field of forensic expertise. In addition, as also noted earlier, DNA testing has in recent years has become more and more important, as illustrated by the enormously increased use of such testing in criminal justice investigation and trials (NPA White Paper on Police, 2017). Finally, it is fruitful to focus especially on DNA reporting and interpretation practices given the enormous authority attributed to DNA evidence in criminal justice.

### 2.1. Procedural context

There has been considerable debate about the question of how to characterize Japanese criminal justice procedure. As also briefly noted in Chapter 1, following World War II, Japan adopted an adversary system that was closely modeled on the US system. Japan thus formally introduced "a style of decision-making in which two contestants argue their cases before a neutral judge".[14] There is a formal separation between the judge as a passive and impartial adjudicator and the prosecutor, who determines the object of proceedings. Furthermore, "the defendant's procedural rights receive some degree of protection to counterbalance the power of government" (Miyazawa, 2002: 2). While Japanese criminal justice is formally set up in line with these requirements, in practice there is an imbalance in power between the parties. Shinomiya has in this regard argued that in Japan "the defendant is not an actual adversary against the police or prosecution in Japanese criminal procedure, but rather more of an isolated 'hostage'" (2002: 115). This characterization, which has also been used by other scholars of Japanese criminal justice, refers to the fact that most suspects are detained in police detention cells rather than detention facilities managed by the Ministry of Justice, so as to facilitate interrogation and the obtaining of a confession (see also Miyazawa, 2002). Significantly, lawyers are not allowed to be present during the interrogations (Miyazawa & Hirayama, 2017: 158–159).[15]

Furthermore, judges in most cases grant Prosecutors' request for detention, although the approval rate has in the past decades gone down, ever so slightly, from more than 99% (in the 1980s and 1990s) to more than 96% (Ministry of Justice, 1980–2017). Prosecutors will in addition charge a person only when they are convinced that they can obtain a conviction, and finally, prosecutors are the ones who, together with the police, conduct the criminal investigation and who disclose the evidence that this investigation has produced. In recent years the rules for disclosure have been changed, allowing the defense to generally get a clearer picture of what evidence has been gathered, as prosecutors are for example required to hand over a list of all the items gathered, if a lawyer requests them to do so (JFBA, 2016). Nevertheless, there is no obligation on the part of the prosecution to disclose exculpatory evidence, no sanction if they fail to do so, and the new rules allow judges considerable discretion in deciding whether to order the disclosure of a particular piece of evidence or not (Ito, 2012: 1265).[16] All in

14 This is Malcom Feeley's definition of an adversary system, quoted in Shinomiya (2002: 115)

15 Lengthy interrogations carried out under these circumstances have in a number of cases led to false confessions, as they also have in the earlier discussed Ashikaga case. The outcry and calls for reform following cases such as this will by June 2019 finally translate into reforms, as at that time a system of mandatory videotaping will be introduced. Significantly, however, the application of this reform is limited to a very small proportion of cases (Miyazawa & Hirayama, 2017: 153).

16 Significantly, Johnson in this regard notes, "Since the 'Conspiracy at Matsukawa' case that resulted in the wrongful conviction of 20 men in 1950 and their subsequent acquittal (. . .), almost every exoneration in Japan has involved the failure of prosecutors to disclose critical evidence to the defense" (2015). In the Matsukawa case three persons were killed as a result

all, one of the adversaries is in practice significantly more powerful than the other, to the extent even that Japanese criminal justice can be qualified as "Prosecutors' justice" (cf. Johnson, 2012; Weber, 2009: 6).

Prosecutors thus constitute one of the parties in an adversary system, one that is very much able to shape the outcome of the adversary confrontation. At the same time, however, they are also representatives of the public interest, in accordance with the Public Prosecutors' Office Law art. 4 (1955, law no. 61). As also discussed in Chapter 3, the new *Principles of Prosecution*, which were formulated following a scandal involving prosecutorial misconduct, also formally reaffirm Prosecutors' commitment to serving that public interest (Supreme Public Prosecutors Office, 2011). These principles are in line with Prosecutors' authority to decide who, in the interest of justice and the suspect in question, should be prosecuted and whose prosecution should be suspended. Prosecutors' wielding of such authority brings into focus their double role in Japanese criminal justice, namely as one of the two parties to the process, and as a more magistrate-like actor.[17] But while prosecutors may have a magistrate-like role at the pre-trial phase, "off stage" (cf. chapters 2 and 3), in diverting certain suspects from trial, when a trial does take place the aim is, of course, to obtain a conviction and to win (cf. Ramseyer & Rasmusen, 2001: 61; Johnson, 2012: 227; Kingston, 2011).[18] As parties to the process they argue their partisan case, much like the defense does, arguing that the defendant is guilty, or rather innocent, deserving of the sentence demanded or rather of a lesser sentence. Scientists' and scientific evidence are accordingly by definition incorporated in a story that aims to persuade, and for the purpose of which some elements are downplayed or omitted, while others are highlighted (cf. Ewick & Silbey, 1995). In this way, trials may develop into wars of science between the two parties, with each party calling on scientific experts to present scientific results in line with their argument.

## *2.2. Institutional context*

Court wars of science are an exception, however, that occurs especially when cases are reopened – again, like the Ashikaga case (cf. Yazawa, 2014). Forensic

---

of a train being sabotaged, in August 1949. Of the twenty persons arrested 19 were Communists or leaders of labor unions. All 20 were initially convicted; five defendants received a death sentence. Ultimately, some 20 years later, all 20 were exonerated. For an insightful account of this case, thought to have been a frame-up case by the investigative authorities, see Johnson (1972).

17 Japanese prosecutors are of course not unique in that respect. See, for example Susan Bandes' description of US Prosecutors' dual role (2006: 483).

18 Ramseyer and Rasmussen note in this regard that "Japanese prosecutors face particularly stark incentives to win cases. (. . .) Prosecutors are part of a national bureaucracy. Within this bureaucracy, some posts are prestigious and some are not. Yet every 2 years, prosecutors find themselves moved from post to post on the basis of their performance" (2001: 61). While the Prosecutors' Office has in the aftermath of various scandals involving prosecutorial misconduct formally committed to emphasizing their role of servants of the public interest – cf. Chapter 3 – this incentive structure has not changed.

tests in Japan are conducted by those working for the National Research Institute of Police Science or a prefectural scientific research institution. In fact, DNA testing for criminal trials is in principle only done at these institutions. In exceptional cases, such as when there are doubts concerning the original test, university forensic laboratory may however also perform such tests (Minaguchi, 2017; Okada, 2006: 17; Hiraoka, 2014: 7). Nevertheless, it is safe to say that forensic investigation in general and DNA testing in particular are monopolized by research institutions affiliated with the police.

At the trial stage one of the parties may request the Court to order a scientist to perform one or another forensic test. In such a case the defense can check and provide input as to whether the material to be tested is the most suitable for that test, what might be the best testing method, and so forth (Honjō, 2017: 14). Most forensic testing however takes place at the investigation stage (Honjō, 2017: 15). At that stage forensic tests are performed at the request of a police officer or an (assistant) prosecutor. Such tests are typically conducted with the aim of finding evidence in support of the case against a particular suspect.

Even if the research institution or the researcher is no party to the process, they do generally perform their tasks in service of one of those parties. In evaluating these tests as evidence, the courts do not distinguish between court ordered tests and tests performed at the request of those carrying out the criminal investigation, the assumption being that as long as those performing the tests are scientists, they will not be partisan (Honjō, 2017: 14). The basis of such trust, beautiful as it is, remains unclear. Tests are conducted at the request of investigative authorities, without the presence of a third, neutral party, at police affiliated research institutions by scientists who are trusted by the courts.

### *2.3. Local reporting and interpretation practices*

The point here is not that scientists working at such police affiliated research institutions are not to be trusted. One problem is however that scientists may not be aware of the bias that may enter their judgment when they are called upon within the context of a criminal investigation. As also noted in Chapter 2, the forensic psychiatrist who examined Toshikazu Sugaya in the Ashikaga case wrote an evaluation whose general gist and conclusion was totally based on the assumption that Sugaya had sexually abused and killed a little girl. In other words, this evaluation was very much carried out as part of an attempt to explain the actions of the perpetrator. In this case "the actions of the perpetrator" constituted the basis on which the forensic psychiatrist performed his evaluation. In this case one could however accuse the forensic psychiatrist of not having gone about his evaluation in accordance with basic criteria for an objective evaluation.

The question is if bias, conscious or unconscious, could also enter more "hard" scientific forensic investigation. In general terms, when forensic research is done as part of a criminal investigation and at the request of those looking to establish guilt, it is hard to categorically deny the possibility of bias, given that criminal investigators select certain items to be tested and others not. There is in addition the possibility that scientists succumb to pressures to represent test results in a biased way. With regard to forensic research undertaken in the police affiliated prefectural scientific research institutions, Hiraoka for example writes that "one cannot say that it absolutely does not occur" that researchers are subjected to demands to make changes in their reports, changes that better fit the story that criminal investigators aim to prove and argue in court (2014: 138).

By itself, scientists' ability to withstand pressure from investigators is not enough to guarantee "objective results". To achieve such results scientists must be seen to comply with methodological requirements and criteria characteristic of a field in question – requirements and criteria that are the product of incessant negotiations between members of a specific discipline (cf. Jasanoff, 1995: 52 and references listed there). Accordingly, as these negotiations continue, with "the progress of science", there is continuous debate and disagreement about things such as methodological requirements and standards that need to be met for a certain conclusion to become viable. The adversary system of course also thrives on such debate, as it often allows for one expert's unequivocal scientific truth to be countered by another one. A lawyer's job is in fact to seek an expert to point out problems in current forensic scientific practice: "they must be out there" (Kobayashi, 2012: 76).

Zooming in on DNA testing practices may serve to prove this point. As we have seen, scientific evidence in general and DNA evidence in particular wield considerable authority in court. Japanese defense lawyers reportedly lose their motivation to fight for their client when there is DNA evidence, while an authoritative Supreme Court report holds, as we have seen, that it is possible to convict a defendant on the basis of only DNA evidence. (Hiraoka, 2014: iv; LRTI, 2013: 138).[19] To an important degree this importance derives exactly from the perception that the results of scientific research, and by extension, forensic investigation, are objective. It is this perceived objectiveness that allows for stories to be presented and perceived as non-partisan.

19 Admittedly, the LRTI document is ambivalent in this regard. On one hand it highlights the objective and reliable nature of scientific evidence in general and DNA evidence in particular, especially when compared with human cognition and statements based on such cognition. On the other hand it also notes as follows: "normally, it is almost always the case that scientific evidence is (. . .) nothing more than circumstantial evidence. It is often the case that what kind of probative value that circumstantial evidence has is something that depends on an overall judgment that combines it with the other circumstantial evidence. The experience-based statements of the victim and witnesses and so on constitute evidence that unfolds like a story (*sutooriiteki na hirogari wo motsu) shōko*), and if the reliability thereof is confirmed it can have a high evidentiary value that is conducive to an overall solution of the case. By comparison, in principle only pinpointed facts can be derived from scientific evidence (. . .). Accordingly one should first of all be aware that scientific evidence has its limits when it comes to what it by itself (shows) in relation to the facts that need to be proven" (LRTI, 2013: 8). Rather than an objective alternative for unreliable human cognition and statements, scientific evidence is here thus depicted as capable of showing nothing more than single facts that only acquire its value in the context of the stories told by other evidence.

Nevertheless, despite its general authority as the golden standard in forensic science, there are studies that have pointed out that DNA evidence is in fact "not insusceptible to error, subjectivity, bias and controversy" (Keijser et al., 2016: 71; Damon-Moore, 2017: 1539). To give just a few examples: Keijser et al. asked experienced DNA experts from different forensic research institutions in different jurisdictions to evaluate an identical forensic case with mixed profiles, the type of profiles that DNA experts commonly encounter in their daily forensic work (Keijser et al., 2016: 73). Obtaining responses (reports) from 19 accredited forensic institutes located in different western countries, they found that reports on findings varied widely in form but also in terms of the content of the conclusions. While for example in one report a suspect was excluded as a contributor to a profile, another report held that it was "209 million times more likely if the victim and the suspect are contributors than if the victim and an unknown person are the contributors". (78).[20] On the basis of examples from among others, case work and analysts' own testimony, Thompson on the other hand observes how analysts "(shift) the purported criteria for a 'match' or an 'inclusion' after the profile of a suspect becomes known", thereby effectively shifting the target (2009, 257). These are just a few examples of a growing body of literature that brings into focus diverging interpretations of the same DNA profiles as well as the impact of DNA analysts' and other forensic analysts' prior beliefs about a suspect's likely guilt or innocence (cf. Dror & Hampikian, 2011; Whitman & Koppl, 2010; Moser, 2013).

Given this literature, the question is to what extent for example confirmation bias in DNA testing exists in Japan, given that such testing is predominantly being carried out by police affiliated research institutions. The problem is that we do not know, and that it is very difficult to check. When it comes to the interpretation of complex DNA profiles judges may have little choice but to go along with the police DNA expert. In fact, that is what the authoritative LRTI report advises them to do, in addition to "cautiously evaluating" the significance of the information presented to them (LRTI, 2013: 118, 123).

## 3. Lay judges, scientists and DNA evidence

As also noted earlier, the most serious cases are as of May 2009 tried before a panel of both lay and professional judges. The previous sections have addressed the question of how professional judges have been making sense of scientific evidence in general, and DNA evidence in particular, and how the scientists producing such evidence are institutionally affiliated with investigative authorities. The question then is: how do lay judges make sense of DNA evidence? How do they assess its reliability? This section addressed these questions on the basis of the records of meetings organized by district courts all over Japan, in which especially

20 Significantly, Keijser et al. further found that the very different reporting styles also translated into very different understandings of the meaning of the report findings among jurists who were asked to interpret the reports (2016: 80).

lay but also professional judges exchanged opinions about their experiences – see the introductory chapter for more details on these meetings.[21]

Recurring in all meetings was the question of whether the lay judges had been able to understand everything that was said in their trial with regard to DNA and other forensic evidence, for that matter,[22] including also the testimony provided by scientists in court. The reason for this recurrence is easily explained, as in all meetings the lay judges were asked if they had understood, by a judge who was informed about the specifics of each trial in which the lay judges had participated. The question of understanding was not specific to the issue of forensic evidence, but was one that actually recurred, as a more or less standard question, in all 468 meeting records – not just the 18 meeting records on which this section is based.[23]

The records show that most lay judges did find the information presented on DNA related issues hard to follow, not in the least because of the details and amount of "specialist information". The following remark from a lay judge is illustrative this regard:

> When it came to investigating the evidence, and if the DNA matched or if it didn't match and all, there were too many specialist things [senmonteki na koto]. I did understand that that's how they do it, but the part about the DNA test evaluation was very hard to understand. It was way too detailed for me to understand. (. . .) I'm sorry but it was like I was attending a lecture

21 The meeting records (363 on 31 December 2017) were searched using the following search terms: DNA (32 hits – used in 32 meetings), *kagakushōko* (scientific evidence) (0 hits); *kagaku* (science) (46 hits); (*kasōken*, commonly used abbreviation standing for prefectural [police] research institution) (13 hits); *kakeiken* (commonly used abbreviation standing for National Research Institute of Police Science) (1 hit). In a total of 18 meetings the subjects of DNA evidence and/or subjects related to *kakeiken/kasōken*, such as the testimony of a *kakeiken* expert, were actually discussed among the lay and professional judges. In the remaining meetings the terms were used only in passing by the judge leading the meeting or by a lay judge. The aim of these searches was to look for any references to understandings of DNA evidence and the role of scientists in presenting such evidence, keeping in mind that forensic investigation and DNA testing in particular is in Japan predominantly done by scientists affiliated with either a prefectural research institution or the National Research Institute of Police Science. The 18 meeting records in which such references were found were examined for commonalities and recurring themes. Of course, given the small number, the question is very much to what extent findings from these 18 meetings reflect a more general picture. Nevertheless, these meetings do give a snapshot impression of how especially lay judges approach the DNA evidence presented to them in the course of the trial in which they participated. The lay judge meeting records (2013–2017) are available at: www.saibanin.courts.go.jp/ikenkoukan/index.html. Website last visited 31-8-2018.

22 The term "forensic evidence" was actually not used. Lay and professional judges instead referred to "expert opinion" (*kantei*) or used other phrasings that typically had a connotation of "specialism".

23 And so this question is indicative of a more general preoccupation with lay judges' ability to understand the issues and terminology used. I will come back to this issue in the following chapter.

> I didn't want to attend, like in the past. And so I think it would be good if they took out only the necessary bits, and only showed us: this is the idea. (Saitama District Court, 22 August 2012)

In commenting on the difficulty of understanding what was said, lay judges also referred to the terminology and phrasing used – professional judges typically also raised this issue – much like in the following quote:

> LAY JUDGE: *In the expert's report there was talk of fragments of human tissue and DNA and so on, and that was hard to understand.*
>
> PROFESSIONAL JUDGE: *Following up, did you understand the fact itself that the DNA taken from the victim's glove was not in contradiction with the DNA of the defendant?*
>
> LAY JUDGE: *That it was not in contradiction with the DNA of the defendant, that way of saying that it is*, in other words, the DNA of the defendant, *because of that sort of thing it was hard to understand. But in the end the judge explained it to me, so I understood.* (Gifu District Court 7 October 2015, my emphasis)

Given the way in which this lay judge phrased his remark, the question remains if during trial he indeed understood the issue at hand, after the judge's explanation. While a recurring theme was accordingly that of the difficulty lay judges had in understanding the information presented to them, the concrete nature of physical evidence nevertheless had a certain appeal:

> LAY JUDGE: *This method of investigation, using what is there, blood stains on clothing and so on, that was easy to understand. That method of what do you call it, physical evidence. Personally, I felt that for a lay person like me, expanding on that type of thing makes for an easy to understand hearing.*
>
> PROFESSIONAL JUDGE: *Wasn't it the case that that was on the contrary too specialist, or that the special terms were difficult, or something like that?*
>
> LAY JUDGE: *No, that* was *an issue, but there were after all things with different kinds of machines – it was so difficult that I don't remember well.* (Tottori District Court 25 May 2012)

All in all, lay judges indicated that they found the information presented hard or impossible to fully understand, questioning the need for detailed explanations and the complicated ways of saying things. Concrete, physical evidence nevertheless had a certain appeal. The meeting records also indicate that judges as well as prosecutors provided additional explanations that they were able to understand.[24] Nevertheless, comprehension of the information provided was an issue, as the

24 Lay judges were in addition given access to a video presentation, provided by the court, on DNA evidence.

quotes also illustrate. One question that presents itself is that of how the lay judges went about deciding what and whom to believe.

One factor relevant in this regard was the conviction and outspokenness with which experts presented their expert opinion. While the example provided here actually concerns fingerprinting, it does provide an insight into matters that may affect the impact of "expert testimony":

LAY JUDGE: *What stuck with me was when an expert on fingerprinting from the prefectural scientific research institution, stated, and I don't know if it was because it was so very much a lay person's [*shirōto*] statement: 'I'm 99% sure'. That was something that became a topic of conversation for us [lay judges] – that a craftsman* [shokunin] *has been working like that [so as to be able to speak out so categorically].* (. . .)

PROFESSIONAL JUDGE: *I see. The fact that a specialist is saying something with that amount of accuracy, that carried much weight when it came to forming a judgment.*

LAY JUDGE: *Yes.*

The testimony of this expert witness accordingly carried much weight exactly because he was so uncharacteristically sure of his case. The typical specialist was perceived to not be outspoken, but so nuanced as to render it difficult what to make of the testimony provided, in line with this professional judge's description:

PROFESSIONAL JUDGE: *The expert was saying: "It is thought that"* (. . .). *With experts it is after all not something like black or white, but there is considerable nuance, and in conveying that sort of thing accurately they do not necessarily speak out clearly.*

LAY JUDGE: *Indeed.* (Tokyo District Court 14 January 2014).

While in court all science may be merely opinion (cf. Luhmann, 1991: 1430), the strength with which that opinion is expressed may determine its weight in the process of judging facts. Still, that does not mean that the nuanced specialist is not believed. The fact that something is written or stated by specialists turns it into something the non-specialist can only accept for what it is:

> If the result comes out: "it's the same person", or "it's not the same person", and there is an explanation to back that up, then from the perspective of a lay person, you just accept the content of what is written as it is, when it says "this is this" and "that is that" and "that is that". The point is that there is no room for you to doubt, or how shall I put it, because you're a person with no knowledge, if it is written then that's how it is. It is not about whether it is easy to understand or difficult to understand, because it is what it is, and you cannot do anything but simply accept that.
>
> (Oita District Court 27 April 2012)

The veracity of the information provided by a specialist can only be questioned by another, even if the lay judge him or herself is not fully convinced:

> The specialist [here: sensei][25] said with full confidence that there was no mistake, but I wasn't sure how we could assess that. If you knew that [the conclusion] doesn't really change even if you bring in another specialist (. . .) and they told you that beforehand, it would have been easier to become fully convinced.
>
> (Tokyo District Court 3 December 2013)

Lay judges' status of non-specialist thus prevented them from independently engaging with the information and professional opinion provided by the expert. At the same time, the specialist's status as a person with specialist knowledge forced upon the lay judges a shortcut for the evaluation of the value of the information provided (cf. Sanders, 2002: 909).[26]

The picture that emerges from the meeting records examined is accordingly one of lay judges who struggle to understand the information provided to them by the "specialists", but who also feel that there is little to do for them other than accepting the specialists' findings or opinion. These meeting records do not show how lay and professional judges subsequently arrive at a combined, "substantive" evaluation of all the evidence presented. This section does however bring into focus a contrast between lay and professional judges. While earlier sections did show that professional judges too may feel that they cannot but rely on forensic scientists' judgment, they also highlighted how these professional judges' feel free to personally evaluate the probative value of all evidence presented to them. Scientific evidence too is subjected to judges' more general, common sense based overall judgment. By contrast, nowhere do the quotes from lay judges presented in this section suggest that these lay judges feel free to form their own convictions with regard to evidence presented by specialists. Instead they simply accept what is presented to them, aiming to understand, under the guidance of professional judges who can enlighten them on "the correct understanding".

## 4. The impact of scientific evidence

One issue that has remained untouched in the previous sections is that of whether the increasing importance of scientific evidence is changing the character of Japanese criminal justice proceedings, in the sense that it would allow for

---

25 The word *sensei* can be generally translated as teacher; master; instructor. The word in any case has the connation of expertise.

26 Here it is important to remember (cf. Chapter 2) that when it came to judgments of whether a defendant was "normal" or rather "mentally disturbed" and accordingly fully or rather diminished or not criminally responsible, lay judges did feel free to draw their own conclusions, illustrating again the extent to which forensic psychiatric conclusions are amenable to common sense, daily life experience based re-evaluations.

less reliance on statements, and in particular confessions of guilt. While the LRTI document highlights the objectivity of scientific evidence in comparison with such statements, it does not encourage its readers, Japan's legal professionals, notably judges, to place more emphasis on scientific evidence. While it highlights the reliability of certain forms of scientific evidence, notably DNA evidence, it at the same time warns against placing too much faith in scientific evidence (cf. note 19).

When it comes to what actually happens in Japan's criminal justice courts, there are no clear indications of change. Legal scholar Makoto Ibusuki states in this regard: "In the overwhelming majority of the cases *the* job for the police is the compiling of statements. And so I do not feel that the reliance on confession statements has changed. When it comes to cases that the Prosecutors' Offices investigate by themselves, the reliance on statements (also) has not changed, as many of these concern finance-related cases for which scientific evidence is not very relevant" (Ibusuki, 2017).[27] Criminal justice statistics are also in line Ibusuki's observations, given that 91.5% of the defendants tried before the District Court in 2016 made a full confession.[28] This percentage does of course not by itself show that the Courts continue to rely on confession statements. It does however show that the cases that public prosecutors bring to court are, as ever, cases of confessing defendants. As such, the percentage is indicative of the continued (perceived) importance of confessions for securing a conviction. Whether scientific evidence will indeed contribute to less reliance on confession statements accordingly still remains to be seen. Important to keep in mind here is that the importance attached to confessions of guilt in court relates to more than their evidentiary value. Regardless of their impact on sentencing, confessions of guilt accompanied by expressions of remorse remain part and parcel or court rituals that are by and large, for practical purposes, about establishing the right punishment for guilty defendants. It is doubtful if the increased importance of scientific evidence will change what criminal trials are and have for such a long time been about.[29]

---

27 Personal correspondence with the author.

28 Here, a full confession of guilt is defined as "admitting all allegations at the final (trial) stage, while not claiming the existence of grounds hindering the legal establishment of the crime, or grounds for an exemption of punishment." (Supreme Court of Japan, 2017: 81).

29 Any evidence, including DNA evidence, can of course also be incorporated in such criminal justice rituals, as illustrated by the following remark from a lay judge who had participated in a rape case in which the only evidence against the defendant was one piece of DNA evidence (the meeting records do not specify the kind of DNA evidence): "If it hadn't been one piece of DNA evidence but on top of that some other one or two things (pieces of evidence) had come out, I have the feeling that he wouldn't have disputed his guilt. And if he hadn't disputed his guilt but he himself had admitted his own guilt, and would from now on be dealing with that, his life would become quite different compared to being made to carry that guilt without admitting the crime. I wanted for the police to have tried a little harder (. . .) getting out of prison having admitted one's guilt, there's also a difference in terms of remorse." (Niigata District Court, 5 March 2014). Given the assumption of guilt, it is also

## Conclusion

If there is anything that stands out in this chapter, it is the confidence in judges' ability to evaluate scientific evidence, even though in criminal trials it is not necessarily clear what the words "scientific evidence" (***kagakutekishōko***) and by extension scientific expertise stand for. In practice this question is deemed not all that relevant, in light of judges' prerogative to substantively evaluate the probative value of the evidence presented to. Remarkably, the fact that judges in practice may have no choice but to rely on outsiders' expertise and the fact that judges have demonstrably been unable to detect mistakes made by these outsiders does not affect their perceived ability to freely form their convictions, and correctly evaluate the evidence. Judges' conclusions, given that they are based on a careful evaluation of the information available at the time, here assume an air of both unavoidability and unassailability.

As confident as the professional judges are to substantially evaluate scientists' findings, as subservient to these findings the lay judges present themselves. While with regard to professional judges all science indeed seems to be merely opinion, for lay judges there is little more to do than to accept that opinion as it is. There is a tension between on one hand professional judges who feel free to subject scientific evidence to their common sense based judgment, and on the other hand lay judges who cannot but accept specialists' judgment for what it is. How this tension is in practice resolved is however something that the meeting records unfortunately did not show. Given professional judges' advisory role on the correct understanding of scientific evidence as well as their status of legal specialist on the other – keeping in mind the respect that the lay judges accorded to specialist opinion – the question is what in the end remains of lay judges' own perspectives and opinions in legal judgment. Chapter 2 already showed that even when lay judges do feel free to engage with experts' opinion, they still find themselves to have little choice but to submit to the authority of forensic psychiatrists, judges, legal principles and jurisprudence. Given the sense of being out of one's depth, so apparent in the meeting records, any impact of lay judges' average citizen perspective on the process of legal judgment in relation to scientific evidence remains doubtful.

The LRTI document illustrates a sociology of knowledge-like awareness of how legal findings are conditioned by the agreed upon scientific criteria valid at one particular point in time. They are of course further conditioned by the frameworks or reigning legal principles and jurisprudence. Or so it would seem, in a country of career judges who all undergo the same training. After all, another thing that stands out from the earlier sections besides judges' confidence in their own ability to substantively judge the probative value of all

assumed to be in the best interest of the defendant to admit guilt and express remorse, while there is also an expectation that the presence of enough evidence will normally result in such an admission of guilt.

evidence is just how much in practice is unclear within the practice of legal judgment. Most importantly: the words "scientific evidence" stand for very different things in different judgments, while judges do not necessarily abide by "reigning principles" that should guide them in distinguishing reliable from unreliable scientific evidence. Judges cannot but rely on or defer to expert opinion while finding themselves free to incorporate that opinion in an overall common sense based judgment that is to variable degrees shaped by legal guidelines.

Legal judgment here reveals the hybrid nature of the knowledge that lies at its foundation. How the different elements of scientific knowledge, legal knowledge and guidelines and common sense based judgment in the end combine to inform judges' conclusions is something that remains obscured by the blanket of "substantive judgment". While for lay judges science is not "mere opinion" – it is an opinion they cannot but accept as it is – professional judges' stance does not allow for such clear-cut answers. Here, neither Luhmann's "mere opinion" perspective nor Foucault's "science redefines legal judgment" perspective do justice to the actual practice of legal judgment.

Despite the lack of uniformity with regard to how judges go about evaluating scientific evidence – except for the fact that everything is evaluated on the basis of a substantive judgment – judges' conclusions are presented as the unavoidable outcome of a careful evaluation of the available information. Nevertheless, the forensic evidence, and especially the DNA evidence on which judges' unavoidable conclusions are based, is analyzed almost exclusively by scientists working at police affiliated research institutions. Their findings are in turn incorporated in the parties' arguments, even if they generally stand in service of the more powerful of the two, the prosecution.

Literature from international contexts highlights the possibility of scientists' unacknowledged biased interpretations of the results of especially mixed profile DNA tests as well as diverging interpretations of the same results. Given what is known about DNA interpretation practices from the context of testing conducted by accredited research institutions, it is difficult to imagine that bias and the multi-interpretability of DNA results are not also issues in the context of forensic DNA testing in Japan. In light of such issues the availability of a third party, one that is not institutionally embedded in Japan's biggest crime fighting organization, might allow for more transparent and verifiable DNA fact finding.

As yet, the increased use of scientific evidence, notably DNA testing in Japanese criminal justice, does not appear to have resulted in less reliance on statements and confessions just yet. It is doubtful, however, if the increased importance of scientific evidence will change the criminal justice script that dictates that prosecutors only indict the guilty, and that lawyers plead extenuating circumstances on behalf of a suitably remorseful and therefore confessing defendant, for the sake of a lenient punishment. To these subjects we will however return in the following chapter.

## References

Asahi Shimbun (2010). Kagaku shōko, saibansho mo kenkyū: ashiri jiken no DNA kantei. *kyōkun*, 24 April.

Bandes, S. (2006). Loyalty to one's convictions: the prosecutor and tunnel vision. *Howard Law Journal* 49: 475–497.

Bernstein, David E. (2001). Frye, Frye, again: the past, present, and future of the general acceptance test. *Jurimetrics*: 385–407.

Damon-Moore, Stephanie L. (2017). Trial judges and the forensic science problem. *New York University Law Review* 92: 1532–1570.

Dreyfus, Hubert L. and Paul Rabinow (1983). *Michel Foucault: beyond structuralism and hermeneutics*. Chicago: University of Chicago Press.

Dror, Itiel E. and Greg Hampikian (2011). Subjectivity and bias in forensic DNA mixture interpretation. *Science & Justice* 51(4): 204–208.

Ewick, Patricia and Susan S. Silbey (1995). Subversive stories and hegemonic tales: toward a sociology of narrative. *Law and Society Review*: 197–226.

Foote, Daniel H. (1991). Confessions and the right to silence in Japan. *Georgia Journal of International & Comparative Law* 21: 415–488.

Foote, Daniel H. (1992). From Japan's death row to freedom. *Pacific Rim Law & Policy Journal* 1: 11–103.

Foucault, M. (1978). *Discipline and punish*, trans. Alan Sheridan. New York: Vintage.

Harada, Kunio (2012). *Gyakuten muzai no jijitsunintei*. Tokyo: Keisōshobō.

Hiraoka, Yoshihiro (2014). *Hōritsuka no tame no kagakusōsa gaido*. Tokyo: Hōritsubunkasha.

Honjō, Atsushi (2017). Keiji tetsuzuki ni okeru kagaku kantei no genjō to kadai: kanteinin no chiiron wo chūshin ni. *Hitotsubashi Hōgaku* 16(1): 1–21.

Ibusuki, Makoto (2017). Personal correspondence with Makoto Ibusuki, between 1-9-2017 en 4-10-2017.

Ito, Kazuko (2012). Wrongful convictions and recent criminal justice reform in Japan. *University of Cincinatti Law Review* 80: 1245–1275.

Japan Federation of Bar Associations (JFBA) (2011). *Ashiri jiken kensahōkokusho*. Available at: www.nichibenren.or.jp/library/ja/opinion/report/data/110506_2.pdf. Website last visited 30 August 2018.

Japan Federation of Bar Associations (JFBA) (2016). *Keijisoshōhōtō ga kaisei saremashita*. Available at: www.nichibenren.or.jp/library/ja/publication/booklet/data/keijisoshohoto_kaisei_01.pdf. Website last visited 30 August 2018.

Japan Innocence & Death Penalty Information Center (2018). *Kuma Michitoshi*. Available at: www.jiadep.org/Kuma_Michitoshi.html. Website last visited 30 August 2018.

Jasanoff, Sheila (1995). *Science at the bar*. Cambridge: Harvard.

Jasanoff, Sheila (2006). Just evidence: the limits of science in the legal process. *The Journal of Law, Medicine & Ethics*, 34(2): 328–341.

Johnson, Chalmers (1972). *Conspiracy at Matsukawa*. Berkeley: University of California Press.

Johnson, David T. (2012). Japan's prosecution system. *Crime and Justice* 41(1): 35–74.

Johnson, David T. (2015). Wrongful convictions and the culture of denial in Japanese criminal justice. *Asia-Pacific Journal* 13(6): 1–10.

Keijser, Jan W. de, Marijke Malsch, Egge T. Luining, Marleen Weulen Kranenbarg and Dominique J.H.M. Lenssen (2016). Differential reporting of mixed DNA profiles and its impact on jurists' evaluation of evidence. An international analysis. *Forensic Science International: Genetics* 23: 71–82.

Kobayashi, Osamu (2012). Kagakuteki shōko wo meguru Q&A. *Keijibengo* 71: 75–78.

Kingston, Jeff (2011). Justice on trial: Japanese prosecutors under fire. *Asia-Pacific Journal* 9(10).

Legal Research and Training Institute (LRTI) (2013). *Kagakuteki shōko to sore wo mochiita saiban no arikata*. Tokyo: Hōsōkai.

Luhmann, Niklas (1991). Operational closure and structural coupling: the differentiation of the legal system. *Cardozo Law Review* 13: 1419–1441.

Mercer, David (2002). The intersection of Sociology of Scientific Knowledge (SSK) and law: some themes and policy reflections. *Law Text Culture* 6: 137–147.

Minaguchi, Kiyoshi (2017). Hōigakukyōshitsu ni okeru DNA kantei no genjō: muzukashii DNA kanteirei wo kenkyū dekiru kankyō ga hitsuyō. *Japan Medical Journal* 4839: 55.

Ministry of Justice (MOJ) (annual). *White paper on crime*. Available at: http://hakusyo1.moj.go.jp/en/nendo_nfm.html. Website last visited 30 August 2018.

Mitsui, Makoto (2004). *Keijitetsuzukihō* 3. Tokyo: Yūhikaku.

Miyazawa, Setsuo (2002). Introduction: an unbalanced adversary system – issues, policies, and practices in Japan, in context and in comparative perspective, in Malcolm M. Feeley and Setsuo Miyazawa (eds.), *The Japanese adversary system in context: controversies and comparisons*. Houndmills: Palgrave Macmillan: 1–11.

Miyazawa, Setsuo and M. Hirayama (2017). Introduction of videotaping of interrogations and the lessons of the Imaichi case: a case of conventional criminal justice policy-making in Japan. *Pacific Rim Law & Policy Journal* 27: 149–176.

Moser, Scott (2013). Confirmation bias: the pitfall of forensic science. *Themis: Research Journal of Justice Studies and Forensic Science* 1(1): 71–81.

National Police Agency (NPA) (annual). *White paper on police*. Available at: www.npa.go.jp/publications/whitepaper/index_keisatsu.html. Website last visited 31 August 2018.

National Police Agency (NPA) (2010). *Ashiri jiken ni okeru keisatsu sōsa no mondaitentō ni tsuite*. Available at: www.npa.go.jp/bureau/criminal/sousa/torishirabe/houkokushogaiyou.pdf. Website last visited 30 August 2018.

Okada, Kaoru (2006). DNA gata kantei ni yoru kojinshokubetsu no rekishi, genjō, kadai. *Reference* 56(1): 7–31.

Ramseyer, Mark J. and Eric B. Rasmusen (2001). Why is the Japanese conviction rate so high? *The Journal of Legal Studies* 30(1): 53–88.

Sanders, Joseph (2002). The merits of the paternalistic justification for restrictions on the admissibility of expert evidence. *Seton Hall Law Review* 33: 881–941.

Sasamori, Manabu (2010). Ashiri jiken saibanin bengo no ayumi: Ashiri jiken no kyōkun kara manabu. *Keiji Bengo* (63): 90–95.

Satō, Hiroshi (2010). "Ashiri jiken no kenshō" no gendankai: muzaihanketsu, keisatsu, kensatsu hōkokusho ni yoru kenshō wa dokomade susundaka; Ashiri jiken no kyōkun kara manabu. *Keiji Bengo* (63): 80–89.

Satō, Hiroshi (2013). Ashiri jiken kara mita kagakuteki shōko ni kansuru shihōkenkyū (kagakuteki shōko to keijisaiban: shihōkenshūsho hen "kagakuteki shōko to kore wo mochiita saiban no arikata" no kentō). *Keiji Bengo* (76): 101–108.

Science Portal (2016). *Shinpo mezamashii DNA gata kantei hanzai sōsa de iryoku no ippō mondai mo "dai 2 kai" saikantei no hoshō jitsugen ni kokumin no kanshi mo*. Interview with Shigemi Oshida 19 February 2016. Available at: http://

scienceportal.jst.go.jp/columns/interview/20160219_01.html. Website last visited 30 August 2018.

Shinomiya, Satoru (2002). Adversarial procedure without a Jury: is Japan's system adversarial, inquisitorial, or something else?, in Malcolm M. Feeley and Setsuo Miyazawa (eds.), *The Japanese adversary system in context: controversies and comparisons*. Palgrave Macmillan: 114–127.

Supreme Prosecutors' Office (2010). *Iwaruru Ashiri jiken ni okeru sōsa, kōhan katsudō no mondaiten tō ni tsuite*. Available at: www.kensatsu.go.jp/content/001148804.pdf. Website last visited 30 August 2018.

Supreme Public Prosecutors Office (2011). *The principles of prosecution*. Available at: www.kensatsu.go.jp/content/000128760.pdf. Website last visited 30 August 2018.

Thompson, William C. (2009). Painting the target around the matching profile: the Texas sharpshooter fallacy in forensic DNA interpretation. *Law, Probability & Risk*, 8(3): 257–276.

Tokunaga, Hikaru (2013). Shihō kenkyū no igi to genkai: kagakuteki shōko he no shinraisei to kyoyōsei no kanten kara (kagakuteki shōko to keijisaiban: shihōkenshūsho hen "kagakuteki shōko to kore wo mochiita saiban no arikata" no kentō). *Keiji Bengo* (76): 84–89.

Tsujiwaki, Yōko (2010). Kagakuteki shōko no kanrensei to shinraisei. *Hōkadaigakuinronshū* 7: 413–443.

Valverde, Mariana (2009). *Law's dream of a common knowledge*. Princeton: Princeton University Press.

Van Krieken, Robert (2004). *Legal reasoning as a field of knowledge production: Luhmann, Bourdieu and law's autonomy*. Available at: https://ses.library.usyd.edu.au/bitstream/2123/967/1/legal%20reasoning.pdf. Website last visited 30 August 2018.

Wada, Toshinori (2011). Idenjōhō/DNA kantei to keijihō. *Keiō hōgaku* 18: 79–136.

Weber, I. (2009). The new Japanese jury system: empowering the public, preservation continental justice. *East Asia Law Review* 4: 125–176.

Whitman, Glen and Roger Koppl (2010). Rational bias in forensic science. *Law, Probability & Risk* 9(1): 69–90.

Yazawa, Shōji (ed.) (2014). *Saishin to kagakukantei*. Tokyo: Nihon Hyōronsha.

## *Japanese legal judgments:*

Supreme Court Second Petty Bench, Shōwa 40 (a) 238. Verdict of 21.2.1966.

## *US legal judgments:*

*Daubert v. Merrell Dow Pharmaceuticals, Inc*, 509 U.S. 579, 1993.

*Frye v. United States* 293 F. 1013 (D.C. Cir 1923).

# 6 Lay judges and sentencing

## Introduction

The previous four chapters each focused on a non-legal professional with a designated role in Japanese criminal justice. By addressing their roles and contributions each chapter also brought into focus how the other criminal justice players interact with these "legal outsiders" and how they incorporate outsiders' contributions into their arguments and decisions.

This final chapter focuses on another species of non-legal professionals, namely that of lay judges. Of course, the previous chapters have already touched upon lay judges' role, in specific connection with the criminal justice roles of forensic psychiatrists, participating victims of crime and scientific experts. This final chapter zooms in on what for practical purposes can be considered one of the most important aspect of lay judges' functioning, namely their role in sentencing.

As noted in Chapter 1, important aims of the lay judge system were to provide criminal justice with a "popular basis" and to infuse criminal justice processes with "society's sound common sense" (JSRC, 2001). Sentencing would seem to present an ideal opportunity for participating lay judges to speak out and to have a democratic say in defendants' sentence. Zooming in on how lay judges make use of the discretionary authority that their assigned role grants them to determine the right sentence is important not only to see what in practice becomes of the reform aims. It is also fruitful in light of the populist elements that, as discussed in Chapter 1, have had a strong impact on criminal justice policy making.

Chapter 1 has highlighted how perceptions and media misrepresentations of rising crime rates, victim interest group lobbying and politicians aiming to meet the perceived demands of the electorate ultimately translated into legal reforms allowing for harsher punishment, notably the 2004 amendments that specified longer prison sentences for different categories of offenders, reforms that affected 104 different offenses As the lay judge system was implemented on 21 May 2009, lay judges have now for a number of years had the opportunity to make use of the possibilities for harsh sentences that the 2004 reforms have allowed for. To what extent have they indeed done so? Do sentencing practices vindicate the politicians who in the people's name pushed for sentencing reforms?

These are the first questions that this chapter will address. It however not only examines the sentencing output of lay judge trials; it also, secondly, looks into *how* lay judges together with their professional colleagues arrived at their decision, on what considerations their decisions were based, how lay judges positioned themselves vis-à-vis the professional judges and vice versa, and finally, how they felt about participating in these judgment processes. In doing so this chapter not only addresses the reform related questions outlined in the previous paragraph, it also brings into focus some of the effects and implications of lay participation for the functioning of Japanese criminal justice in more general terms.

The questions outlined in the previous paragraphs are specifically linked to Japanese criminal justice practice and context. An examination of sentencing practices in Japanese lay judge trials however also speaks to a third, more general topic, namely that of the exercise of discretionary authority. Being included in processes of sentencing also means being asked to exercise discretionary authority. "Discretionary authority" (*sairyōken*) is here understood to refer to the authority that (lay) judges formally have to make a decision that is appropriate in a given case for a given defendant, within the room that Japanese law provides. Formally speaking, that room is considerable, especially when it comes to the category of serious offenses tried in lay judge trials. To give an example: according to Criminal Code Article 199 murder is punishable by a prison sentence no less than five years, an indeterminate prison sentence or the death penalty. Depending on the circumstances, however, the sentence may be reduced to fewer than five years, and in case it is reduced to fewer than three years, suspended. For persons charged with murder, in other words, the sentencing possibilities range from a suspended sentence to the death penalty.

As the Japanese Criminal Code does not stipulate any formal sentencing criteria, judges have referred to the guidelines formulated in the *draft* of the revised Code of Criminal Procedure. Article 48 of this Code states that punishment should contribute to the prevention of crime and the offender's rehabilitation, and that the punishment imposed should correspond to the defendant's culpability, giving due consideration to the offender's age, character and circumstances (etc.). However, article 248 of the Code of Criminal Procedure, which contains criteria for the suspension of *prosecution*, also forms an important formal legal point of reference (Endō, 2011: 53–54; cf. also Chapters 1 and 3). In sentencing, (lay) judges are in addition required to take into account legal precedent as well as "going rates" (Harada, 2011: 114–124; 2004: 1–26; Oka, 2012: 3–5). Nevertheless, little is known about how in lay judge trials sentencing decisions are in practice made. By examining how lay and professional judges together arrive at a sentencing decision, this chapter will also do just that – that is: studying what happens in practice, when lay and professional judges are called upon to exercise their discretionary authority.

## 1. The lay judge system and sentencing trends

Before getting into the topic of sentencing trends it is fruitful to first refresh our memory on the lay judge system itself. The introduction of this new system was part of juridical reforms that ranged from an overhaul of the legal education system to measures facilitating access to the courts and legal expertise. With specific regard to criminal justice, the Justice System Reform Council (JSRC) that issued the recommendations for reform noted that the people had to grow out of their "excessive dependency" on the national government and their mindset of "governed objects", and that they had to bring about "public awareness in themselves" (2001). The JSRC decided that one way to help accomplish this aim was to introduce lay participation in criminal justice.

In doing so the JSRC thus also introduced what had before been discussed as a way to change the character of Japanese criminal justice. Hirano famously diagnosed Japanese criminal justice as diseased and hopeless, in view of among other things the requirement of a high level of suspicion for indictment, as a consequence of which the "real substance" of Japanese criminal procedure had come to lie in the pre-trial stage of this procedure, that could be characterized as an inquisitorial process performed by prosecutors and police (Hirano, 1989: 131; cf. generally Chapter 1). In Hirano's and other reform minded scholars' and practitioners' view, reinstating a jury system could help "cure" Japanese criminal justice.

The cure that was introduced in May 2009 came however in a watered down form. The new system introduced in 2009 was after all a mixed lay participation system in which lay judges and professional ones together decide on a defendant's guilt or innocence, and the sentence a guilty defendant should receive. To be more precise: six lay judges randomly selected among those eligible to vote and three professional judges together make these decisions on guilt and sentencing.[1] The Act on Criminal Trials in which Lay Judges Participate (No. 63, 18 May 2004) art. 67 furthermore specifies that in order to reach a decision a majority consisting of both lay *and* professional judges needs to agree. What is more: only a limited range of the most serious offenses is tried in this way. Accordingly, as significant as the introduction of this system is, in quantitative terms its impact remains limited, as only about 2.5–3% of the cases are tried under this system.[2] These 2.5–3% do however represent the most serious cases. Death sentences, for example, are now exclusively handed down in lay judge trials.

### *1.1. Overall sentencing trends*

Before examining sentencing trends in specifically in lay judge trials, now, it is fruitful to have a look at sentencing trends in more general terms. Doing so will

1 In simple, uncontested cases panels may also consist of four lay judges and one professional judge.

2 There are two categories of offenses:

a offenses for which by law the (possible) punishment includes the death penalty and imprisonment with or without hard labor for an indefinite period (e.g. murder, robbery causing death, robbery causing injury, rape causing death, arson of an inhabited building, etc.).

b among the offenses that require a trial by a panel of three judges, those offenses where the victim was caused to die because of an intentional criminal act (e.g. murder, robbery causing death, injury causing death, dangerous driving causing death, etc.). See Supreme Court of Japan (2009a).

allow us to what extent trends in lay judge sentencing are in line with more general sentencing trends. These general trends furthermore allow us to examine the extent to which professional judges have made use of the opportunities to impose harsher sentences that the 2004 reforms allowed for. Graph 6.1 shows these overall sentencing trends for Criminal Code offenses tried in District Courts.

Looking at the sentences that have been meted out over the past 30 years in District Courts, the courts of first instance, it becomes clear that the 2004 amendments have had very little impact on overall sentencing trends. Important to note, first of all, is that these had already started to shift from the early 1990s on. From 2004 to 2007, judges did admittedly mete out slightly more sentences of the higher category of lower than 10 and higher than 5 years than they did both before and after these years, totaling 1.8% in 1991, 4.1% in 2004 and 2.5% in 2016, respectively. The biggest shift however occurred between the sentencing categories of less than 3, more than 2 years on one hand, and less than 2, more than 1 year on the other. The sentences falling within the first category almost doubled, going from 16.3% in 1991 to 33.6% in 2016, while those of the latter category dropped almost 10%, going from 53.7% to 42.2% in the same period.

Importantly, though, these statistics make no distinction between suspended and non-suspended sentences. Graph 6.2 shows that suspended sentences in the range of less than 3, more than 2 years have gone up significantly, from 7% to 18%, while the rates for the categories of less than 2, more than 1, and less than 1 year have gone down. The noted rise of the percentage of sentences in the

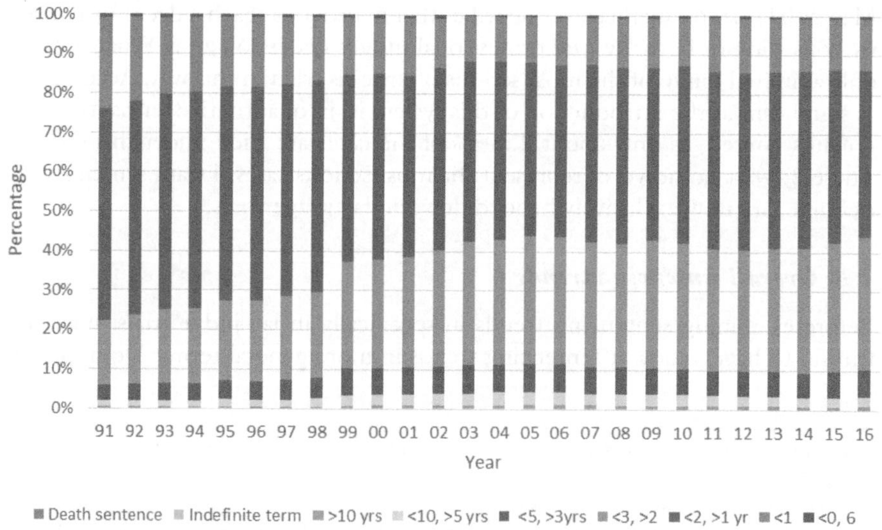


*Graph 6.1* Sentencing trends 1991–2016 Criminal Code offences (*keihōhan*) tried in District Courts

Source: This graph was generated on the basis of data from the MOJ White Papers on Crime 1992–2017.

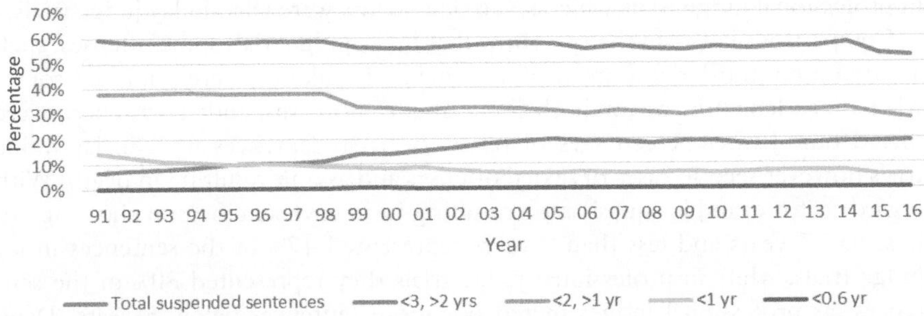


*Graph 6.2* Rates of suspended sentences 1991–2016 Criminal Code offences tried in District Courts

Source: This graph was generated on the basis of data from the MOJ White Papers on Crime 1992–2017.

range of less than 3, more than 2 years was thus largely caused by the rise of *suspended* sentences in this range. Here it is important to note that the overall rate of suspended sentences has as of 1991 been decreasing slightly, but has remained by and large stable, in "penal populist" times. All in all, Japanese sentencing practices have accordingly not shown a clear trend toward increased punitivism.

## *1.2. Sentencing in professional and in lay judge trials*

What then, about sentencing patterns in lay judge trials? The sentences meted out in lay judge are included in the overall rates shown in the previous graphs, but given that they only represent 2.5–3% of the cases, their potential to make a clearly visible dent is limited, and so it is useful to zoom in on sentencing practices in lay judge trials only, to also see if they are in line with or rather diverge from the general trends seen in especially Graph 6.1, but also how they compare with the sentences that professional judges have been handing down for the same types of offenses.[3]

Such a direct comparison has been for three years been possible, as in the stage of transition from trials with professional judges only to trials with lay and professional judges, there were case that had started and prosecutions that had been filed shortly before May 2009, when the lay judge system was introduced. These cases were processed like they would have been before the introduction of the new system, that is, through trials led by professional judges only. This has allowed for a comparison between the sentences imposed in professional judge trials and lay judge trials, between April 2009 and May 2012, and between

3 Since the cases adjudicated in lay judge trials all concern relatively serious offenses, comparing rates of suspended sentences, which are not available for prison sentences of five years and higher, comparing rates of suspended sentences is not fruitful.

May 2009 and May 2012, respectively. In this period 2,290 defendants were tried in professional judge trials while 4,316 defendants were tried in lay judge trials.

Comparisons between the two show that in lay judge trials some offenses, such as attempted murder and arson of an inhabited building, were punished somewhat more leniently, as for both for example more suspended sentences were meted out. Larger percentages of relatively harsh sentences were in lay judge trials however seen in cases of sexual offenses and assault resulting in death. With regard to for example (quasi) rape resulting in injury[4] sentences in the range of less than 7 years and less than 9 years represented 47% of the sentences in lay judge trials, while in professional judge trials they represented 30% of the sentences, as professional judges meted out more sentences below 5 years. Drug offenses were punished more or less the same, while sentences for robbery resulting in bodily injury were in lay judge trials punished both more leniently (more suspended sentences) and more severely (more relatively heavy sentences) when compared with professional judge trials.[5] The overall image, however, was one of relative continuity, when lay and professional judges together took over from professional judges (Supreme Court General Secretariat, 2012: 83–90).

Some years have passed since then, and comparing verdicts of professional judges and lay judges is no longer possible. There are however offenses that are as of 2009 almost exclusively tried in lay judge trials, such as murder and robbery resulting in injury, robbery resulting in death and robbery and rape.[6] In order to appreciate the significance of lay judge sentencing for these specific offenses in the years from 2009 on, it is fruitful to here briefly zoom in on the developments before 2009, that is: before the introduction of the lay judge system in 2009. Graph 6.3 shows that sentences for murder have for a long time been getting stricter, in the sense that for example the percentage of sentences in the more than 10 years range has been increasing, going from 13.4% in 1992 to 31.6% in 2009. The graph however also shows that this increase had already started before the advent of Japanese style penal populism in the late 1990s. From 2009 on sentences in the range of more than 10 years have gone down slightly, hovering at around 30%.

When it comes to robbery resulting in injury or death/robbery and rape, the picture shown in Graph 6.4 is similar. Here too, the percentage of sentences longer than 10 years has been increasing since the early 1990s, going from 6% in 1991 to 10% in 2001, and 12% in 2009. This up-going trend continued until 2011, when the lay judge system had been running for one and a half year. From 2011 on sentences have become slightly more lenient, similar to the trend witnessed for the offense of murder. Accordingly, as in Graph 6.3, the trend toward increased severity in sentencing started before the introduction of the lay judge system. Both graphs do however show that sentences started rising especially

4 The addition "quasi" here refers to cases in which the victim has lost consciousness or is unable to resist (cf. CC art. 178).

5 For an overview of comparative sentencing data, see the Supreme Court of Japan General Secretariat Report on the Functioning of the Lay Judge System (2012), page 84 and following.

6 These three offenses are in overall graphs, i.e. graphs not limited to lay judge offenses, represented as "robbery resulting in injury or death/robbery and rape" (*gōtōchishishō/gōtōgōkan*).

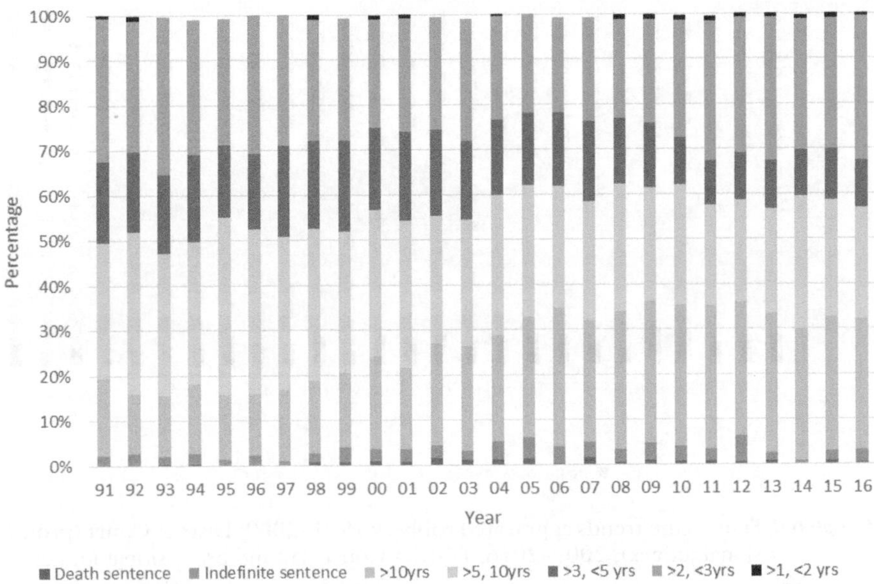


*Graph 6.3* Sentences meted out for murder 1991–2009: District Court (professional judges); 2009–2016: District Court (lay and professional judges)

Source: This graph was generated on the basis of data from the MOJ White Papers on Crime 1992–2017.

from 2001 on, allowing for the possibility that the penal populism and moral panic that started in the late 1990s did affect the sentences meted out for this offense.

Scholars talking about the developments that have taken place in the late 1990s and early 2000s – media misrepresentations of rising crime rates, victim interest group lobbying and politicians aiming to meet the perceived demands of the electorate ultimately translating into legal reforms allowing for harsher punishment – have done so in terms of penal populism or popular punitivism (Miyazawa, 2008a; 2008b; Hamai & Ellis, 2008). The term used in Japanese is that of *genbatsuka*, a term that simply refers to punishment getting increasingly harsh. These graphs show that to the extent that punishment has indeed been getting harsher *for specific offenses*, such harshness had already started before the moral panic surrounding rising crime rates of the late 1990s. These graphs furthermore show that the 2004 legal changes allowing for the imposing of harsher punishment have not translated in trend-breaking harsher sentences from 2004 on.[7] Most importantly,

7 All this does not mean that judges have not made any use of the room for harsher sentencing that the amendments allowed for. Between 2005 and 2016 sentences in the range between 15 and 30 years, that was now available to a much greater range of offenses than before, comprised 0.2% to 0.37% of all sentences meted out. Judges thus did make use of the extra room for harshness, but only in a fraction of the cases that came before them.

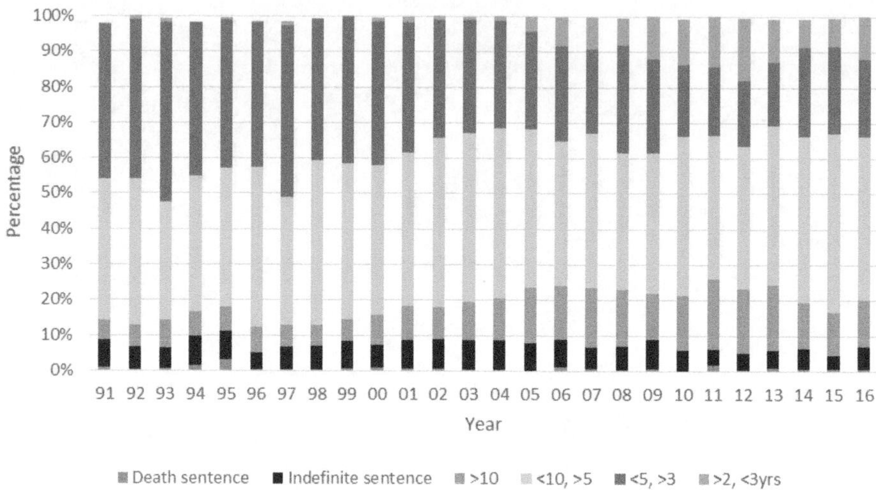


*Graph 6.4* Sentencing trends aggravated robbery 1991–2009: District Court (professional judges); 2009–2016: District Court (lay and professional judges)

Source: This graph was generated on the basis of data from the MOJ White Papers on Crime 1992–2017.

Note: This graph shows the combined percentages for three lay judge trial offenses: robbery resulting in injury (*gōtōchishō*), robbery resulting in death (*gōtōchishi*) and robbery and rape (*gōtōgōkan*). These three offenses are in overall graphs, i.e. graphs not limited to lay judge offenses, represented as "robbery resulting in injury or death/robbery and rape" (*gōtōchishishō/ gōtōgōkan*).

they show that the sentences meted out after the introduction of the lay judge system in 2009 have also been in line with existing trends.

It is important not to dismiss the differences that can be seen since 2009. After all: the Supreme Court comparisons showed that lay judges did mete out higher sentences for sexual crimes than their professional counterparts. Nevertheless, the overall picture, supported also by the more recent graphs, has been one of relative continuity. How can such continuity be explained? Here we need to turn to the question of how sentencing decisions in lay judge trials come about – how, in other words, lay and professional judges together go about making use of their discretionary authority to decide on the right sentence in each particular case.

## 2. The conceptualization of discretion

It is important to note first of all that lay and professional judges can make use of a (non-public) database of sentencing decisions, originally set up by the Supreme Court in 2008 to assist lay judges when making their decisions, although prosecutors and lawyers can also make use of the terminals connected to this database, set up at the 60 district courts and branches nationwide (Shiroshita, 2010: 246; Sugeno, 2012). Very little is known, however, about how exactly the lay judges together with their professional counterparts make use of this database, and how they go about making their sentencing decisions.[8] By focusing exactly on how lay and professional judges make their sentencing decisions this chapter accordingly sheds new light on an important yet little researched aspect of the functioning of the lay judge system.

Discretion has been predominantly conceptualized in binary opposition to law, where "more law means less discretion, and less discretion means more law" (Pratt & Sossin, 2009: 302). Dworkin's famous "hole in a doughnut" too is in line with such conceptualizations, as it evokes the image of a hole that is after all untouched by law, even if that hole is surrounded by a legal belt of restriction (Dworkin, 1977: 52). As a result, discretionary authority is easily understood as a potential source of arbitrariness and as potentially standing in the way of achieving certainty and consistency in legal decision making.[9]

Nevertheless, the limitations of such understandings of discretion are increasingly being acknowledged. It has been noted, first of all, that while decisions may be entirely discretionary in legal terms, they may nonetheless be very much patterned and predictable, raising doubts about the hole/belt of restrictions binary (cf. Baumgartner, 1992).[10] Those studying the exercise of discretion have furthermore recognized various degrees of discretion and the diversity of ways in which discretion is embedded in and overlaps with legal rules, (cf. Pratt & Sossin, 304). What is more, in contrast with Dworkinian conceptions of discretion as an undetermined space, it has been noted that it is rather the "rules" that are "inherently malleable, indeterminate and discretionary while 'discretion' is inherently patterned, ordered and rule-governed". Accordingly, within actual legal decision making practices, rules and discretion may easily become mutually indistinct, rendering the law-discretion or rules-discretion binaries neither valid nor relevant (Tata, 2007: 430).

As a consequence, however, the question of how to conceptualize discretion remains. After all: even if from the perspective of an observer of legal practices the distinction between "rules" and "discretion" is neither valid nor relevant, that obviously does not mean that the distinction is invalid or irrelevant for e.g. those

8 On the basis of talks with former lay judges Vanoverbeke, however, provides a brief account of sentencing practices, noting the emphasis placed on precedence by professional judges during the deliberations on sentencing between lay and professional judges (Vanoverbeke, 2015: 173–174).

9 The perceived risk of inconsistency does not only result from the room that "the hole" provides, but also from the possibility that discretionary decision making is not necessarily characterized by a consistent reference to agreed-upon goals. In this regard Walker, referring to the US criminal justice system, in fact goes notes that "there has never been consensus over the goals of the justice system" (Walker, 1993: 14).

10 While Baumgartner was referring to discretionary authority in administrative law, this observation is very much in line with the observations by Harada and Oka, referred to earlier, about "going rates" in the context of sentencing in Japan.

making the decisions or for those whom these decisions concern. One question that accordingly presents itself is how to understand the significance of the label "discretionary authority" – the significance, in other words, of decisions being categorized as falling under the realm of discretion. As will become clear, this question is very much relevant when trying to make sense of the ways in which (lay) judges make their sentencing decisions.

The label of "discretionary authority" in any case allows for an adjustment of sentencing practices, or in any case an adjustment of the explanations provided for such practices, in accordance with prevailing sentencing philosophies. Discretionary authority might for example allow for more emphasis to be placed on the goal of rehabilitation rather than retribution, or it could be used to refer to actuarialist risk management-type considerations, that might seem to actually diminish decision makers' discretionary authority.[11] An examination of the significance of the label "discretionary authority" furthermore brings into focus the political dimensions of discretion, as the framing of the exercise of discretion is inevitably linked to highly political considerations and discussions regarding sentencing goals. By zooming in on how (lay) judges exercise their discretionary authority in sentencing, the next section will address both what such discretionary authority in practice entails within the context of Japanese lay judge trials, and how the significance of the label of "discretionary authority" as applied to (lay) judge sentencing practices can be understood.

## *2.1. Professional and lay judges and the use of discretion*

This section is based on transcripts of 50 of 363 meetings organized by the Japanese Ministry of Justice, in which six to eight lay judges answered questions and were generally invited to offer their opinions on their experiences. The meetings typically lasted around 2.5 hours and were led by a judge familiar with the cases in which the lay judges had participated.[12] Use was in addition made of surveys that

11 Actuarialist sentencing philosophies are in fact often linked with limitations on discretion, as practitioners' decision making is perceived to be supplanted with structured decision-making templates informed by actuarial risk technologies. See (2009), and references provided there. Based on interviews with Canadian correctional workers Hannah-Moffat, Maurutto & Turnbull note, however, that "risk tools are not simply imposed on criminal justice practitioners; instead, practitioners actively resist and embrace risk technologies and temper the impact risk tools have on their discretionary decision making" (393). See also Tata (2007) for similar observations.

12 See also the book Introduction. Meeting records were searched using the term *ryōkei* (sentence/sentencing) (363) hits. The meeting records that were searched were the records that were available on 30 December 2017. More meetings have been held since then. As the topic of sentencing was discussed in each of the 363 meetings and it was not feasible to analyze the records of each meeting, 50 meeting records were randomly selected. Questions, statements and responses were searched for commonalities and recurring themes with regard to sentencing practices. Meeting records can be accessed at: at: www.saibanin.courts.go.jp/ikenkoukan/index.html. Website last visited 31–8–2018).

the Supreme Court has since the introduction of the lay judge system each year held, so as to get an insight into how the citizens who participated in lay judge trials viewed their experience. These surveys all include a section that provides an overview of participants' responses to open questions. In these responses the former lay judges invariably referred to sentencing practices, thereby supplementing the data gathered from the meeting records. The remarks about sentencing are in the Supreme Court surveys noted as representative responses among the responses given to specific questions.

As noted in the Introduction of this book, the meetings proceeded according to a fixed agenda. The lay judges were first asked to introduce themselves and provide their general impression of their experience as a lay judge, after which the talks and questions successively focused on court hearing procedures; deliberations; "a message for future lay judges" and questions from the press. While lay judges often raised sentencing issues in different part of the meetings, sentencing procedures were in any case each time discussed in connection with deliberations, during which sentencing decisions are made.

### 2.1.1. *Arguments and anchor points*

The meeting records show that the first clue with regard to the sentence to be imposed came from the public prosecutor and defense lawyer, who in their arguments indicated what sentence, in their view, was appropriate. The arguments in which the prosecution and defense express their views in this regard were and are made in their respective "closing arguments" (*ronkoku* and *benron*). Until these arguments were presented, the lay judges had no idea as to what sentence might be appropriate in their case[13]:

> I had absolutely no idea what the sentence was going to be. When at the end the prosecutor had demanded a sentence of life imprisonment, it was after that, that I finally understood it was going to be something like that.
>
> (Osaka District Court, 18 March 2015)

The records also show that for most this was the first time they were told about the reasoning behind a sentence demanded or recommended. Most lay judges indicated that they had had no difficulty following the reasoning of the prosecutor or defense lawyer, in terms of the ways in which sentences were calculated. The (former) lay judges indicated, in other words, that they understood how an application of legal conventions and rules to the case at hand translated into the punishment demanded or recommended. The amount of punishment, typically, imprisonment with hard labor, was nevertheless a source of bewilderment

13 As a result of the fact that proceedings are structured this way, where only at the end it becomes clear what sentence the public prosecutor demands, (lay) judges accordingly also do not know if "theirs" is a capital trial. See in this regard Johnson (2010).

(*tomadoi*) and questions, as it was not necessarily clear how, beyond laws, conventions and precedent, this amount actually made sense in the case at hand. As one former lay judge remarked:

> Toward the end the prosecutor stated the sentence he demanded. To me that was something utterly incomprehensible. The amount of time to be spent in prison, was that the amount of time that would be effective for the defendant? Was that the amount of time that would allow him to atone for his crime, or to rehabilitate? It was impossible to assess that.
>
> (Aomori District Court, 21 March 2013)

The amount of punishment demanded by the public prosecutor was in any case the first number the lay judges were confronted with, and that accordingly "had a big impact". Lawyers often would not recommend a specific number, but the lay judges discovered that when they did, the sentence recommended was typically not that different from that demanded by the public prosecutor.[14] When two numbers were available, together these created the impression of an upper and a lower limit for lay judges to keep in mind.

Nevertheless, for a number of reasons the lay judges overwhelmingly indicated being convinced by the prosecution's arguments, rather than those presented by the defense. This appeared to have something to do, first of all, with the earlier referred to perception that lawyers to a great extent simply went along with the public prosecutor's arguments, rather than assertively opposing them, or raising issues in defense of their client. In addition, public prosecutors presented the lay judges with material – typically an overview of the case in connection with a summary of their arguments – that lay judges indicated was easier to understand than that presented by the defense. In the words of one former lay judge:

> This trial was about determining the sentence, but the defense lawyer hardly offered any opinions. It was more like he in any case did not object to anything, while the material provided by the prosecutor was very easy to follow. There was a timeline, it was in color and easy to read. The lawyer's material was in black and white, and was really like "We admit [to the crime]. However, the defendant has a child", and so "doesn't that mean that there are extenuating circumstances?" – it was that kind of material. Overall, as the prosecutor's material was very easy to read, I was swayed in that direction.
>
> (Chiba District Court, 21 January 2015)

The difficulty that lay judges had in trying to understand what the defense lawyer was getting at was in fact a recurring theme.[15] These observations now have to be interpreted in connection with some key characteristics of Japanese criminal

14 Lay judges referred to differences between four and one years. Many in fact indicated they were surprised by the extent to which defense lawyers went along with the arguments presented by the public prosecutor.

15 In line with these lay judges' observations, reports on the functioning of the lay judge system published yearly by the Supreme Court of Japan show that of the three legal professionals

justice discussed in the previous chapters. As also noted in Chapter 1, conviction rates in Japan have for years been around 97–98%. In lay judge trials too the conviction rate has hovered around the same percentage (Supreme Court of Japan, 2017b, 2018).[16] This percentage is to an important extent the result of the high level of suspicion required for an indictment (Hirano, 1989: 129–131), as only those cases in which a conviction is "guaranteed" go to trial. In a very large percentage of the cases, typically more than 90% (cf. Supreme Court of Japan, 2017a: 119; 2017b: 81), defendants confess to all or part of the charges, as a result of which many trials are, for all practical purposes, more about determining a defendant's sentence, rather than his or her guilt.

Under such circumstances, presenting an alternative argument, alternative to that presented by the prosecution, may be difficult, and for lawyers there may not be much left to do besides arguing extenuating circumstances. As a result, criminal defense is less than appealing for those seeking to make a lawyering career, and is said to attract especially young lawyers with relatively little experience and older lawyers.[17] In addition, public prosecutors have the benefit of being supported by an organization with resources geared to criminal prosecution, in preparing for their case defense lawyers may be very much left to their own devices. In any case: meeting records show that especially the sentence demanded by the prosecution formed the basis (*tatakidai*) for further debates on the sentence, that would take place during deliberations.

### *2.1.2. Sentencing principles and going rates*

Meeting records show that before the start of these deliberations judges would explain "the basics" of sentencing, which, as was reiterated throughout the meetings and as voiced by one professional judge is about:

> looking at what that person has done, the motive, nature and consequences of the crime. In doing so you by and large determine the sentence margin. Then, for the rest you look at whether [the defendant] is remorseful, and

(judges, prosecutors and lawyers) lay judges find lawyers the most difficult to understand (Supreme Court of Japan, 2009–2016).

16 In 2016, 1,104 defendants were tried in lay judge trials. Of these 12 were found innocent; two were transferred to the Family Court, the remaining cases ended in a guilty verdict (MOJ White Paper on Crime). In 2016 the conviction rate was accordingly just under 99%. Of the 11,152 cases tried since the lay judge system was introduced 10,827 ended in a guilty verdict (= 97% conviction rate) (Supreme Court of Japan, 2018); 88 persons (0.7%) were found innocent. In 2016 53,247 "ordinary" cases were tried in first instance in District Courts. Of these 52,106 (= 97.6%) ended in a guilty verdict. 105 persons (= 0.02%) were found innocent. Here it is important not to translate the percentage of defendants found innocent in the conviction rate. The gap between defendants found guilty and those found innocent is filled with persons transferred to other courts, notably family courts, cases dropped, no jurisdiction, etc., etc. (Supreme Court of Japan, 2017b).

17 Johnson notes in this regard: "older lawyers are attracted to criminal defense work because that is where their comparative advantage lies. In most criminal cases they can do about as much for the accused as can their more energetic, mentally agile juniors. Which is to say, *not much*" (2002: 72–73, my italics).

> depending on the case also [his or her] age and whether s/he has compensated the victim, and so on. The facts and circumstances separate from the facts of the crime are factors on the basis of which you make adjustments within that by and large determined margin.
>
> (Chiba District Court, 5 September 2014)

Through such explanations, lay judges were informed about how sentencing works, about the line of thinking to be adopted, regardless of what one, as an individual, might think. In the words of another (professional) judge:

> Given that one is applying the law, one has to follow that line of thinking.
>
> (Fukuoka District Court, 20 June 2014)

In this way lay judges were educated about the do's and don'ts of sentencing. Lay judges in fact explicitly indicated that they felt they were being educated – that they were given a crash course in sentencing. Many indicated how grateful they were to receive such explanations:

> The explanation we received was so good, I felt we should be paying tuition.
>
> (Nagano District Court, 28 November 2013)

As a result of such explanations, however, it also became very clear just how much judges knew about making a sentencing decision, and how little, if anything at all, the lay judges knew. A topic that in fact recurred in each meeting was that of the difference between the judges as knowledgeable legal professionals and the lay judges as laymen and -women[18] who knew next to nothing about the law and about sentencing. As the lay judges thus became very much aware of their lack of knowledge, they also became concerned about their ability to make "the right decision":

> When it came to deciding on the sentence to some extent I experienced pressure because I, as lay judge who is a lay man when it comes to law, had one vote, just like the judge. It's ok to express one's opinion based on one's own perspective. But I felt that I wanted to leave the judgment concerning the final conclusion up to the judge.
>
> (Supreme Court, 2016 (2009–2017): 187)

The sentence demanded by the public prosecutor and recommended by the defense lawyer did, as indicated earlier, provide the lay judges with a baseline for their deliberations. Besides the explanations given by judges on sentencing principles, the professional judges further "helped" their lay colleagues by showing

18 The word used in Japanese is *shirōto*, a word that generally conveys a lack of expertise, and is used in opposition to the words for "expert" and professional.

them graphs of sentencing decisions imposed for similar cases, created by inserting information ("more than 10 relevant factors" – Inoue, 2012) on the type of offense, number of victims, age of the defendant, the type of weapon used in the database of sentencing decisions referred to earlier. This database thus allowed the lay judges to see how similar cases had been dealt with before, but also – with the help of the judge(s) – to check the line of reasoning and legal precedent on which the sentencing decisions in these cases had been based, and to contextualize the arguments presented by the prosecution and defense.

For many lay judges the database, graphs and information on legal precedent were a source of relief, as they facilitated their participation and welcomed them to join the sentencing process, as exemplified in the following quote:

> [The information provided] gave me the feeling that they were actually looking for the opinion of an average elderly woman like me.
>
> (Kobe District Court, 10 September 2014)

Lay judges also expressed relief as the information would allow them to make a sentencing decision that was fair and in line with the sentence received by other defendants, in similar cases (cf. (Supreme Court, 2014 (2009–2017): 185). The information provided also raised doubts among the lay judges, however, about their role in and contribution to the sentencing decision making process:

> Amongst each other we said during the [deliberation] break: "There is a script! What's that then! What a charade!" [chaban] (. . .) We're rank amateurs, and on top of that we don't get to see all the evidence.[19] It's under such circumstances that we're asked to decide on the sentence. And if we're then told, after having decided: "well, no, legal precedent says something different, you see", you wonder what that is all about.
>
> (Yokohama District Court, Odawara branch, 17 February 2015)

In the words of other lay judges:

> If the idea is for us to decide on the sentence on the basis of sentencing data, I wonder if there's any sense in us participating. That's what I kind of felt toward the end. I couldn't help think about the aim [of participating].
>
> (Chiba District Court, 5 September 2014)

19 In the case of lay judge trials pre-trial proceedings are held, during which the defense and prosecution determine, in front of a judge, which issues they will dispute and what evidence they will present in court. The selection of evidence is said to be aimed at reducing the burden placed on lay judges, who will not have time to (e.g.) read all the statements compiled during the pre-trial investigation. This procedure does however obviously imply that lay judges will have to base their judgment on a selective presentation of the available evidence. See Supreme Court of Japan (2009b).

And:

> I felt that if the sentence is decided on the basis of legal precedent, you don't really need lay judges.
>
> (Supreme Court of Japan, 2017 (2009–2017): 189)

And finally:

> I felt like it was a run race. I feel that sentences that constitute guidelines are necessary, but also that our talks proceeded so as fit in that framework.
>
> (ibid., 197)

Lay judges were thus either before but mostly during sentencing deliberations informed about legal precedent and "going rates". Meeting records show that typically the judges and lay judges would discuss their views on the case and the sentence they felt to be appropriate, and that after it had thus become clear where everybody stood, the professional judges would provide the information from the legal database. While different judges provided information at different moments, different judges also followed slightly different decision making procedures. In some cases discussions reportedly continued until everybody agreed with the sentence to be imposed; in other cases sentencing decisions were taken on the basis of a majority vote, where, as indicated earlier, one judge had to agree with lay judges' conclusion.

These quotes thus show how lay judges were given a baseline for their deliberations, how they were "educated" on how to go about making a sentencing decision, and how they were presented with information on relevant verdicts and sentencing decisions in similar cases. As part of their education on the do's and don'ts of sentencing, they were also informed about the importance of fairness in sentencing, meaning that similar cases called for similar sentences. Unsurprisingly, as shown, this way of involving lay judges has led to sentencing patterns that show great similarities to those found in professional judge trials. Studying how lay judges made use of their discretionary authority thus shows that their exercise of such authority was especially about learning to discern the correct bandwidth within which decisions should be made. It is however by virtue of such discretionary authority that the lay judge system can be represented as aiming to reflect "the sound common sense" of the people.

### *2.2. Continuity and change*

The previous section brought into focus the emphasis placed in lay judge deliberations on reaching sentencing decisions in line with legal precedent. Such emphasis in turn explains the relative continuity in sentencing practices in lay judge trials. When it comes to such continuity, however, there is another question to consider, namely that of how professional judges' ideas about sentencing relate to those of Japanese citizens. In 2007 the Supreme Court run Legal Research and

Training Institute (LRTI) published an extensive research report on this issue, that however focused on just one offense, namely that of murder. As the research for this report was done in 2005, one year after the 2004 legal amendment of the Criminal Code that allowed for harsher punishment, and following years of victim activism and a moral panic surrounding a perceived rise in crime, the results of this report are here significant. One thousand men and women were selected on the basis of random sampling among those eligible to vote from eight different parts of Japan. All citizen participants would accordingly also later become eligible to participate in the lay judge system. Judge participants were all judges who in District and High Courts handled criminal trials. All were asked various general questions on sentencing as well as questions in relation to five hypothetical cases.

To give a brief overview of some of the findings of the report: the percentage of citizens who find it *irrelevant* if crime victims desire a harsh punishment is much higher (50%) than that of judges (20.1%) (LRTI, 2007a: 25). A much greater percentage of citizens find it *irrelevant* for the sentence if a defendant admits the crime and shows remorse (35.2%) than that of judges (5.5%) (2007a: 33). A large percentage of the judges would impose "a lighter sentence" in case the defendant has apologized to the victim or the victim's family and provided compensation (60.4%, as opposed to citizens' 19.3%); 36.4% of the judges would in that case impose "a somewhat lighter punishment", as opposed to 34.6% of the citizens. Most citizens (39.3%) however indicate that they would neither impose higher, nor lower punishment, as opposed to judges' 1.4% (2007a: 35). These results thus suggest that citizens are much less swayed by both crime victims' wishes and defendants' apologies than judges are.

When it came to the hypothetical cases, however, judges' and citizens' sentences were quite similar, even if the sentences that citizens meted out were slightly heavier than those of the judges. In the report legal scholar Masahide Maeda remarks in this regard, on the basis of the results: "it looks like the people who are scheduled to take part (in criminal trials) as lay judges will, on average, be meting out slightly heavier sentences, but (. . .) it is expected that that will not result in a large change of the current situation" (2007a: 173). So, yes, lay judges find themselves having to decide in conformity with existing precedent. That does not necessarily mean however, that the end result would have been very different if they were not.

Different from what one perhaps might expect, in light of this discussion, lay judge trials do from time to time result in sentences that are perceived to go beyond established margins. When this happens, but more generally, when the parties do not agree with the sentence imposed, they can still appeal the verdict on the grounds of an "unjust sentence" (*ryōkei futō*).[20] While the possibility of

20 The appeal rate in all lay judge trials combined, i.e. all lay judge trials held since 2009, the verdict was appealed in 36.1% of the cases. In ordinary cases tried in first instance in District Courts the appeal rate was 12% (Supreme Court of Japan, 2018; Ministry of Justice 2017).

appeal of course allows for the correction of e.g. fact finding mistakes and faulty (legal) reasoning, it also means that deviations from the margin, based on "the sound common sense of the people" can also be neutralized, and the impact of citizens' input limited.

In its verdict of 24 July 2014 the first petty bench of the Supreme Court directly addressed this controversial issue. The case concerned a robbery for which the prosecution had demanded 10 years imprisonment, but the (lay) judge court had imposed 15 years. The Supreme Court overturned the original verdict, noting that:

> The lay judge system was introduced to adopt citizens' perspectives in criminal trials. Accordingly, with regard to sentencing too, it had been foreseen that fitting [sōō] change in the assembled results of legal precedent would be effectuated. (. . .) However, it goes without saying that, lay judge trial or no lay judge trial, in comparison with other trials a suitable fairness [kōheisei] has to be maintained. With regard to deliberations, it should be said that what is demanded is a deliberation that is suitable for the case at hand, where the point of departure is a shared acknowledgement of basic trends in sentencing up until now.[21]

While it is not exactly clear what "fitting change" stands for here, the Supreme Court verdict in any case implies that any change is only acceptable as long as it is still based on an acknowledgment of – or put differently: in dialogue with – existing jurisprudence. In the end, in order not to be overturned on appeal, lay judge sentencing decisions need to be embedded in existing frameworks regarding fair punishment.

## 3. Effects and implications

Earlier paragraphs of this chapter already referred to the fact that in Ryūichi Hirano's and other like-minded scholars and practitioners the "real substance" of Japanese criminal procedure had come to lie in the pre-trial stage of this procedure, which could be characterized as an inquisitorial process performed by prosecutors and police (Hirano, 1989: 131; cf. generally Chapter 1). The percentages noted in the previous paragraph illustrate that the high suspicion requirement has not disappeared and that accordingly much of the "real substance" still lies in the pre-trial stage of Japanese criminal procedure. After all, it is at this stage that prosecutors select the winnable cases, and in doing so by and large determine who is to be found guilty in court, keeping in mind the conviction rates that still hover around 98%, in both ordinary and lay judge trials. Given also that the lay judge system is only available for a very small percentage of all cases, this system could of course not be expected to fully "cure" Japanese criminal justice, as Hirano had

21 Supreme Court first petty bench verdict of 24 July 2014, p. 7.

hoped. Be that as it may, the introduction has in various ways had a big impact, though be it not in terms of conviction rates or net sentencing results.

From the time it became clear that a lay judge system was going to be introduced in Japan, this system has been the subject of considerable attention and debate, in academic and non-academic fora alike. Some studies, for example, questioned the extent to which the new system could be expected to transform criminal courts and improve the rights of the accused, while others highlighted the increased transparency and checks that the new system would in any case provide for (Weber, 2009; Soldwedel, 2008; Fukurai, 2002). Comparisons were and are still made between the (proposed) Japanese system and previous Japanese jury systems.[22] Mock trials – organized to familiarize people with the new system as well as for research – were used to examine matters such as the extent to which people felt free to state their opinions during deliberations (finding that people felt more free to speak out when they expected that the deliberations would reflect their opinion – cf. Fujita, 2004, 2008).

Different studies have also highlighted the societal impact of the system, noting for example the enormous public attention for and discussion about issues of criminal justice, as well as lay judges' commitment to their task – their concern, for example, about the rehabilitation of the offender as well as the rights of the accused (Hirayama, 2012: 129–130). Vanoverbeke furthermore highlights the impact of participation on lay judges personally, and how the experience, the personal involvement in their trial, induces them to become more civically aware and engaged (2015: 175–185).[23] Reichel and Suzuki further highlight the increased reliance of oral testimony in court, as well as the increased transparency resulting

22 Between 1873 and 1875 a jury system – with 12 jurors who determined the defendant's guilt or innocence after which three professional judges determined the sentence – was used in exceptional cases. In 1929 a jury system was again introduced. 12 jurors (men older than 30 who paid at least 3 yen per year in taxes, i.e. less than 10% of those eligible to vote) decided on the guilt or innocence of defendants who, depending on the charge, could choose between trial by jury or trial by a judge. On 1 April 1943 the system was discontinued as it was found to be used only very infrequently, and as citizens were expected to "focus on the war effort" (Vanoverbeke, 2010: 110, see also Dobrovolskaia, 2007, 2010).

23 Meeting records are in line with these findings, as lay judges repeatedly referred to how by participating they felt they had fulfilled their duty as citizens. The meeting records as well as the Supreme Court surveys also show how participating in lay judge trials, and especially deciding over another person's life and liberty, personally affected them. The following quotes are illustrative in that regard, but also as an expression of lay judges' personal involvement in the process, in their trial: "After all, I experience(d) deciding on people's punishment and the sentence as a burden [*futan*]. I have the feeling that from now on too I will wind up wondering if my judgment was right, and that presses on me [*ki ga omoi*]" (Supreme Court of Japan General Secretariat, 2012 (2009–2017): 156). And: "When I saw the expression in the defendant's face when the verdict was pronounced I wondered if the sentence was appropriate, and that feeling sometimes gnaws away at me. On the other hand, I at the same time thought that I'd like for him to somehow atone for his crime, and make a great return to society [*rippa ni shakai ni fukki shite hoshii*] (Okayama District Court, 9 September 2014).

from changes in the rules of the disclosure of evidence (2015: 257; cf. also Chapter 5). Indeed, the introduction of the lay judge system has in various ways had an enormous impact.

A recurring theme in the literature is in this regard also that of the surveys, which the Supreme Court has held each year since the introduction of the lay judge system, to which the previous sections already referred. Statistics from these surveys that are invariably highlighted are those on the ideas about participating that people had beforehand, and their ideas after participation. These statistics show that many people are initially not too eager to participate, but that they do evaluate their participation as a very positive one. According to the 2017 survey, for example, of the 5,392 respondents 62% found the experience "extraordinarily good" (*hijō ni yoi*), while another 34.3% found the experience good, in spite of the fact that beforehand a total of 50% either did not really (30.8%) or simply did not want (16.2%) to participate (Supreme Court of Japan, 2017 (2009–2017): 131–132). These statistics are important to bear in mind, in light of the previous sections, as well as the previous chapters, which highlighted lay judges' confrontation with existing rules, principles and frameworks that they found themselves having to conform to.

The statistics on people's evaluation of their experience are important, as they convey participants' satisfaction about their participating experience, and by extension the system in which they participated. In this sense these positive statistics would appear to provide a stamp of approval from the people, the *demos*, who participated. At the same time, however, it is important to note that these statistics are very much focused on the *experience* of participating. As such they are indicative of the attention that especially the courts have given to indeed ensuring a satisfactory "lay judge experience". The questions regarding the overall experience of participating and the attitude people had before participating are part of a much larger range of questions aimed at a sort of "customer satisfaction". Participants are for example asked about whether the court provided sufficient information, and for each legal professional whether they were easy to understand, did not talk too fast or spoke unclearly. Participants were asked if the intentions behind and content of the questions asked to witnesses had been understandable, and whether it was easy for them to express themselves during deliberation.

The Supreme Court surveys accordingly bring into focus the legal professionals as providers of a service, a performance that is evaluated through the surveys. The meeting records too show this evaluative approach when, for example, one of the legal professionals would ask about how his or her performance was received, or whether there were any points that could be improved. For example:

> LAWYER: *I'd like to ask lay judge number seven: I let a friend of the defendant appear in court as a witness in relation to the circumstances surrounding this case, and s/he indicated that s/he would help with the rehabilitation [of the defendant]. Could you tell me if that was enough as a way of proving that?* (Sapporo District Court, 14 February 2013)

And:

PUBLIC PROSECUTOR: *listening to how I read the statements out loud, could you tell me if that was too long or something, or if there were things that you didn't understand because I left out too much?* (Kushiro District Court, 12 March 2014).

Here, the lay judges are the clients who together with the professionals look back on an event in which the lay judges participated, but that was run and presented to them by the professionals. These professionals let the laymen and women in on the rules and principles, and then they got to have a go at joining the process of criminal justice decision making themselves. This service orientation is also illustrated by books published by the earlier mentioned Legal Research and Training Institute on, for example, explaining difficult legal concepts to lay judges (LRTI, 2007b) and how legal professionals should approach sentencing processes in lay judge trials, where "what is important, is to always, in each separate case, determine what kind of form is the appropriate form for a criminal justice trial in which lay judges (. . .) participate, and *how and what one should have the lay judges judge* [*saiban'in ni nani wo dono yō ni handan shite morau beki nanoka – my italics*]" (LRTI, 2012: preface). This last quote also conveys a sense of guardianship over criminal justice processes: the professionals know how things are done, and now it is a question of getting the lay judges to be "appropriately" involved.

This does not preclude lay judges' contribution to or impact on the end results, but it is clear that this impact is carefully monitored by the professionals who bring the people the lay judge experience. Lay judges earlier mentioned self-conscious self-labeling as non-specialists, laypersons (*shirōto*) who could not hope to compete with the professionals, further reinforces the character of lay judge trials as the professionals' world in which the lay judges briefly come to visit. The professionals nevertheless aim to make the experience one that is as fruitful as possible, hence the effort to monitor and improve the operating of the lay judge system on the basis of the opinions and subjective views of the laypersons who participated in it (Supreme Court of Japan, 2017 (2009–2017): 1). Thus, "client satisfaction" is added to the wide range of criteria in reference to which justice is administered in Japanese lay judge trials.

## Conclusion

Studying sentencing statistics shows us just how much Japanese criminal justice practices are characterized by continuity, rather than change. The changes that the graphs do exhibit are longer term trends, showing that overall sentencing trends are not clearly affected by either penal populism, reforms allowing for the imposing of stricter sentences or the introduction of the lay judge system, although these may have reinforced long term trends of increasing severity in sentencing for specific offenses.

Japanese criminal law grants judges, lay and professional alike, considerable discretionary authority in deciding what sentence is appropriate in the case at hand, for a particular defendant. When it came to applying that authority lay judges were taught, by their fellow professional colleagues, how to apply relevant principles and contextualize their thoughts and decisions in terms of previous, relevant cases. Lay judges were thus taught how to position their line of thought in pre-existing frameworks of principles and knowledge. Accordingly, lay judges were taught to perform a judge's job, a job that came with a binding description: "given that one is applying the law, one has to follow that line of thinking" – regardless of what one, as an individual, might think (Fukuoka District Court, 20 June 2014 – see previous text). The framework structuring lay judges' exercise of discretionary authority was thus presented as non-negotiable.

As a result, the decisions taken in lay judge trials by and large do not exceed the margins of tolerance of the existing frameworks of sentencing principles and jurisprudence. When they do, the possibility for appeal and review by a higher court ensures that the integrity of the existing frameworks is maintained. Nevertheless, the sentencing decisions taken in lay judge trials do arguably have the effect of altering the margins of such decisions, thereby allowing for accumulating changes in sentencing trends.

Valuable as the changes in sentencing decisions can be said to be – after all: for certain offenses changes can be discerned – what stands out from the accounts of the deliberations on the sentence to be imposed is the effort made and felt to make lay judges conform with pre-existing sentencing practices. All this raises doubts about the meaning of the officially professed ambition, referred to earlier, to infuse processes of fact finding and sentencing with "the sound common sense of the people".

The fact that sentencing decisions in cases of the highest public interest – after all, the most serious and publicity attracting cases are dealt with in lay judge trials – are now demonstrably a joint product of professional judges and members of the general public does in any case provide these decisions with an apparent added democratic flavor, and accordingly with an added sense of legitimacy. Discretionary authority – authority formally labeled as "discretionary" – is a prerequisite of such legitimacy, as it is obviously only when lay judges are formally given the authority to make a decision that is appropriate in a given case for a given defendant, that the sentencing decisions taken are also theirs. Regardless of the content of discretionary authority based sentencing decisions, such authority has allowed for renewed attention for and reinvigorated societal discussions about criminal justice, which may ultimately translate into citizens' redefining sentencing margins and frameworks.

Lay judges are overwhelmingly very positive about their experience. We know this to be the case because of the Supreme Court's constant monitoring of lay judges' opinions and sentiments. Lay judges' positive experiences go a long way in representing the introduction of the system as a success, irrespective of case outcomes.

The monitoring of lay judges' satisfaction with their experience is indicative of how "client satisfaction" is added to the criteria in reference to which justice is administered in Japanese lay judge trials. The previous chapters brought into focus the myriad of conflicting perspectives and aims in reference to which Japanese criminal justice is administered, such as general and special prevention, social defense, "offenders' best interests", victims' perspective and "reliable scientific evidence". Chapter 1 highlighted how criminal justice can characterized as a complex, internally differentiated whole, whose different elements are nonetheless interrelated (cf. Garland, 1990: 279). The assumption in this book has been that given the myriad perspectives, points of reference and aims, criminal justice should in fact be seen as an overdetermined field. The addition of "client satisfaction" as a point of reference here still further determines this already overdetermined field. Within this field the different perspectives and aims coexist.

There is nothing extraordinary about criminal justice players pursuing, for example, different aims at the same time. Nevertheless, tensions do exist between them. The question is how this tension is in practice resolved and how, and with what consequences. This is one question that the conclusion, on the basis of all previous chapters, will address.

## References

Baumgartner, Mary Pat (1992). The myth of discretion, in Keith Hawkins (ed.), *The uses of discretion*. Oxford: Clarendon Press: 129–162.

Dobrovolskaia, Anna (2007). An all-laymen jury system instead of the lay assessor (saiban'in) system for Japan? Anglo-American-style jury trials in Okinawa under the US Occupation. *Zeitschrift für Japanisches Recht*: 57–80.

Dobrovolskaia, Anna (2010). *Japan's past experiences with the institution of jury service*. Available at: http://blog.hawaii.edu/aplpj/files/2011/11/APLPJ_12.1_dobrovolskaia.pdf. Website last visited 31 August 2018.

Dworkin, Ronald M. (1977). Is law a system of rules?, in Ronald M. Dworking (ed.), *The Philosophy of Law*. Oxford: Oxford University Press: 38–65.

Endō, Kunihiko (2011). Jitteihōki kara mita ryōkei kijun, in Osaka Keijijitsumukenkyūkai (ed.), *Ryōkei Jitsumu Taikei*. Vol. 3. Tokyo: Hanrei Taimuzusha.

Fujita, Masahiro (2004). Mogisaiban hyōgi no keiken ga saiban'in seido ni taisuru hyōka ni oyobosu eikyō. *Hō to Shinri* 3(1): 68–80.

Fujita, Masahiro (2008). *Shihō he no shiminsanka no kanōsei: nihon no baishinseido/saiban'in seido no jisshōteki kenkyū*. Tokyo: Yūhikaku.

Fukurai, Hiroshi (2002). Japan's newly proposed quasi-jury system and the introduction of checks and balances into the Japanese legal system. *Sociology of Law*: 195–215.

Garland, David (1990). *Punishment and modern society: a study in social theory*. Oxford: Oxford University Press.

Hamai, Kōichi and Thomas Ellis (2008). Japanese criminal justice: was reintegrative shaming a chimera? *Punishment & Society* 10(1): 25–46.

Hannah-Moffat, Kelly, Paula Maurutto and Sarah Turnbull (2009). Negotiated risk: actuarial illusions and discretion in probation. *Canadian Journal of Law and Society*: 391–409.

Harada, Kunio (2004). *Ryôkeihandan no jissai*. Tokyo: Tachibana Shobō.

Harada, Kunio (2011). *Saiban'insaiban to ryōkeihō*. Tokyo: Seibundō.

Hirano, Ryūichi (1989). Diagnosis of the current code of criminal procedure. *Law Japan* 22: 129–142.

Hirayama, Mari (2012). Lay judge decisions in sex crime cases: the most controversial area of Saiban-in trials. *Yonsei Law Journal* 3: 128–160.

Inouye, Masahito (2012). *Saiban'in seido ni tsuite.* Powerpoint presentation available at: www.google.com/url?sa=t&rct=j&q=&esrc=s&source=web&cd=4&ved=2ahUKEwjpvYLwhJzdAhXIJlAKHZhjAwsQFjADegQIBxAC&url=http%3A%2F%2Fsocial.judicial.gov.tw%2FLayJudgeAttach%2F030D%2F%25E4%25BA%2595%25E4%25B8%258A%25E6%25AD%25A3%25E4%25BB%25813.pptx&usg=AOvVaw2gCbVExyHli3f-NOCTVMTF. Website last visited 31 August 2018.

Johnson, David T. (2002). *The Japanese way of justice: prosecuting crime in Japan.* Oxford: Oxford University Press.

Johnson, David T. (2010). Capital punishment without capital trials in Japan's lay judge system. *Asia Pacific Journal* 8(52): 1–38.

Justice System Reform Council (JSRC) (2001). *Hōkokusho.* Available at: www.kantei.go.jp/jp/sihouseido/report-dex.html. Website last visited 31 August 2018.

Legal Research and Training Institute (LRTI) (2007a). *Ryōkei ni kansuru kokumin to saiban no ishiki ni tsuite no kenkyū.* Tokyo: Hōsōkai.

Legal Research and Training Institute (LRTI) (2007b). *Nankai na hōritsugainen to saiban'insaiban.* Hōsōkai.

Legal Research and Training Institute (LRTI) (2012). *Saiban'insaiban ni okeru ryōkeihyōgi no arikata nitsuite.* Hōsōkai.

Ministry of Justice (MOJ) (annual). *White paper on crime.* Available at: http://hakusyo1.moj.go.jp/en/nendo_nfm.html. Website last visited 31 August 2018.

Miyazawa, Setsuo (2008a). The politics of increasing punitiveness and the rising populism in Japanese criminal justice policy. *Punishment & Society* 10(1): 47–77.

Miyazawa, Setsuo (2008b). Will penal populism in Japan decline? (symposium: globalized penal populism and its countermeasures). *Japanese Journal of Sociological Criminology* 33: 122–136.

Ōka, Shin'ichi (2012). Saiban'in saiban ni okeru Ryōkei Handan Kentō no Igi, in Japan Federation of Bar Associations (ed.), *Saiban'in Saiban no Ryōkei.* Tokyo: Seibundō: 2–7.

Pratt, Anna and Lorne Sossin (2009). A brief introduction of the puzzle of discretion. *Canadian Journal of Law and Society* 24(3): 301–312.

Reichel, Philip L. and Yumi E. Suzuki (2015). Japan's lay judge system: a summary of its development, evaluation, and current status. *International Criminal Justice Review* 25(3): 247–262.

Shiroshita, Yuji (2010). Current trends and issues in Japanese sentencing. *Federal Sentencing Reporter* 22(4): 243–248.

Soldwedel, Arne F. (2008). Testing Japan's convictions: the lay judge system and the rights of criminal defendants. *Vanderbilt Journal of Transnational Law* 41: 1417–1474.

Sugeno, Akira (2012). Ryōkei ni kansuru shinri/tetsuduki no henka, in Nihon Bengoshirengōkai (ed.), *Saiban'in saiban no ryōkei.* Tokyo: Gendaijinbunsha.

Supreme Court of Japan (2009–2017). *Saiban'in nado keikensha ni taisuru ankeito.* Available at: www.courts.go.jp/saikosai/iinkai/saibanin_kondan/index.html. Website last visited 31 August 2018.

Supreme Court of Japan (2009a). *Saiban'in seido no shōkai*. Available at: www.saibanin.courts.go.jp/introduction/index.html. Website last visited 31 August 2018.

Supreme Court of Japan (2009b). *Kōhanseiri tetsuzuki ni tsuite*. Available at: www.courts.go.jp/vcms_lf/20903007.pdf. Website last visited 31 August 2018.

Supreme Court of Japan (2017a). *Keiji tsūjō daiisshin jiken no gaikyō*. Available at: www.courts.go.jp/vcms_lf/hokoku_06_03keiji.pdf. Website last visited 31 August 2018.

Supreme Court of Japan (2017b). *Keijitsūjō dai'ichijiken no shūkyokukubunbetsujin'in (jitsujin'in)*. Available at: www.courts.go.jp/app/files/toukei/505/009505.pdf. Website last visited 31 August 2018.

Supreme Court of Japan (2018). *Saiban'in saiban no jisshijōkyō nit suite (seido shikō: heisei 30nen 5gatsumatsu/sokuhō)*. Available at: www.saibanin.courts.go.jp/vcms_lf/h30_5_saibaninsokuhou.pdf. Website last visited 31 August 2018.

Supreme Court of Japan General Secretariat (2012). *Saiban'in seido jisshi jōkyō no kenshōhōkokusho*. Available at: www.saibanin.courts.go.jp/vcms_lf/diagram_1-55.pdf. Website last visited 31 August 2018.

Tata, Cyrus (2007). Sentencing as craftwork and the binary epistemologies of the discretionary decision process. *Social & Legal Studies* 16(3): 425–447.

Vanoverbeke, Dimitri (2010). *Recht en instellingen in Japan: actuele thema's in een historische context*. Leuven: Uitgeverij ACCO.

Vanoverbeke, Dimitri (2015). *Juries in the Japanese legal system: the continuing struggle for citizen participation and democracy*. Vol. 13. London: Routledge.

Walker, Samuel (1993). *Taming the system: the control of discretion in criminal justice, 1950–1990*. Oxford: Oxford University Press.

Weber, Ingram (2009). The new Japanese jury system: empowering the public, preserving continental justice. *East Asia Law Review* 4: 125–176.

***Verdicts:***

Supreme Court of Japan First Petty Bench, Heisei 25 (a) 689. Verdict of 24.7.2014.

# Conclusion

The previous chapters have examined the roles played and contributions provided by different non-legal professionals in Japanese criminal justice, both in connection with the roles played by legal professionals and against the background of the changes that either gave birth to or affected the roles played by "outsider". In doing so, these chapters have also painted a picture of Japanese criminal justice policy making and practice. In view of the focus on different players and both long-term and very recent developments, this picture looks somewhat like a collage of different pieces that one can twist and turn so as to make visible what from one point of view would remain out of sight. This picture is of course not complete – leaving aside the question of the possibility of a complete picture. It does not aspire to say everything. It does, however, say many things at the same time, thereby highlighting the diversity of perspectives, points of reference and aims of criminal justice that make it into such an incredibly complex, internally differentiated whole of interrelated elements. It is not surprising, therefore, that the previous chapters do not allow for unequivocal bottom lines or yes or no binaries. They do, however, bring into focus a number of recurring themes relevant to understanding the role and contributions of the legal outsiders that are the focus of this book. This conclusion addresses these themes and their implications for understanding outsiders' roles in Japanese criminal justice.

## Social, technological and legal change

The previous chapters have been about social and legal change. These changes have been triggered by the political lobbying and pressuring exercised by non-legal players such as the Japan Business Federation (***keidanren***) and victims' rights groups, but also by lawmakers' perceptions of a public desire for harsher punishment and the measures they deemed necessary to curb rising crime rates or perceptions thereof. International trends and developments also played their part. The increased visibility of victims of crime and awareness of their rights in Japan, for example, cannot be understood separately from international trends of growing recognition of crime victims' rights. Similarly, the increased use of DNA testing and other "scientific evidence" in Japanese criminal justice is in line with relevant worldwide technological and scientific advances in these areas.

Here I will not again go over every specific source of reform. The point here is rather that of noting that outsiders' role has been generally tied up with very different sources of change; change that resulted from both social and technological developments, changes that were part of grand plans to overhaul the Japanese legal system and redefine its role in Japanese society, as well as changes that were initiated on a short term basis in response to very specific events and developments. By addressing of the role of legal outsiders, this book has allowed for an examination of the contexts of change and an inquiry into what in practice came of such change and why.

The introduction of the Medical Treatment and Observation Act (2005), discussed in Chapter 2, points to an increased role for legal professionals in assessing who is to be or remain forcibly admitted to a mental institution. The recently introduced manual for forensic psychiatrists, aimed at standardizing their evaluations of suspects and defendants, has resulted in an increased reference to legally relevant factors. Evaluations have become increasingly colonized by the language of the law in determining what aspects of a suspect's thinking and acting is relevant. These evaluations have accordingly become more forensic in the sense that they now more explicitly than ever stand in service of legal professionals' judgments, even if it is not clear that such juridification has affected the impact that psychiatrists' evaluations have on judgments and decisions made by legal professionals. At the pre-trial stage, forensic psychiatrists' evaluations by and large determine whether a suspect will be prosecuted or not. In the courtroom, changed social and legal understandings of mental illnesses, among other factors, have led to fewer and fewer defendants being found diminished responsible or criminally insane in court, although mental disturbances are considered at sentencing even if formal labels are not regularly applied.

While psychiatrists' judgment has in any case become increasingly legally colored, social workers' input, which has only very recently become institutionalized, is much more ambivalent in terms of its forensic quality. Input is determined first and foremost by considerations of their client's best interest. While a social worker's rehabilitation plan for a client, for example, can be incorporated to support lawyers' arguments or factor into Prosecutors' decision making, social workers may and do resist providing direct input about prospects of recidivism or other frameworks used by legal professionals.

Social workers' contributions do allow for suspects and defendants who would otherwise have been sent to prison to be diverted. For now, these suspects and defendants constitute a small percentage of all persons passing through the criminal justice chain each year, although the exact number of suspects or defendants receiving support from a social worker is unknown. As the number of elderly offenders keeps on rising in Japan's aging society, much like the influx of inmates with a mental disturbance, it is to be expected that social workers' criminal justice role will also become increasingly important. The question is whether an increased awareness of the problem of elderly, and often mentally disturbed, repeat offenders will also translate into different legal evaluations of their criminal responsibility.

Pursuant to legal changes made in the Code of Criminal Procedure in 2000 and 2008, crime victims' participation in Japanese criminal justice has been formally institutionalized. Crime victims who make a statement of opinion in court or who participate under the victim participation system do so out of their own accord, as opposed to being called upon to provide input in service of the arguments and decision making processes of the legal professionals. In spite of such *relative* independence – victims' participation in each separate case remains formally subject to judges' approval, even if in practice such approval is typically granted – victims in practice literally, that is, physically, side with the prosecution, as it is on the prosecution's side that their seat in court is reserved. What is more, their input lends support to the prosecution's argument and position, reinforcing the "traditional" Japanese criminal justice script and division of roles, which dictates that defendants remorsefully throw themselves at the mercy of prosecutors and judges for the sake of a lenient disposition. Be that as it may, it is unclear whether such teaming up of crime victims and prosecutors has any effect on professionals' decisions.

The role of those providing input in relation to forensic evidence, notably DNA testing, has in recent years vastly expanded. With advances of relevant technologies, increased use is being made of these forensic scientific experts. The impact of their input does not allow for unequivocal conclusions, as this input is included in the whole of factors that Japanese judges freely evaluate. Judges, lay and professional alike, may on one hand find they have no choice but to accept what the expert tells them. On the other hand, they confidently assess both the scientific reliability and probative value of experts' input. While DNA testing involves science-based procedures and techniques that do not allow for juridification, they may nevertheless allow for scientists to "paint the target around the arrow". To what extent this occurs in practice is as yet impossible to ascertain, as forensic research remains the nontransparent domain of police institutions.

Scientific evidence, however defined, may have the potential to change Japanese criminal justice practices, and allow for the king of evidence, the confession of guilt, to become a little less authoritative. Notwithstanding highly publicized wrongful convictions in which false confession statements have played an important part, scientific evidence has as of yet not translated into a clearly discernable break with the reign of confessions of guilt, while crime victims' new role has translated into a reinforcement of existing criminal justice scripts, rather than a redefinition thereof.

Lay judges' new role and input, made possible by the 2009 introduction of the lay judge system, is not easily qualified. Given that any decision on guilt, innocence or sentencing requires an agreement between both professional and lay judges, these are joint decisions. The relative continuity in terms of both conviction rates and sentencing trends, when compared to professional judge-only trials, does by itself not tell us anything about the impact of the lay judge's voice. After all, as long as prosecutors select only the slam dunk winnable cases to go to trial, lay judges may find little room to come up with a different, "independent" evaluation of the evidence. Furthermore, there is the possibility that sentencing practices before 2009, before the introduction of the lay judge system, were by and large in line with popular opinion, as research conducted by the Supreme Court in fact suggests. Chapter 6, however, has shown how lay judges found they had no choice but to position their input within the existing frameworks of legal principles and especially also legal precedent when making their decisions on sentencing as well as when evaluating the input of forensic psychiatrists and crime victims. Nevertheless, sentencing decisions taken in lay judge trials do have the effect of altering the margins of such decisions, allowing for accumulating changes in sentencing trends.

When it comes to how in practice the various social, technological and legal changes have played out, the picture is accordingly mixed. Depending on one's perspective, the criminal justice picture that presents itself when examining legal outsiders' roles in context can accordingly be characterized by continuity or change, or both. Legal outsiders' new or redefined roles do affect charging decisions, fact finding processes as well as sentencing decisions. Nevertheless, public Prosecutors' suspended prosecution rates have by and large remained stable, and their charging decisions have remained as careful as ever. Courtrooms remain places where guilt is confirmed. Sentences are meted out in accordance with legal precedent, allowing for only incremental change. Neither penal populism driven criminal justice policies and reforms nor legal outsiders' roles have done much to change that.

When considering such by and large continuity in numerical terms, however, it is important to keep in mind, as already briefly noted, that with the exception of forensic scientists, legal outsiders as yet play their roles in only a small percentage of all criminal cases. While this percentage may well expand when it comes to forensic psychiatrists, social workers, victims of crime and forensic scientists, for that matter, the role of lay judges will remain limited. In accordance with a design that could never have resulted in the cure for the "diseased state" of Japanese criminal justice that Ryūichi Hirano was hoping for (1989), lay judges are conferred with the responsibility of co-deciding on facts and sentencing in only 3–4% of all cases.

This book's interest in the role of the outsider goes beyond highlighting the resilience of criminal justice practice. The legal reforms related to psychiatrists' and social workers' criminal justice role are significant in the first place for the suspects and defendants who are evaluated and supported, forcibly sent to a mental institution or prison, or perhaps otherwise diverted. The institutionalization of social workers' involvement is significant in that it implies increased importance being assigned to rehabilitative rather than punitive considerations, after years of policy making aimed at allowing for more punitive dispositions. Crime victims' institutionalized participation allows for victims' voices to be heard, communicating a powerful message: namely that the criminal trial is also theirs, that the conflict, to use Christie's term, is still their conflict. Scientists' contributions, notably in the shape of DNA testing, have demonstrated how both apparently incontrovertible scientific evidence and confessions of guilt may still allow for an innocent person to be convicted. Forensic evidence accordingly highlights the errors that can be made in pursuing confessions in an investigative environment that very much enables that pursuit, the room for error in both the gathering and evaluation of forensic evidence. Ironically, therefore, techniques that appear to allow for increased certainty in fact finding processes highlight the need for an acknowledgment of uncertainties in these processes. Finally, lay judges' participation has sparked enormous public attention for, interest in and debate on issues of criminal justice, matters that may in time translate into further democratic input in criminal justice through legal change, a subject we will return to below.

## The drama and play of criminal justice

This book is full of words that belong to the realm of theater and play, something which is not surprising given the parallels that exist with criminal justice. The goal of invoking these words was however not simply to highlight the parallels, but to draw attention to their implications. The preceding chapters showed just how much court hearings are staged events with actors playing out performances so as for partisan narratives to be most convincingly presented. As we can see from the records of opinions exchanged between lay judges and legal professionals, lawyers and prosecutors sought feedback on whether the tools of the trade they had employed in court had been effective, thereby explicitly acknowledging the performative aspect of court proceedings.

Prosecutors rehearse in-court statements with victims, and both prosecutors and lawyers select the evidence, information and presentation format that will maximize the impact of their narrative. In lay judge trials, these selection processes are formally integrated in criminal procedure in the form of a pre-trial conference in which the parties determine, before a judge, which issues they will dispute and what evidence they will introduce or not introduce to do so. There is much in court proceedings that is scripted. As mentioned in the previous section, in addition to the points of dispute that are agreed upon beforehand, there are pre-rehearsed witness testimonies, questions and statements by the parties, and the traditional scripts regarding appropriate courtroom behavior by the defendant. One can further add the decision-making scripts outlining legal principles and precedent that are provided to lay judges, who are shocked, surprised and relieved to find that "There's a script! What a charade!"

Invoking the stage metaphor is not meant to suggest that court hearings are just for show, even if we can by and large predict how the courtroom drama will end, namely with a confirmation of the guilt of the defendant and a sentence in line with legal precedent. The stage metaphor brings into focus the contrast between the by and large predictable world of public court hearings and the off-stage, behind the scenes world of charging practices, pre-trial psychiatric evaluations, social workers' advice to public prosecutors, forensic investigation, and also the black boxes of judges' deliberation and working chambers. The off-stage part is, of course, where opinions are formed, on the basis of which most criminal justice decisions are made, keeping in mind that the majority of cases, even those in which there is sufficient evidence to indict, do not go to trial.

We do know what factors prosecutors find relevant in making their decisions, and as highlighted in social workers' reports, when it comes to "support at the entrance", considerations regarding the seriousness of the offense formally weigh in more heavily than the best interests of the offender. Statistics do show, however, that prosecution is also suspended in serious offenses. During the pre-trial investigation, prosecutors reportedly make charging decisions in line with forensic psychiatrists' evaluations. Yet exactly how all these decisions were made, on what considerations and reasoning they were based, remains hidden behind the scenes. What goes on in the judge's working chambers, and heads, for that matter, remains unclear. Defendants' motives, reasoning and actions, the admissibility of a confession statement, or a piece of scientific evidence: these are matters that do not speak for themselves. They necessitate professional and lay judges' interpretation and reasoning. Of course, these are outlined in court verdicts, supported by relevant legal argumentation. It is striking, however, how Japanese courts manage to find mentally disturbed perpetrators of serious offenses fully criminally responsible, thereby preventing their acts from going unpunished, and how in the free evaluation of evidence, including scientific evidence and confession statements, issues of admissibility and reliability become mixed, in that the latter play a role in determining the former, preventing evidence perceived to have probative value from being thrown out.

Verdicts show how judges defend their conclusions. Of course, they can only reach conclusions that are indeed legally defendable. That does not mean, however, that the verdict gives those who hear and read it access to how judges freely evaluate the information brought before them to reach their conclusions. The off-stage metaphor accordingly alerts us to what we do not know, and normally remains beyond scrutiny.

Given that most outsiders provide their contributions on stage, these contributions would seem to be preconditioned to either stand in service of or prevent a likely conviction and a sentence in conformity with legal precedent. The idea of outsiders serving the dichotomy of unpredictable off-stage decisions and predictable ones on stage, however, ignores the communicative aspect of what happens on stage. What happens on stage serves to show what is formally qualified as relevant in publicly adjudicating defendants. "What is formally qualified as relevant" is, however more generally part of the realm of criminal justice practice and policy referents, to which the next section will turn.

## The multitude of Japanese criminal justice points of reference and goals

In zooming in on non-legal professionals' role in the administration of Japanese criminal justice, the previous chapters have highlighted some of the many points of reference and criminal justice goals that shape players' actions. One could focus on one or a few of these so as to highlight a specific emphasis on certain goals that then characterize Japanese criminal justice, in explicit or implicit comparison with criminal justice practices in other parts of the world, allowing one to highlight, for example, Japanese officials' benevolent paternalism, their dedication to uncovering the truth of a case and to dealing with different cases differently, and similar cases similarly (Foote, 1992, Johnson, 2002, cf. Chapter 3). In the conclusion of his book on Japanese criminal justice, David Johnson expresses the hope that his book reflects how "the Japanese way of justice seeks confessions, consistency, corrections and convictions, and often obtains them, but also . . ." (2002: 278). Johnson's "but also . . ." points to the fact that his portrait of Japanese criminal justice is, like any portrait, framed by assumptions of what matters and what does not, and that unavoidably much, much that others might consider important was not included in this portrait. One of the aims of this book has been to emphasize the overdetermined, multifaceted quality of Japanese criminal justice, the ever present "but also . . .". Still, this book has focused on outsiders' and insiders' roles from the stage of the pre-trial investigation to the moment a verdict and sentence are handed down. Accordingly, there are legal outsiders whose role this book has not, or only in passing, looked at outsiders whose roles would have brought into focus still more dimensions of Japanese criminal justice. There is more to say, for example, on volunteer probation officers' role in supporting persons released from prison than said in Chapter 3. The same goes for the Prosecution Review Commissions, which have been given more power than before to review Prosecutors' decision not to file charges, as also briefly noted in the same chapter. These belong to the "but also . . . realm" of this book.

Returning to the matter at hand: in highlighting a multitude of criminal justice practice referents and goals, the aim of this was not just to highlight that multitude, but to show especially also how criminal justice practices are about pursuing different goals at the same time; goals that are often in one way or another at odds with each other. Chapter 2 has highlighted, for example, how processes of responsabilization of mentally disturbed offenders allowed for such offenders to be held legally responsible and accountable for their actions, in line with changed perceptions of such offenders as responsible, purposively acting persons. The same chapter also highlights how processes of responsibilization went hand in hand with legal reforms aimed at keeping society safe from these all in all dangerous offenders by increasing the options for their non-punitive institutionalization. Similarly, Chapter 3 brings into focus the recognition of the problems that holding elderly and often mentally disturbed offenders criminally responsible generates in the prisons in which they receive their just desserts. Pursuant to that recognition the aim is now to divert them and rehabilitate them, to the extent allowed by the retributive principles of criminal responsibility. So the official explanation goes, in a criminal justice system that diverts most offenders with the aim of rehabilitation, without, however, providing rehabilitative support except to said small group of elderly and often mentally disturbed repeat offenders, within the limits set by retributive principles. The will of the people and victims' rights and interests have become important policy and practice points of reference, but it remains unclear to what extent these have actually affected sentencing decisions, within the whole of factors considered in the process of sentencing, regardless of all the often dramatic attention they receive in court hearings and verdicts.

Given this lack of clarity concerning the concordance of courtroom or policy attention and actual dispositions, it is tempting to become cynical about the significance of Japanese courtroom practices. Of course, as already briefly mentioned, such practices are also about communicating what is formally recognized as important or relevant in administrating justice. At the same time, this quality of courtroom practices as communicative acts whose translation in actual dispositions is not necessarily clear, reinforces the character of these communicative acts as scripted performances and moral dramas with a sui generis reality. Accordingly, to ask the question of whether Japanese criminal justice is *really* or actually about bottom line dispositions rather than what goes on in criminal courts is to confuse different dimensions of criminal justice. This question and the idea of courtroom drama with a sui generis reality does, however, alert us to the importance of being mindful of these different dimensions that are so highly relevant when trying to make sense of outsiders' roles.

The previous section referred to different off-stage elements in legal decision making processes that remain beyond scrutiny, and how legal verdicts do not necessarily tell us how legal decisions come about. Rather, these verdicts are the reports written to account for and justify the conclusions arrived at. The Luhmannian idea that within legal processes the contributions of outsiders are merely opinions that need to be constituted as legal facts is in line with how the law communicates about its own processes (1991: 1430). Such communication is crucial for the representation of the law as a system of rules that is systematically and impartially applied to specific cases, with results that simply follow from that application of rules. That a Luhmannian representation of fact finding and sentencing processes and that the role of lay and specialist opinion does not exactly conform to legal practice is something the law and legal specialists in legal terms cannot communicate. Again, regardless of whether judges or prosecutors have any notions about what should happen with a certain defendant, keeping in mind his or her best interests or public sentiments, "on stage" at least, these notions need to be legally explainable and defendable. Outsiders' perspectives do in different ways inform fact finding and sentencing practices as well as the legal communication about those processes. The Foucauldian notion that outsiders' perspectives and knowledge redefine legal judgment thereby characterizes legal judgment as ever malleable (1978: 19–22). If there is anything that the previous chapters have shown, however, it is that legal decision-making processes are not easily redefined, given, for example, the importance attached to the principles of criminal responsibility and legal precedent. Rather, these perspectives are added to the multitude of points of reference and the hybrid knowledge that informs and factors into criminal justice legal practice. It is this quality of legal decision making that provides it with its capacity for variation in accordance with the case and the social circumstances at hand.

## Legal outsiders' role and the resolving of tensions between conflicting goals

Legal outsiders add to the already multilayered and multifaceted quality of Japanese criminal justice, thereby altering what administration of justice practices, especially courtroom practices, signify as "part of an authoritative, institutional discourse which seeks to organize our moral and political understanding and to educate our sensibilities" (cf. Garland, 1990: 252). Garland was here talking about sentencing practices, but it can be said that everything that goes on in courtrooms becomes part of this authoritative discourse in that verdicts are publicly communicated and disseminated for all to read and see what is relevant and what is not, and what is worth emphasizing and taking note of. Nevertheless, the fact remains that the previous chapters have also told a story of continuity in terms of the prevailing of courtroom scripts, the emphasis attached to confessions of guilt, conviction rates and sentencing dispositions, despite legal change. There are several factors contributing to such continuity. The most important of these is Prosecutors' authority in deciding which defendants are to be indicted and which are not, meaning that important criminal justice decisions, notably those on guilt and innocence, continue to be effectively made off stage, out of reach of professional and lay judges. Another relates to judges' role: as long as judges continue to emphasize legal precedent as they do, changes in lay judge sentencing trends will remain incremental, though not absent. And as long as prosecutors continue to indict mostly confessing defendants, and judges abide by the principle of freely forming convictions, forensic psychiatrists' scientists' contributions, as well as confession statements, for that matter, will remain subject to a substantive, common sense based judgment.

The previous section already noted that legal decision-making processes are not easily redefined, in view of the importance attached to principles of criminal responsibility and legal precedent. Given the importance attached to these principles, Prosecutors' adherence to their careful charging policies and judges' prioritizing of their prerogative to substantively evaluate the probative value of evidence, regardless of formally defined a priori conditions concerning the admissibility of evidence, trend breaking change in substantive decision making, or in courtroom scripts, for that matter, are unlikely. Prosecutors' and judges' dedication to this way of going about their jobs thereby turns them into guardians of continuity within the Japanese administration of justice. Important as such guardianship is, it is not complete. The roles of the outsiders that have been the subject of this book are firmly integrated in criminal justice practice, meaning that such practice is no longer what it was before. Judges, prosecutors and lawyers will continue to engage with the input provided by forensic psychiatrists, social workers, forensic scientists and lay judges. In doing so, the exact impact of such input on legal decision making may not always be clear even to the professionals, when engaging, for example, with input they are not in a position to verify. How outsiders' role will develop in the years to come and with what accumulative effect will remain to be seen, but with their contributions Japanese criminal justice will never be the same.

## References

Foote, Daniel H. (1992). The benevolent paternalism of Japanese criminal justice. *California Law Review* 80: 317–390.

Foucault, Michel (1978). *Discipline and punish*, trans. Alan Sheridan. New York: Vintage.

Garland, David (1990). *Punishment and modern society: a study in social theory.* Oxford: Oxford University Press.

Hirano, Ryūichi (1989). Diagnosis of the current code of criminal procedure. *Law Japan* 22: 129–142.

Johnson, D.T. (2002). *The Japanese way of justice: prosecuting crime in Japan.* Oxford: Oxford University Press.

Luhmann, Niklas (1991). Operational closure and structural coupling: the differentiation of the legal system. *Cardozo Law Review* 13: 1419–1441.

# Index

Note: Page numbers in *italics* indicate figures and in **bold** indicate tables on the corresponding pages

For Product Safety Concerns and Information please contact our
EU representative GPSR@taylorandfrancis.com Taylor & Francis
Verlag GmbH, Kaufingerstraße 24, 80331 München, Germany